To[m] —

with warm regards.

Managing Contemporary Conflict

Westview Studies in Regional Security

Wm. J. Olson, Series Editor

Managing Contemporary Conflict:
Pillars of Success,
edited by Max G. Manwaring and Wm. J. Olson

Gray Area Phenomena:
Confronting the New World Disorder,
edited by Max G. Manwaring

Suppressing Insurgency: An Analysis of
the Malayan Emergency, 1948–1954,
edited by John Coates

Low-Intensity Conflict:
Old Threats in a New World,
edited by Edwin G. Corr and Stephen Sloan

The Military, the State, and Development
in Asia and the Pacific,
edited by Viberto Selochan

The Comandante Speaks: Memoirs of an
El Salvadoran Guerrilla Leader,
edited by Courtney E. Prisk

Uncomfortable Wars: Toward
a New Paradigm of Low-Intensity Conflict,
edited by Max G. Manwaring

U.S. Strategic Interests
in the Gulf Region,
edited by Wm. J. Olson

Managing Contemporary Conflict

Pillars of Success

EDITED BY

Max G. Manwaring
and Wm. J. Olson

WestviewPress

A Division of HarperCollins*Publishers*

Westview Studies in Regional Security

Copyright © 1996 by Westview Press, Inc., A Division of HarperCollins Publishers, Inc.

Published in 1996 in the United States of America by Westview Press, Inc., 5500 Central Avenue, Boulder, Colorado 80301-2877, and in the United Kingdom by Westview Press, 12 Hid's Copse Road, Cumnor Hill, Oxford OX2 9JJ

A CIP catalog record for this book is available from the Library of Congress.
ISBN 0-8133-8969-0

The paper used in this publication meets the requirements of the American National Standard for Permanence of Paper for Printed Library Materials Z39.48-1984.

10   9   8   7   6   5   4   3   2   1

Contents

PART THREE
THE THIRD PILLAR: AN APPROPRIATE MANAGEMENT
STRUCTURE FOR THE CONDUCT OF CONTEMPORARY
CONFLICT

PART FOUR
ADDITIONAL CHALLENGES IN CONFRONTING THE
NEW WORLD DISORDER

Editors' Note

This is the third book in a series aimed at revitalizing our strategic thinking on "uncomfortable" contemporary conflicts, that is, conflicts other than major wars. The main theme of this volume is that conflict, regardless of level of discomfort, must fit into an overall foreign policy structure that identifies supportable ends, adequate means, and clear purpose.

Ambassador David Miller identified the essential principles that must help us to operationalize that structure. This volume is built around that essay, which, updated, is reprinted here as Chapter Two. He argues that, although we face many new problems in a more problematic setting, success in the contemporary security environment will be constructed of the same fundamental components as those developed in the past. These "pillars of success" include a sound theory of engagement; the development and use of appropriate instruments of national power to support the theories of engagement; and the promulgation of an executive branch management structure to ensure the effective implementation of the theories of engagement and the coordination of the various civil and military instruments of power.

By coming to grips with the lessons of success and failure that we should have learned over the past several years, decision makers and their staffs should be able to develop the conceptual, operational, and organizational instruments necessary to win contemporary conflicts, once a competent decision has been reached to engage US purpose and power.

The editors wish to thank the contributors whose knowledge, experience, analytical powers, wisdom, and many hours of work made this book possible. We also want to thank Aileen Moodie, our professional editor, for making us sound wiser and more consistent that we might have, and Sandra Rush, our professional word processor, who made it all look easy.

We respectfully dedicate the volume to General John R. Galvin who has been an inspiration and a thoughtful strategist on behalf of his country.

Neither this book nor the individual chapters in it should be construed as reflecting the official positions of the United States Government, the Department of Defense, or the Department of State. We and the various contributors alone are responsible for any errors of fact or judgment.

Max G. Manwaring   Wm. J. Olson
Carlisle, PA   Chevy Chase, MD

Foreword

We face a new and difficult task: How to define for ourselves what our purpose should be in a world much changed. Although the Cold War era held many disturbing threats to our interests and survival, it also gave us a certainty of purpose and coherence to planning that is no longer there. We find ourselves the only superpower in a world growing steadily more diverse; a world in which our power is increasingly ill-fitted to deal with the problems we face.

In the years of US-Soviet rivalry, the number of states added to the family of nations grew rapidly. Great European empires disappeared into a sea of new nations, many with little ability for self-government beyond the desire. Self-determination moved many of the world's ethnic and religious groups to seek a country of their own, a movement of people and ideas that became one of the dominant themes of world politics, often lost on us as we struggled with the perplexities of the threat from the Soviet Union to our immediate survival and well-being. The fashioning of these new states raised the expectations of many groups for similar outcomes. Unfortunately, there were and are more aspirations than there is geography to accommodate them. In addition, many of the governments of the newly created states were not up to the task of governing. Either through mismanagement or maliciousness some of these governments have made the lives of their citizens miserable.

The politics and economics of despair have spawned the growth of informal and illegal economies, particularly the rapid expansion of major criminal organizations, that have further undermined the stability of many of the world's fledgling states. The demands on the international community to rescue failed or failing states have grown phenomenally in just the last few years as even once seemingly stable political orders, as in Yugoslavia, disappeared into the nightmare of civil strife and ethnic cleansing.

It is in this environment that we must now find our way. We must begin to assess our purpose as we pass into 21st century and what, if anything, we can and are prepared to do to come to terms with a world troubled by so many problems. Although we face a new order of challenges, most of which do not present themselves with the clarity of the Cold War, we are not

without experience or insight. On the whole, the United States did remarkably well in the years of the Cold War, managing its own affairs and dealing
with a host of Herculean troubles. That we emerged successfully from the
Cold War with our political institutions and ideals intact, and that we did
so while superintending a process that prevented a major world war are
eloquent testaments to our abilities and our perseverance. We are not babes
in the bull rushes. We have the acumen and the capabilities to deal with the
new order in which we now find ourselves. The issue is whether we have
the will, the stamina, and the understanding to deal wisely with the many
complex and often ambiguous circumstances that now demand our
attention.

The present volume is one effort to address that issue. The authors, with
long, collective experience in the formation and implementation of US
foreign policy, here make a major contribution to our efforts to frame the
questions and the answers necessary to help us to define our place and our
purpose. This work is the third in a series of volumes that trace the nature
of the new order and its many challenges. This volume, building upon an
earlier contribution by Ambassador David Miller, focuses on how we can
use the experience and the knowledge gained from the Cold War to
construct an effective program for the future. It includes the elements for a
theory of engagement and it identifies the management concepts that must
instruct our foreign policy, and develops a coherent set of ideas that must
inform the implementation of such a policy.

The arguments of the editors and their co-authors are straightforward.
First, the general threat they outline is that of the collapse of civil society
and legitimate government in many parts of the world, and the corresponding rise of violence, disruption, dislocation, and social chaos. They then note
the nature of specific challenges, such as the rise of major criminal and other
non-state actors, the proliferation of conventional weapons and weapons
of mass destruction, religious and ethnic challenges to existing order, and
the burden that these many problems place on an already over-taxed
international system.

In developing the picture of a world in turmoil, they delineate concepts
and ideas that should chart our future course. In particular, they note not
only the need for sound thinking and workable concepts of action, they
underscore the basic importance of sustaining political will. No policy,
however well conceived, is worth much if it cannot engender public
support. As the authors make clear, in the more ambiguous circumstances
of today's world, winning that support has grown more problematic. While
the American public is no less concerned about securing America's place in
the world, the public is paying closer attention to a cost-benefit analysis.
Policy makers would do well to temper future efforts based on a thorough
understanding of this pragmatic accounting mixed with traditional Ameri-

can idealism. The approach outlined in this volume offers the means to do that.

As the contributors argue, success in the future will be a combination of understanding our past and responding with finesse to unfolding circumstances. Those with the difficult but urgent task of developing US security policy and strategies would be well served by heeding the guidelines developed here.

Lawrence S. Eagleburger
Washington, D.C.

INTRODUCTION

1

A New World, A New Challenge

Wm. J. Olson

Has such been the fate of the centuries which have preceded our own?...has man always inhabited a world like the present, where all things are not in their proper relationships, where virtue is without genius, and genius without honor; where the love of order is confused with the taste for oppression, and the holy cult of freedom with a contempt for law; where the light thrown by conscience on human actions is dim, and where nothing seems to be any longer forbidden or allowed, honorable or shameful, false or true?

—de Tocqueville

Pick up any major newspaper or news journal and you cannot miss the fact that the world is a troubled place. Despite the end of the Cold War, regional wars persist, and violence remains endemic, while refugees and starving victims of government excess people our front pages and prime time. In the last several years, millions have died in wars, revolutions, and ethnic strife; this violence has rendered tens of millions more homeless, orphans of chance on international relief. There are few encouraging signs that this condition will change for the better anytime soon.

As concerned as Americans might be for the plight of refugees and the victims of violence brought home to us nightly on CNN, the issue for us is when, where, how, and, most important, whether to engage American force or capabilities in dealing with the many problems manifest in waves of refugees, wars, and instability in disparate locations and situations. Already the two post-Cold War presidents, George Bush and Bill Clinton, have committed the United States to such situations—with notable success in Kuwait, with disaster in Somalia, with mixed results in Rwanda, with deep caution in Yugoslavia, and with consequences yet unclear in Haiti.

This paper reflects the views of the author and not the views of the U.S. Government, the U.S. Senate, or the Caucus on International Narcotics Control.

Such decisions to call upon American resources and resolve on foreign shores in risky environments have never been easy or taken lightly, but in the post–Cold War environment, the rationale for engaging US force in defense of interests is far less clear or easy to justify. One has only to review the debates leading up to the Gulf War or the intervention in Haiti to be reminded of just how uncertain things are and how divisive such decisions can be when the interests and purposes are unclear.

In the past, we intervened with the notion of defending democratic order against communist threats. We wanted to preserve certain basic values and interests, not to mention our own survival, in the face of particular threats to order and those interests. We were lucky, at least in the sense that the enemy was generally clear, the interests mostly understandable, and the purposes explainable to a public concerned about security against a certain, impending menace. The risks and costs seemed commensurate with the issues involved. The circumstances requiring intervention in the future, however, are likely to be less precise; and intervention, if it comes, is likely to be on behalf of preserving order against chaos, a far more dubious and ambiguous concept upon which to base justifications for action and risks. It is going to be more difficult to demonstrate the link between the sacrifices demanded and the rewards achieved. It is going to be more difficult also to realize or recognize success.

The nature of threats in the future are likely to arise from two sets of problems. The first set involves order in particular states, their stability and governability, and the forces that threaten both. The second set involves threats to international order from regional powers made bolder by the retreat of the superpowers and the disappearance of the bipolar rules of the road that gave some measure of coherence to international politics for the last half century. American foreign policy makers will have to decide how best to deal with both these sets of problems.

Governability

The majority of problems in the future, as in the past, that will levy demands on our attention are likely to occur in various parts of the developing world, in Asia, Latin America, Africa, the Caribbean, and now the states emerging from the ruins of the Soviet empire. Unlike earlier demands, however, we no longer have the singular threat that the Soviets and an international communist movement once provided for making us, willy nilly, a player in the complexities and vagaries of international politics and regional conflicts. Indeed, the collapse of the Soviet Union and the end of the containing features of bipolar politics now contribute to making those environments yet more complex and ambiguous, especially for determining with any certainty what US interests are, how they should be protected, where, by whom, and with what.

The problems are multiple. One of the most significant problems besetting the developing world is the issue of governance itself. This has two faces. There is the question of basic competence: Is the government able to govern, to provide the essential security, stability, and equity upon which sound social, economic, and political policies can be developed. In many areas of the world, government is simply not up to the task. In far too many cases, corruption and malfeasance of every invention have sapped government not only of its vitality but of the essential public confidence that must underlie good governance. The consequences can be seen in governments unable to provide basic services, to maintain decent roads, education, health, and public services. It can be seen in the inability of governments to provide basic security and a functioning legal system that protects civic rights and a sense of equity. It is seen most painfully in the decline in basic honesty, integrity, and the instinct for virute in office that must underpin decent government.

In addition to the basic competence of government there are the consequences, often growing out of the first issue, of government made desperate by its inabilities to maintain control. Faced with disparate ethnic, political, or religious groups insistent upon establishing a separate identity, if not a separate establishment, governments have reacted with violence, often thuggish and brutal. In some cases, regimes have come to power based on the notion of the superior rights of some elect ethnic, political, or religious group and have used the power and the authority of the state to suppress rival groups and claims to equal status and civil rights. The results in many areas—Rwanda, Russia, Burundi, Iran, Yugoslavia, the Sudan, Cambodia, and Angola, to name only a few—have been waves of "cleansing" violence that have torn states apart or created on-going internal wars and a host of internal and external refugees. Thus, in many areas and for a divergent set of reasons, government has become an enemy of the people.

The third major problem grows out of the fact that the ability of many of these ethnic, religious or political groups, to resist government is far greater than it once was, whether they are victims of government injustice or not. The ready availability of arms on the international market now makes it possible for various groups to resort to the means of violence with greater facility, to resist government more effectively. Whether they buy arms directly from suppliers or acquire them from friendly allies or steal those provided to government forces, resistance movements worldwide of whatever character and motivation can claim access to a useful assortment of weapons that make resistance more possible. Global media coverage has added to the ability of these groups to attract international attention and support. This access to sources of support both physical and psychological often complicates efforts to find peaceful solutions and makes the search for solutions to political differences more violence prone, a readier tool available to anyone. And there are far more groups now seeking some form of distinct identity.

The fourth major problem complicating the international scene is the spread of the idea of self-determination to more and more groups. The overwhelming majority of states today are not homogeneous, composed of the same ethnic or religious groups. Most states harbor significant minorities. Many of these groups, influenced by what they can see happening in other countries and made to feel alien and unwelcome by ruling authorities, have found their own desire and voice for separateness. These groups, with greater access to arms and aid, are better able to resist governments, often enfeebled by their own incompetence. If this were not enough, such groups can now call upon a variety of support groups—non-governmental organizations or UN agencies—to sponsor their grievances in the face of governments. It is no wonder that the very concept of sovereignty as a legitimizing norm for states is under assault.

In most cases, such groups cannot overwhelm the power of states, at least in the short run. But many of these groups have a strategy for protracted conflict, relying on time and international pressure to help them prevail. Even this strategy has not been particularly successful, but it has succeeded enough—Eritrea, Afghanistan, Mozambique, Angola, to name only a few—to lend support to those who believe in the inevitability of their success because of the righteousness of their cause. Even short of success, however, they can severely disrupt normal social, political, and economic life for many countries for extended periods, and their actions can create climates of threat and violence that spawn waves of internal and external refugees. One indicator of the degree of the problems created by such situations is the fact that the United Nations has undertaken more peacekeeping missions in the last 5 years than it did in the previous 45 years.

The fifth major problem likely to demand attention results from the rise of a variety of non-state actors, who have grown more powerful and daring in a world of weak and weakened states. In part, some of these actors are the ethnic and religious separatists who challenge states—operating as insurgencies or international terrorist organizations. One has only to look at the bombing of the World Trade Center in New York or the Tokyo subway gas attack to understand how conscienceless such groups can be and how disruptive of the civil peace and public trust. But there is another class of actors who are wholly separate from states and who, unlike the ethnic and religious groups, generally harbor no desire to replace government only to benefit from its incapacity. These groups are the emerging major criminal organizations in various parts of the world.

It is generally hard for those brought up on the ideas of a world organized around nations to conceive of a situation in which criminal groups can be anything but marginal actors. It is interesting to note that neither academic theorists of international relations or practical politicians have any real grasp of the nature and extent of the threat from such groups to local political order and the fate of democratic institutions. Yet, as the plight of

Italy, Russia, Colombia, and Mexico vividly show, criminal groups and the corruption they entail can undermine democratic processes and public confidence and, in the worst case, undo political regimes either by threat or bribery. While the aim of such groups, in the past at least, has been to make money and not to seek to replace the existing government, their operations nevertheless can have serious, long-term consequences for the possibility of decent, competent government. Indications of links between various criminal groups with each other and of these groups with terrorist and insurgent organizations only raise the level of possible instability such groups can foster within given countries.

Further, since many of these groups operate globally in defiance of any and all norms of international practice, and traffic in goods and services—people, drugs, arms—in defiance of local law, often resorting to violence and corruption, they help to promote a climate of lawlessness that is destabilizing. With growing evidence that at least some of these groups may be trafficking in nuclear weapons, the destabilizing influence of such groups on national and international politics goes well beyond traditional thinking about the nature of organized crime or its marginality.

The sixth major problem is less concrete than the others but it is of no less concern. It involves the erosion of international norms of behavior and practice along with the collapse of states or their increasing disabilities. Although often honored in the breach, over the years the interactions of the individual members of the international community have built up certain patterns of behavior governing their relations with one another. In particular, this evolution has led to a variety of rules regulating war and the conduct of war—particularly rules concerning the use of chemical and biological weapons, and the treatment of civilian populations and prisoners of war— appropriate forms of political and economic relationships, rules concerning human rights, and a large body of precedent and tradition on the proper conduct of inter- and even intrastate relations.

In particular, the views underpinning the growth of this international civil society argue that individual human rights are prior to any claims of group authority, especially that of the state—the implication being that there are limits to state power; that war should be an option of last resort in self defense and its conduct rule governed; and that government should be limited, democratic, and based on the rule of law. These norms have not always prevailed, but they have been increasingly the standards to which states have been held accountable. This accountability has gone some way towards modifying state behavior for the better, particularly in reducing the occasions of major international conflict and in providing regular means for adjudicating such conflicts when they do occur. It is this body of practice, along with the stability of the individual members of the international system, that are at risk in the present environment of spreading ungovernability.

Indeed, many of the sub-state and non-state actors responsible for challenges to individual states are hostile to the very notions underpinning international society. Many of these groups have no stake and little interest in the rules governing the present distribution of power among nations. Their objective is to destroy this system and, if they have thought so far ahead, to replace it with one more compatible to their notions of fairness and equity, whatever these disparate ideas happen to be.

Such groups as Islamic fundamentalists directly and major criminal organizations indirectly threaten the cohesion of these ideas. They have learned, and taught one another, how to defy individual states, how to destabilize them. Moreover, as the warlords in Somalia showed, you do not have to be a superpower or even a state to frustrate a superpower. All you have to do is maximize the ambiguity and raise the level of risk for loss of life. In the US case, the number of lives the country currently seems prepared to risk is vanishingly small.

International order, such as it is, is based on a variety of understandings and a host of agreements that the individual members—nation-states— adhere to and enforce. In dealing with sub-state and non-state actors, however, there is no treaty system nor any enforceable set of agreements that apply group to group. The enforcement mechanisms are extremely attenuated and vulnerable, especially given the weakness of some member countries, who are the main enforcement mechanism for dealing with localized groups. There are no enforceable agreements, for example, that apply to terrorist or criminal organizations on the proliferation of small arms, not to mention chemical, biological, or nuclear weapons. In fact, in a world of weakened states and multiplying centers of power, the ability to contain such proliferation is singularly weakened. The implications for domestic peace and international order, for the ability to uphold standards of decent conduct applicable to all, are sobering.

To what degree, how far off or close the realities of this bleak description are for any particular situations is unclear, a further part of our problem, but the combination of these forces and threats add complication to the world that we must make our place in. They not only threaten the stability of individual governments, the nature and prospect of government itself, they offer a variety of distinct and yet ambiguous challenges to US interests. They also challenge our ability to understand the nature of the menace and our patience in developing responses. But these are not the only threats and ambiguities that we must deal with.

Rogue States and Regional Powers

The second major set of problems confronting us involves the actions of more traditional players on the international scene—other countries, their ambitions and anxieties. It also involves our own understanding of our predicament, our purposes, and our will. While these concerns are more familiar, they too will unfold with a difference in a post-Cold War world.

On of the major changes in the international scene with the demise of the Soviet Union has been the end of bipolarity. This factor has certain implications. We can say with reasonable certainty that US-Soviet rivalry had a profound influence on the nature of international order and how it evolved in the last 50 years. Bipolarity imparted specific features to the overall tone of international relations and developments and not just to the specifics of US-Soviet dealings. We can note both positive and negative influences. We can cite particular confrontations and proxy fights, tense moments, and a host of summits and lesser meetings that helped to frame much of the context of international relations. But we cannot determine with any exactitude just what that influence was or how it manifested itself in particular situations.

Just how much and how US-Soviet rivalry—and the rules of the game that developed over the years between the two superpowers that kept them from nuclear war—influenced particular regional developments is not easy to decipher. It is not clear just how this rivalry helped to shape decision making in various capitols, how it influenced leaders and people in the choices they made to act or not act, how it helped to establish a framework for relations not just between the superpowers but also between and among them and their respective allies and enemies. We can discern outlines but few distinct features in any detail. If these details are blurred, just how the ending of US-Soviet rivalry is going to affect the future evolution of the international environment is even less apparent. We can say with some confidence, however, that there will be a host of consequences. We can also reasonably assume that most of these will arise in localized situations the result of actions by regional actors.

As various regional states and actors, and the United States and the successors to the Soviet Union, adjust to new circumstances and explore the possibilities opened by the ending of the Cold War and the rules that governed bipolarity, it is reasonable to assume that we can anticipate a variety of changed and changing patterns of relations, although we cannot be certain of their nature or direction. Since even political leaders in the United States are unsure of how to proceed in the present environment, are uncertain how to employ force, what interests to protect, what capabilities to develop, how to relate resources to commitments, and how to explain and justify courses of action, it is reasonable to assume that similar uncertainty abounds in many quarters. Everyone must now struggle with a political reality that offers a new set of opportunities and liabilities accompanied by a host of enigmatic changes in patterns of relationships and power.

The first major issue for US policy in the new international environment, then, is how to deal with a novel fluidity and more ambiguity as to intentions, capabilities, and actions. There are also a lot more actors and potential actors. We have traded bipolarity for multipolarity, whatever that means or is likely to become. In essence, it means that there are a number of local power centers—such as China, North and South Korea, Thailand, Indonesia, India, Brazil, South Africa, Iran, Iraq, Egypt, Israel, Russia, Mexico, Britain, France, Germany, Japan—where decisions and actions are likely to take on greater importance now that they are out from under the shadow of US-Soviet rivalry.

It means that many of the former ties that bound them to certain political realities—treaty commitments, alliances, relics of the Cold War—are likely to lose much of their force, freeing these actors, and others, to pursue interests and policies that are no longer strongly influenced by the wishes of Moscow or Washington. It means that the superpowers are no longer in a position to command or enjoin their subordination. It means as well a decline in the ability of either Washington or Moscow to enforce any discipline on former allies or to overawe with threats and cajolery local leaders bent on their own outcomes. It is likely to mean that these and other local leaders will explore with greater enthusiasm and boldness the new freedom born of the end of the Cold War. A new assertiveness. To date, it has also meant a greater role for the United Nations and a greater emphasis on multilateral operations.

For those states that share in the traditions of the current international regime, most will act responsibly, if more independently. This independence in regional matters is likely to lead to a host of new regional struggles and changes in local balance of power relations, but it will at least take place in a familiar context bound by certain rules and practices. For some state actors, however, the opening up of this brave new world is an opportunity for escaping the constraints of the international system.

The second major problem for the United States in the new world order involves dealing with rogue states. Such countries as Libya or Iran, Syria or North Korea have already demonstrated a willingness to violate the norms of international practice to pursue their own political and ideological goals. They are likely to find the present circumstance an invitation to even greater activity and their success is likely to encourage others to dabble in the same troubled waters. The demise of bipolarity is likely to give such actors greater opportunity—in a world where the constraints have been diminished—to engage in sponsoring terrorism; in trafficking in arms, especially nuclear, biological, and chemical weapons; in drug smuggling; in subversion; in counterfeiting, and in a host of other practices separately or in conjunction with one another or various non-state and sub-state actors. These activities will be harder to suppress, both because the superpowers are not there to enforce discipline, and because the control mechanisms of the international community will have become less effective in a multipolar environment.

In addition, the spread of conventional weapons and chemical weapons capabilities, and the likelihood that the conventions governing the spread of nuclear weapons will erode even further, mean that regional powers, including rogue states, will be more formidably armed and better able to deter international intervention in their own internal affairs or to check them in regional adventures. The third major issue for the United States in promoting and protecting its interests in the new world order, then, will be how to deal with regional states grown more powerful and assertive.

The fourth major concern for the United States lies in its own determination of just how much pain it is interested in enduring and for what interests in a world grown more complex and ambiguous. The 1992 presidential campaign seemed to signal a domestic impatience with foreign affairs and a public unwillingness to see American power engaged overseas. If this remains true, it is going to be very difficult for political leaders to articulate policies and strategies for engagement that are likely to have popular backing. This will complicate the development of any coherent or lasting consensus on what policy should be. This in turn will make suspect US reliability as a partner in dangerous situations. It will open up questions of US commitment and staying power—a problem for allies and an opportunity for enemies. It also creates problems for determining our own best course of action. Uncertainty as to purpose and interest means that we are muddled as to what sort of defense we should have and how much to spend on it. Thus, we are not just a "consumer" of problems but also a "producer". The question for all of us is whether we are also a producer of solutions.

What's New?

As complicated as the new world order now appears to be, as ambiguous and diverse, none of the many challenges it poses are entirely unfamiliar to us, nor are we without experience or expertise. This is not the first time, either, that we have debated among ourselves over what our purposes should be. The development of the containment doctrine itself, the architecture of our post-World War II policy, was the result of vigorous debate, both at its inception and over the many years it remained the essence of our efforts. We have faced quandaries before. Thus, our present circumstance, while offering many new challenges, is not without precedent.

What is new is that we are not faced, at least as yet, with an immediate, direct threat to our physical survival. This is a relief. It is also the source of many of our present quandaries. With the threat of nuclear holocaust removed, what other challenge seems worthy enough to engage our attention or require sacrifice and effort in foreign fields? While there may be many problems, dangerous and difficult, and without solution, so what? What is there in the present international situation that truly deserves our attention? What justifies intervention overseas? Risks? Loss of lives? After years of being a superpower engaging a truly dangerous foe, what in all these niggling problems uncovered by the end of the Cold War truly concerns us? These are the questions that we are now grappling with as a nation. The effort to answer them are likely to trouble us for many years to come. Yet, we, the authors of this present volume, believe that it is essential to come to an answer and with some dispatch.

In that regard, we have attempted to help shape the terms of the debate over what a post-Cold War America national security policy should look like. This is the third volume in a series that we hope will help to frame the questions and outline some of the answers that we believe to be most relevant to finding our way to a reasonable consensus and a coherent policy. The first volume, *Low-Intensity Conflict*, sought to contribute to the conceptualization of the major issues confronting us. The second volume, *Gray Area Phenomena*, carried this effort forward by looking more closely at specific issues and problems. This volume addresses more practical concerns. Building on those earlier discussions, it focuses on what we know about what to do. Its concern is with what a US foreign policy should look like and how we need to go about implementing it. Each of the following chapters looks at specific aspects of implementing a US policy based on the framework developed by David Miller in his chapter. That chapter, revised and enlarged, is reprinted here as the capstone to the subsequent sections that deal with the need to develop a theory of engagement, the appropriate weapons systems to support it, and the implementing structure necessary to carry ideas into action. It also develops principles that should govern our consideration for national security policy and intervention.

2

Back to the Future: Structuring Foreign Policy in a Post–Cold War World

Ambassador David C. Miller, Jr.

Low intensity conflicts again dominate the press and television. After the collapse of the Soviet Union, there was an illusion, held mainly by experts on the United States–Soviet confrontation, that peace was about to break out. But for those who had served in the Third World, been engaged in the numerous low intensity conflicts that have been waged over the last decade, and who had witnessed the rise in religious tensions and seen the impact of the disparity of global income distribution, there was never any illusion that the end of the superpower confrontation would have as a necessary corollary the decrease in military confrontation and violence.

My concern, and that of others, has come from reading the profusion of editorials and listening to television commentaries in which foreign affairs "experts" and observers seem to have discovered for the first time that the ethnic tensions in the Balkans had never really gone away; that social collapse, starvation, and ethnic warfare in Africa has been getting steadily worse for a decade; and that the serious fault lines within the former Soviet Union, to say nothing of the growing estrangement of some Moslem leaders from the West, promise to produce continuing violent confrontation, terrorism, and potentially major confrontations in a number of Middle East countries. Those of us who have worked in these areas simply wonder where the commentators have been and what they have been thinking about for a decade. We must also wonder how many of these pundits believe the United States can remain aloof or unaffected by these situations.

The level of concern rises rapidly when the lack of a national framework to deal with these issues becomes apparent. Our most senior national leaders, foreign policy experts, and, indeed, average citizens all quite correctly pose the question of whether and when the United States should involve itself politically or militarily in the many conflicts where, almost inevitably, it is arguable that an American military effort could help resolve the situation. If we intervene in Somalia on humanitarian grounds, a country to which we have no historical ties, then why not intervene in Liberia, a country that we helped establish and with which we have maintained active ties for more than a century? If, in the former Yugoslavia, Moslems were pursuing a policy of ethnic cleansing and "removing" or "eradicating" Christian populations, would we still be pursuing the relatively hands-off policy that we see today? Given the support of the insurgencies in Afghanistan and in Angola, what is our responsibility to help those countries achieve stable governments after our short-term military goals have been met?

Thus we return to the most basic question facing military and foreign policy decision makers. Where should we risk American lives? Where should American taxpayers' money be spent? What roles or missions are appropriate and acceptable to us as a people? All this might seem academic if so many young Americans had not recently returned from DESERT STORM, or had not been deployed in Somalia in OPERATION RESTORE HOPE; or if we were not currently engaged in trying to restore decent government to Haiti. Past and present experience make it clear that we risk failure and lives when we became involved in situations requiring the use of force without adequate intellectual framework or discipline, without appropriate means or planning, and without public understanding or support.

Thus, the purpose of this book: to look more closely at what we can learn from the end of confrontation with the Soviet Union as we look to this new and confusing era; and, to review the lessons to be learned from the past that we can apply to the low intensity conflict problems of today. There is much to absorb. The balance of this chapter will discuss how to apply what we learned in the United States–Soviet confrontation to the management of these new low-intensity engagements.

Learning from the Past

The United States prevailed in its confrontation with the Soviet Union (that is, avoided both a massive conventional military conflict and an accidental or planned nuclear exchange), I believe, because of three fundamental strengths:

- the development of theories of engagement;
- the development of appropriate weapons systems with safeguards and controls; and

- the development of an Executive Branch management structure to implement the theories of engagement using both civilian and military assets wisely.

First, we worked hard to develop theories of engagement. A great deal of intellectual energy, national debate and writing, to say nothing of war gaming, went into the question of how and under what circumstances we would use nuclear weapons or other weapons of mass destruction, and how we could and should employ our combat forces. Second, we worked very hard to develop the technology and manufacturing capability to produce major weapons systems, both offensive and defensive, to be deployed with adequate safeguards and controls. Third, we developed an Executive Branch management structure to implement the theories of engagement that brought both military and civilian assets to the field in the confrontation with our superpower rival.

These three components ought not be considered relics of a bygone era. Indeed, those assigned the difficult but urgent task of developing U.S. defense and foreign policy in the future would be well served by studying these components and how they were developed and employed in the past. We need to examine these components in more detail.

Basic Components

The gravity of our ideological rivalry with the Soviet Union linked to the risk of thermonuclear war led this country to devote much of its best intellectual capability to winning the Cold War. The leadership of the uniformed services, the Department of State and related agencies, the Central Intelligence Agency, the national laboratories and leaders of the American academic community all wrestled with how to contain, control, and prevail in both conventional and nuclear confrontations. Academic debate on the use of nuclear weapons was fierce and the crisis-management system and war-gaming capabilities of the uniformed services grew increasingly sophisticated. The net result was a carefully devised and structured concept of engagement understood by the national leadership, perhaps most coherently expressed in George Kennan's theory of containment found in his 1947 *Foreign Affairs* article, and re-defined in NSC 68, a national security blueprint developed in the Truman years that laid the foundations for U.S. Cold War policy.

It is worth noting, as will be discussed below, that virtually the entire low intensity conflict spectrum was viewed as a sub-set of the United States– Soviet confrontation. Vietnam (for a period of time), Afghanistan, Angola, and Central America were undertaken as components of the global struggle with the Soviet Union.

The second critical component of our victory over the Soviet Union, based on the concept noted above, was to develop, produce, and sustain the deployment of weapons systems and other tools of national power superior to those of our adversary. It is arguable that the ability of our economy to sustain this effort while also producing civilian prosperity was the key to the ultimate economic and political demise of the Soviet Union. Offensive and defensive systems as well as detection capabilities and command-and-control structures reflected the very best technology available in our country, with cost a secondary consideration.

The third critical component of our success, integrating ideas and weapons, lay in the development of effective management and decision-making structures. Beginning with the National Security Act of 1947, both the Executive Branch and Congress struggled with the issue of providing effective decision making, management and intelligence capabilities with appropriate Congressional oversight. Elaborate command and control structures within the military, checks and balances and oversight of intelligence activities, modification of business-as-usual rules in the Department of State and the Agency for International Development (AID) led to the ability of the president of the United States, working with Congress, to manage effectively the struggle with the Soviet Union. Throughout this period, then, there was a reasonably close fit between ideas, methods, and systems, and a creative and constructive relationship between the Executive Branch and Congress.

What do we face today? I believe, as the chapters in this book illustrate, that in all three areas that were critical to our success in the confrontation with the Soviet Union we find ourselves in a state of confusion. We are groping for theories of engagement, our weapons systems are inappropriate, and our ability to manage low intensity conflicts is poor.

The Need for Reassessment

For various reasons the foreign policy community seems hesitant to grapple with when and where the United States should commit resources in the low-intensity arena. Some views advanced appear to be based more on our capability to execute a mission than on the necessity to do so. It is clear that the rigorous intellectual framework devised to confront the Soviet Empire is inadequate when faced with the confusion of the low intensity conflict environment. The integration of ideas and structures linked by a cooperative atmosphere and sustained by a public consensus that saw us through the Cold War is lacking here. Unless and until we develop such a framework for the environment of tomorrow our efforts will be inadequate and fraught with peril.

American voters will not long tolerate the death of their children in combat or the expenditure of their tax money unless they believe that the engagement is in response to a direct threat to their well-being that they can perceive readily. They knew that losing a global struggle to communism would harm them and their children. They supported massive weapons systems, regional wars (Korea), low-intensity engagements (Afghanistan, Angola, and Central America), and even Vietnam when the cost seemed reasonable. The American people will not sustain support for an unclear or vague policy, but they will support action if the issues are well defined in terms of the national interest, and I believe that the basis for the use of force and the expenditure of substantial amounts of taxpayers' resources will rest ultimately on the same type of bedrock principles that supported our engagement with the Soviet Union.

There are four areas that I believe meet this requirement today: the proliferation of weapons of mass destruction, not only nuclear but also chemical and biological; threats to vital economic interests; a large flow of economic refugees into the United States; and interdiction and suppression of narcotics trafficking and international criminal enterprises as they threaten the United States. These represent basic threats to the nation's perceived long-term well-being and offer the foundations for a clear policy and strategy.

Weapons of mass destruction in the hands of states, such as North Korea or Iraq or Iran, either hostile to the United States or politically unstable pose a direct threat to the well-being of the United States and its allies. The use of military force to prevent the development of serious threats in this area will, I believe, be supported by the American taxpayer, the Congress, and our allies.

As DESERT STORM dramatically showed, the United States was able to create and lead a United Nations coalition not only to maintain international law but, more important, to prevent the emergence of a dominant and hostile power in the Middle East that could disrupt the stability of the international economy. I believe that Americans will support efforts to sustain the key economic interests of the United States and the international community as whole.

Further, it is coming home to American taxpayers that an unchecked flow of refugees into the United States, most of whom are driven by economic reasons and not political persecution, will have a direct effect on the economic well-being of the United States and its citizens. This issue was dramatized by the massive arrival of Haitian refugees fleeing a country whose economy has collapsed through decades of mismanagement and corruption. Assuming that the American taxpayer does not wish to seal the border, a virtual impossibility at any rate, support for intervention in situations such as Haiti, when critical interests are more clearly engaged, to restore a decent and responsible government will, I believe, also have the support of the American taxpayer.

The rise of major criminal organizations, particularly those that traffic in human beings and in drugs, also pose a threat to the well-being of Americans and to the interests of the United States that the public has consistently recognized. This is an area where the government can and must develop consistent programs to counter the rise of criminal groups that target the United States directly and that threaten our interests indirectly by undermining the functioning of democratic institutions around the world.

The unrestrained growth of coca bushes in Peru and the explosive growth of poppy cultivation in the Golden Triangle have produced more casualties among American youth than any recent war, by a wide margin. As drug addiction spreads to other countries, notably Europe, our allies will likely join our citizens to demand that something be done to stop the avalanche of narcotics reaching our countries. While much of the solution lies in domestic programs aimed at decreasing drug addiction, ultimately the taxpayer will have to consider using military force more aggressively in the interdiction missions or to deal with solutions in which local authorities lack either the will or capability to control the territory in which drugs are grown and processed.

Although this is hardly an exhaustive list of issues that directly affect our citizens' welfare, they are the four key issues that I believe pass the test of committing military law and intelligence resources in this new, unstable world that the American public can and will support. Assuming that the country can develop a theory of engagement, it is necessary to focus on the second issue, appropriate response systems.

When drug traffickers murdered a presidential candidate in Colombia, President George Bush responded within a week with a $65 million emergency military assistance package for the Colombian government. The response clearly demonstrated the president's commitment and our ability to come to the aid of an ally, but the nature of what we responded with illustrates a basic problem: finding appropriate equipment to support national strategy. In Colombia, we struggled to find old, slow, inexpensive aircraft and other equipment appropriate to the situation. One C130 Specter, our state-of-the-art gun ship, for example, cost more than the entire military aid package we authorized and could not have been operated by Colombian air crews without a great deal of training. But finding old C-47 gun ships proved difficult. In area after area, we found that we had to make do with equipment, often very expensive, designed for other purposes. While we are very good at such "field expedients," the point remains that we faced a demanding situation with the wrong resources. Nor was this the only example. U.S. Naval and Coast Guard vessels, charged with interdicting drug ships, found themselves searching boats, where, without a tip, there was little chance of finding narcotics, or trying to catch smaller, wooden-hull vessels, difficult to detect with radar.

The intelligence and law enforcement communities found themselves installing small computer systems for data management and rudimentary SIGINT equipment to track down fugitives, providing armored cars and body armor to protect judges and simple encryption and security devices to protect information. Thus, suddenly the United States had to produce inexpensive, easy-to-operate equipment for an ally on the edge of losing complete control of the country to narcotics traffickers. Put simply, the United States has limited equipment that can be used by Third World allies or our own troops in unconventional situations.

At the same time and at the opposite end of the technology spectrum, for example, we find the United States struggling to develop and use high-technology systems to counter terrorism and narcotics. How, for example, could the best assets of the American intelligence community be thrown at Pablo Escobar for a year-and-a-half and still have him elude capture? We face a whole range of demands: How can we detect two kilos of SYMTEX, a plastic explosive, in a package—or worse yet in a shipping container? Is there any practical non-intrusive way to screen shipping containers for their contents, be it weapons or drugs? How can we use the National Security Agency's capabilities to keep track of the movement of money, a key component of both drug and terrorist activities? What technical manner of destruction of coca bushes and poppies might be used that would be acceptable to the host country? Could the precursor chemicals purchased by the drug cartels in massive quantities be altered adequately to destroy cocaine hydrochloride in the processing activities? Could we place non-obtrusive tags on civilian aircraft—from a distance? Can we force the termination of a light aircraft flight without causing a crash?

The high technology systems designed to fight a sophisticated and massive Soviet threat are simply too expensive and sometimes inappropriate to the low-intensity engagement or Operations Other Than War. On the other hand, we must develop new technologies for the detection of chemical and biological weapons, narcotics, terrorist devices, and so on.

We must, moreover, do this in situations that are frequently controlled by "law enforcement" rules of engagement and almost inevitably controlled by civilian-political concerns. There is a clear imperative to develop new technical systems and capabilities appropriate to this law enforcement environment we are likely to face. Our past successes grew from our ability to be both creative and responsive. Surely we can rise to this challenge as well.

The interface between intelligence collection capabilities and law enforcement collection capabilities presents a similar challenge. If we presume that the drug war was basically a law enforcement activity, then the gathering of information and the use of national assets had to occur within the framework of the judicial process. This too had the effect of limiting what we could do.

The most painful example of this last point, which puts it all in perspective, is straightforward. There are in fact both chemical agents and biological agents available today that could destroy coca bushes, with probably less damage to the environment than that caused by the cocaine industry. We have the technical means to locate coca fields. We have the technical means to deliver these agents. But we have not been able to convince civilian governments—notable Peru—that using these agents would be appropriate.

The third component in our ability to respond to future conflicts lies in organization, in unity of effort. While those who have been involved in the development of the military command-and-control structures have labored long and hard to produce excellent systems, these, like our weapons systems, were geared for a different ratio, for major conflict. Sadly, command and control in most low-intensity conflicts is not nearly as well defined. The inability of the American government to develop an effective management structure for this type of engagement has been and will continue to be frustrating if we cannot find the formula for appropriate command and control.

Our traditional systems leave much to be desired. The State Department, for example, by charter has the lead overseas, but the Department has failed to do a very good job with this assignment. Again, typically in low-intensity engagements, the military role is limited, which results in immense frustration when an agency of greater managerial capability is asked to put some of its personnel at risk in a situation that it does not control. Tensions mount as roles and missions collide.

Moreover, the rules and regulations that govern USAID, our main economic tool, make effective use of our aid programs virtually impossible, as noted in the essay by William Olson in *Gray Area Phenomena*. But this is not all. Illustrative of the situation is Ambassador William Walker's experience in El Salvador. At the height of the insurgency in El Salvador, it still took him the usual 18 months to get the approval from Washington for any new AID program. In a fast-moving guerrilla or counternarcotics effort, this is appallingly slow.

Nor are we well structured for quick, effective responses by the intelligence community. Traditional Central Intelligence Agency activities have justifiably had a very complex set of rules and regulations to protect sources and methods. And by the nature of their business, they move slowly and carefully. Further, the CIA is most comfortable as a white-collar espionage agency, one focused until recently on the Soviet threat. Its situation and operating ethics still reflect an old orientation that makes it slow in responding to new challenges. Habits die hard.

Finally, the multitude of United States government agencies necessary to succeed in low intensity conflicts, such as the counternarcotics program, are brought together effectively only at the National Security Council (NSC), and then, after dropping many bureaucratic layers, at the level of a country team in a United States mission. If you assume that the NSC should rarely be operational, then the coordination of these efforts is left to a regional assistant secretary of state. Sadly, for a variety of reasons, assistant secretaries, and the State Department itself, simply do not carry the horsepower to force a multitude of agencies to sing from the same sheet of music. Presidents since Dwight Eisenhower and John Kennedy have tried creating White House special offices, special boards, special advisory groups, and on and on in an effort to manage low-intensity or non-conventional conflicts they faced during their terms.

The last example of this effort was the creation of the Office of National Drug Control Policy by President Bush. William Bennett became our first "drug czar." If anybody could have made this office, which in reality had pathetically little authority, work successfully, it would have been Bill Bennett and his assistant, John Walters. As we took the drug war overseas under the framework of NSD-18, the national drug strategy, we asked Bill Bennett, among other things, to get Secretaries James Baker and Richard Cheney, and CIA Director William Webster to sing as a trio. Without the support of National Security Advisor Brent Scowcroft and the NSC Staff, it would truly have been an impossible mission. Even with the support of General Scowcroft, it was a very difficult and not always effective mission.

No one would go to war without united command and clear lines of authority, without the right equipment or management structure. Yet, we typically engage in low intensity conflict with few of these elements in place in the mistaken belief that our preparation for one type of conflict prepares us for others, no matter how different. We cannot afford such an approach in the future.

What remains clear is that the three factors that led to success in the confrontation with the Soviet Union will be required to successfully confront the low-intensity conflict environment of the next decade, provided that we learn to apply the principles in keeping with the reality of the situation. We have done remarkably well in the past in responding to low-intensity conflict on the margins of the rivalry with the Soviet Union. That is now history. The many unforgiving and complex situations of the future require more. We face a growing surge of challenges and demands on our limited resources. We face a daunting future that requires a new look, a restructuring of past practices, and greater flexibility in our institutions.

The Road Ahead

While we have begun a national dialogue concerning theories of engagement in low intensity conflict, President Clinton took office with pressure to intervene in a host of conflicts with little consensus on a national framework for intervention. If Somalia, why not Liberia? If not Yugoslavia, what level of human outrage will prompt intervention? If not Haiti, are we willing in our own neighborhood to forcibly exclude thousands of refugees fleeing from countries where the economy is collapsing?

The president and his secretary of defense, in an era of shrinking defense budgets, face the intriguing challenge of developing the lower, slower, and less expensive assets required by our own troops and allies in sustaining low-intensity engagements, while maintaining capabilities for larger engagements. At the same time, the Department of Defense and the intelligence community face the challenge of developing higher-technology detection systems to protect our open border against biological, chemical, and smaller nuclear weapons.

Finally, the president must deal with precisely the same challenge of Executive Branch management that faced his predecessors for decades. Assuming that most low intensity conflicts involve a multiplicity of Executive Branch agencies with the military playing a key role but not necessarily in control, who will manage the engagement? Will President Clinton opt for a more operational National Security Council? Will yet another president attempt to make the State Department into an effective conflict-management organization? As awkward as these challenges appear, if we can learn from the past, we can succeed in the future.

Signposts

Three recent involvements—Afghanistan, Angola, and Central America—each achieved U.S. objectives established for them, although the latter case involved considerable heartache. Somalia was a classic failure. While there are many examples to make the point, these three situations, I believe, clearly show the underlying elements that led to achieving national objectives. Rather than discussing the specific cases in detail, we can identify the six essential elements critical to success.

The first involves a clearly perceived national interest. In both Afghanistan and Angola, the Executive Branch and Congress agreed that there was a clear act of Soviet expansion that had to be countered. Soviet troops in Afghanistan and up to 50,000 Cuban troops in Angola provided a substantive basis for a national consensus to support anti-Soviet insurgencies. The Mujahadin and UNITA were fighting our enemy and both received sustained "covert" support with Congressional blessing.

In Central America, conversely, a bitter dispute over the nature and degree of the Soviet or communist threat divided the Executive Branch and Congress and lay at the heart of many operational problems. The lack of Soviet troops or their surrogates was a key factor in the debate concerning the appropriateness of our response. Were communist governments or insurgencies in Central America a legitimate expression of local social inequities or part of a larger anti-American strategy? Ambiguity as to the threat led to uncertainty in the response and significant tension in Executive Branch–Congressional relations.

Clearly, average citizens and their elected representative must perceive sustained engagements in such cases as being in the national interest. Defining the threat and the national interest is likely to become more difficult in the future. First, there is no longer a Soviet enemy to make clear what we are fighting. While internal struggles in Russia may ultimately not produce the democratic, market-oriented society that we hope to see, it seems unlikely that Russia will engage in the global expansionism of the Soviet Union, which led to such situations as Afghanistan and Angola and peripherally to Central America. Thus, the likelihood of having a clearly defined low intensity conflict driven by a global geopolitical confrontation seems unlikely. This will make developing strategy and appropriate responses more uncertain. Whatever potential engagement is under consideration, however, decision makers had best be certain that the American public, the Congress, and the media understand the purposes of American power, the nature of the threat, and agree substantially on the need for engagement in particular situations.

Clearly defined purpose is not the end of the story. Another critical element in sustaining our efforts is to make sure that we are working with legitimate partners. In Afghanistan's case, for example, an overwhelming majority of Afghans wished to see the Soviets withdraw and their puppet government fall. They supported the resistance. Likewise, in Angola, there was no doubt that Jonas Savimbi was an effective and charismatic leader of the Ovambo people. Similarly, success or failure of our various efforts in Central America depended heavily on the perceived legitimacy of the governments or insurgencies that we supported. Support for the government of El Salvador was sustained; in contrast, support for the Contras in Nicaragua was limited and equivocal. Finding situations in the future with a convergence in our interests and local partners, however, will not be easy.

During the Soviet occupation of Afghanistan, it is worth admitting with candor, we occasionally had to deal with partners whose virtues were often hard to find. Shortcomings were overlooked as part of the global confrontation with the Soviets. The cause, however, was unambiguous. That may not hold for the future, and it seems likely that the American public will hold the national leadership to a higher standard, expecting the United States to risk lives only where local partners reflect many of the values we hold dear. It is worth remembering that during the celebration of the success of DESERT STORM the American media and the public asked very direct questions about the wisdom of restoring Kuwait's ruling family to power. Although the specifics of the test may be somewhat unclear and the circumstances not always accommodating, I am convinced that future local partners will have to pass a relatively severe litmus test.

The third consideration in sustaining effective involvement is to ensure the support of regional allies. In most cases, before the issue of U.S. military intervention must be decided, low-intensity situations have festered for some time. Issues such as the procurement of weapons of mass destruction, active involvement in narcotics production and trafficking, and threats to vital economic interests do not develop overnight. Thus the level of concern in the "neighborhood" should be relatively easy to discern. Further, international and regional organizations, such as the United Nations, the Organization of American States, or the Organization of African Unity, should already have offered some level of support. Equally important is some degree of assurance that immediate geographic neighbors will also support our efforts or at least will not seek to undermine them. To a considerable degree, the success of our efforts in Afghanistan and Angola depended on the support of regional allies such as Pakistan, Saudi Arabia, and South Africa. For different reasons, our regional allies had a heavy commitment, coincident with our own, to see our policies succeed. These regional allies provided not only a geographic base but also military and diplomatic support. Had we enjoyed such broad support in Central America, it would have been immensely easier to sustain and support our policies. Without such support it will be difficult in the future to bear or justify an extended effort.

The next essential element in the mix of things needed to underwrite effective action is simplicity of management and effective unity of effort. Our efforts in Afghanistan and Angola benefited from the fact that we managed the effort through a single agency, The Central Intelligence Agency. In part we were able to do this because we were supporting insurgencies and did not have to engage the full panoply of host-nation support that accompanies support efforts to governments, as in El Salvador. In such cases, it becomes difficult to provide effective management or coordination. While limiting agency involvement is not always feasible, too often we drift into situations and allow management of them to play catch up. We cannot afford to be so offhand in the future. Selecting and supporting regional allies, working with legitimate local partners, and defining success all presume an Executive Branch management structure capable of integrating all U.S. government assets. As noted above, this has so far eluded the Executive Branch, the national drug war being a case in point. Although we are adept at integrating large-scale efforts during a crisis, we seem constitutionally unable to provide a corresponding degree of purposeful coordination in small-scale, protracted environments. The future and the American public are likely to be less forgiving of continuing inadequacies on this point.

The deployment of sophisticated American weapons to Afghanistan, to counter Soviet weaponry, demonstrated the value of understanding the nature of the situation and bringing the right equipment to the game. Our ability to support UNITA against conventional Soviet weaponry, at a level appropriate to the environment, makes the same point. The fifth element we must have in place before we commit ourselves in the future, then, is to identify the nature and type of weapons systems that will help to ensure success. Weapons requirements can be analyzed carefully before an engagement. It should be possible to define these requirements not only for our troops but also for our allies and to identify appropriate training and support requirements. Over the years of the Cold War, the Department of Defense developed sophisticated methodologies for designing, testing, and acquiring systems to meet our major war needs. DESERT STORM proved decisively how well that system worked. We need a similar effort, however, to give us the same degree of sophistication in responding to environments short of major war. In addition, we need the intelligence gathering and analytical capabilities to ensure that our efforts are informed and focused. Along with many other areas, however, our intelligence needs in a future, uncertain world have not received due attention and existing capabilities have been allowed to decline.

Finally, and perhaps most important, we need to be able to define what success looks like. The days of delimiting it as military or political victory against a Soviet surrogate or keeping some ally in power are over. The American public expects major U.S. involvement overseas, especially if it occasions the use of military force, to leave the world a better place. A classic illustration of the problems encountered when the objectives are murky came in the wake of JUST CAUSE. While the immediate objective was to remove General Manuel Noriega, it immediately became clear that, having achieved this, there was much more that had to be done in order to restore Panama as a responsible member of the international community. It did not take long for the press and the public to begin asking whether our intervention had made things better than before. If there is as much drug trafficking and money laundering today as there was under Noriega, then what did we achieve? Similarly, if the Royal Family in Kuwait continues to resist moves toward democracy, it will call into question the success of our effort to expel Saddam Hussein. Values as well as interest must be a component in our calculations about intervention. Winning militarily will not suffice if the follow through does not resonant with American values of equity and democracy. Our calculus for involvement, then, must win the hearts and minds of the American people if they are to continue to support foreign involvement and hefty military budgets.

While not exhaustive, these are the key elements that must guide thinking about how, where, and when we use American's strength overseas. In today's environment, there are many demands on our moral and physical resources. These are likely to grow, and they will demand our best judgment and our patience as we work in the fog of incomplete information, the shifting sands of public perception, and the swamp of interagency management. Without the Soviet threat, it will be more difficult in the future to justify or sustain U.S. involvement overseas. Success depends upon understanding the world we face and what criteria we must use to devise credible and effective responses to meet the challenges that confront us.

Looking to the Future

Looking forward requires a brief examination of the Clinton Administration's foray into low intensity conflict. The first major initiative of the Administration in this area, Somalia, was a textbook catastrophe. It involved virtually every classic failure, including mission creep, an awkward and dysfunctional command structure, and objectives that were misunderstood, unclear, and ultimately unachievable. It gives the author no pleasure whatsoever to point out that this result was forecast in the *Gray Area Phenomena*.

The one ray of hope that we can take away from Somalia is that reality began to overtake ideology in at least some quarters of the administration. Some decision makers recognized that working under a UN structure raised a range of difficulties that need more careful consideration; that our effort required an overall "project coordinator" with the power and authority to direct the effort; and that goals needed to be defined and articulated to the American public before American lives were put at risk. It needed consistent leadership that could prevent the expansion of the mission. These improvements could be seen in the Haiti operation, at least in terms of the employment of military force.

Whatever one might say about the wisdom of that effort, the military operation to restore Aristid was a good example of a well-coordinated projection of national power, including effective diplomacy and the use of military force. Sadly, the long-term results in Haiti will probably not justify the rhetoric that preceded the intervention. The recent elections did not go well and the signs are that there has been no fundamental change in the basis of power or the nature of political relationships despite US efforts. Attracting investment and restructuring the economy will prove difficult, especially if violence and instability return. The level of long-term American commitment may be adequate to stem the flow of refugees but clearly not adequate to move Haiti onto a track toward sound economic development or political maturity. While the military aspects of the mission meet the requirements outlined in this and subsequent chapters, the political aspects of the effort remain vague and largely unachievable. Haiti, however, is not the only dubious engagement looming.

As this book goes to press, the prospect of intervention in Bosnia has appeared large on the horizon. There is no one who has not and cannot be moved by the horrible scenes brought home to us on the evening news of the atrocities committed in that unfortunate corner of the world. However moving the images have been, virtually every principle enunciated by this author and a number of his colleagues argues against any active military engagement. The amazing, convoluted drift which has lead to our current position illustrates all of our fundamental concerns.

There is no clearly defined US national interest which the President has been able to articulate to the satisfaction of the Congress or the public. Agreement among local partners or international agencies is non-existent or evanescent. Even if these existed, the prospects for an intervention achieving any desirable outcome in any reasonable time frame are remote at best. The resources, whether in materiel or will, to sustain the type of long-term commitment that intervention will create are lacking. The ability of the local actors to escalate the conflict and level of pain is beyond control or influence, advocates of strategic or precision bombing to the contrary. Beyond some vague notion of ending the present violence there is no clearly outlined end state that the intervention is planning for and no clear idea what level of intervention is required to deliver such an end state. In short, put sadly and crudely, if for some reason this Administration chooses to pursue an active military involvement in this conflict, it will be primarily because television image-making has overcome its ability to run a national foreign policy based on coherent principles. The prospects for success in such a situation are less than encouraging.

That said, there is a requirement for an active, pragmatist involvement in the Balkans. The amazing tenacity of the various people of the region to nurture hatred over centuries and find opportunity to slaughter each other with the slightest excuse is truly remarkable and should give anyone contemplating intervention pause. But, it would be foolish to ignore this European tinder box. Thus, a strategy should be crafted to isolate and contain the current conflict. Efforts between US and European powers to assist in the resolution of ethnic clashes in populations in Macedonia, Albania, and other countries where the level of violence has not escalated beyond hope should be pursued. Steps should be taken now to make sure that the military force is in place and capable of response if the actors in Serbia should seek to extend the conflict beyond the borders of the former Yugoslavia. Provisions need to be made for the trial of war criminals. Relief efforts to aid refugees need to be continued in truly safe areas. But, not until the local combatants have reached a stage where they are willing to talk to one another will it be possible for outside forces to once again act as peacemakers.

So we come to the end of this chapter with a road map for the future based on our travels of the past. As the other chapters in this volume argue, the murky and confusing world we face, with competing pressures for us to intervene, or not intervene — to do more or do less, to save lives or stay home — can be sorted out and decisions rationally made if we stick to the basics.

We must meet the three basic component tests:

1. Do we have a coherent theory of global involvement in this new world?
2. Can we develop and deploy weapons systems and national tools of power that are smarter and more sophisticated to counter new threats?
3. Can we rethink and reorganize the Executive Branch to effectively merge the diverse assets required to prevail in low intensity conflicts and create the necessary unity of effort?

If we can meet these big tests, we must take up six key considerations before committing to any specific engagement:

1. Do we really have a national interest?
2. Do we have regional allies?
3. Do we have the appropriate weapons systems and national tools of power? Including adequate intelligence capabilities to provide an accurate picture?
4. Do we have a legitimate partner?
5. Do we have a management structure and people to run the effort?
6. Do we have a realistic and achievable definition of success and thus an end state in mind compatible with capabilities?

In political affairs, no yardstick can be applied dogmatically, but without some means to take the measure of the problems we face and our ability to respond, we risk failure and we put lives at risk without clear purpose or demonstrable results. This is a failure of leadership. In the present uncertain environment, where we have not direct threat such as the Soviet Union to give our policies the immediacy they once had, we cannot afford to squander our resources in dubious battle. Decisions to act or not to act are always hard and involve unwelcome consequences, but to act without a sense of purpose or due regard to interests and capabilities is to act unwisely. We do not have the luxury.

PART ONE

The First Pillar of Success in Contemporary Conflict: A Theory of Engagement to Deal with the New World Disorder

3

Confronting the New World Disorder: A Legitimate Governance Theory of Engagement

Max G. Manwaring and Ambassador Edwin G. Corr

With the ending of the Cold War, many new challenges at home and abroad are emerging that demand attention and action at a time when it seems unclear what should be done. The confusion in the current environment stems in part from the quixotic hope that the disappearance of the Soviet Union has automatically moved the world from war to peace. It did not. The world changed in unexpected ways, and the promise of a peace dividend degenerated into the "new world disorder." The contemporary chaotic strategic environment reflects a lack of legitimate governance in many parts of the world, and the instability and ambiguous threats that thrive under those conditions. The new world disorder and the confusion with regard to it are the product of a radically changed international environment and the lack of a central strategy to deal with it.

Thus, this chapter will outline a new core to U.S. security policy that addresses the changed central strategic problem. In developing a strategy to deal with the instabilities and threats generated by a lack of legitimate governance, we will do essentially what George Kennan did in his famous Mr. "X" article. He sketched the problems of the post–World War II strategic environment and proposed the containment theory of engagement to manage that environment and the Soviet threat.[1] We will outline the verities and implications of the contemporary security environment; analyze the threat and the resulting challenge and tasks; and propose a follow-on theory of engagement.

The genius of Kennan's theory of engagement is that it combined the realism of power politics with the pragmatism of U.S. idealism. It went beyond the defensive idea of containment in the struggle against Soviet dictatorship and hegemony and promoted the proactive concepts of democracy and freedom "which must eventually find their outlet in either the break-up or the gradual mellowing of Soviet power."[2]

To ensure that America's and the world's embrace of freedom and democracy is sustained and enhanced following the victory over communism, we move forward to a "legitimate governance" theory of engagement. Legitimate governance is defined as governance that derives its just powers from the governed and generates a viable political competence that can and will manage, coordinate, and sustain security, and political, economic, and social development. Legitimate governance is inherently stable because it has the political competence and societal support to adequately manage internal change and conflict affecting collective and individual well-being. As a result, legitimate governance is not just a relic of U.S. democratic idealism. Like Kennan's theory of engagement, the legitimate governance theory is also a very pragmatic foundation for national and international stability and well-being in the international security arena.

This theory is drawn from observation of and empirical research on the many Third World conflicts and small wars that have occurred over the past five decades.[3] It addresses the core governance problem that is prevalent in much of the world and the resultant instabilities that generate the multidimensional and complex threats facing the international community now and in the future. Like the containment theory, this theory is intended to help U.S. policy- makers and the American public understand the nature of the current security environment and to provide the basis for focused and coherent action when responding to specific threats to U.S. interests.

Verities and Implications of the Contemporary Security Environment

The primary verities and implications of the new world disorder are clear. First, the world has seen and will continue to see a wide range of ambiguous and uncomfortable threats in the shadow area between war and peace. These threats—manifest by transnational organized crime, corruption, terrorism, warlordism, insurgency, civil war, regional wars, humanitarian problems such as large scale refugee flows and famine, and the horrors of ethnic cleansing—are the consequences of root cause pressures and problems perpetrated and/or exploited by a variety of internal and international political actors. What these threats have in common is that they are generated and complicated by misguided, corrupt, insensitive, and/or incompetent governance.

Second, acting separately and together, the threats arising out of a lack of legitimate governance increasingly undermine the capability of governments to govern, to provide meaningful development, and to provide adequate and acceptable security measures. These instabilities generate further disorder, violent internal conflicts that resist easy solution, and mushrooming demands by ethnic and regional groups for political autonomy. Success in dealing with these challenges or threats is not determined exclusively or primarily by the results of police or military actions. Instead, success in dealing with these instability problems depends on a protracted, multistage use of political, economic, and moral as well as physical efforts to gain influence over or control of the society and its political system. In short, success depends on the ability to achieve political competence and legitimacy.

Third, in this environment of "unstable peace," legitimacy issues— aggravated by religious, ethnic, racial, ideological, and financial profit motivations and coupled with easy access to armaments and external state and non-state support—translate themselves into constant, subtle and not-so-subtle struggles for power that dominate life in many countries and regions today. These kinds of destabilized situations become an opportunity for exploitation by virtually any political actor—large or small, internal or external, national or transnational, or conventional or unconventional. In this context, legal national boundaries have little or no meaning. Ultimately, the spillover effects of national and regional instabilities place demands on the international community, if not to solve the problems, at least to harbor the victims.

Fourth, in addition to its traditional interests in the current international security arena, the United States has vital interests in the internal social, economic, and political well-being in a number of countries and regions. When what mattered most were military bases, preserving access to sea lanes of communication, choke points, and raw materials, and denying those assets to the Soviet Union or its surrogates, the United States could generally ignore internal conditions in other countries. If, however, the United States is also seriously concerned about the need for a nonhostile disposition toward the United States, the capacity to buy U.S. products, the continued development of democratic and free market institutions and human rights, and cooperation on shared problems like illegal drugs, the environment, and refugees—then the United States must concern itself with the nontraditional internal causal legitimate governance aspects of contemporary national and regional instability.

Fifth, the days of delineating a successful strategic end-state as simple short term self-protection or short-term compassion for a human problem are over. The American public expects U.S. efforts, especially if they involve the expenditure of large amounts of tax revenue and/or the expenditure of even a few American lives, to make the world a better place. Thus, U.S. policymakers have an obligation to go beyond simple self-protection or compassion and to advocate and defend the principles for which America stands. To do this they must combine realism, pragmatism, and idealism to secure "an organized and effectively enforced system of general international peace."[4] In these terms, it is necessary to understand that contemporary conflict—at whatever level—is essentially a sociopolitical matter. It is also necessary to rethink ways, means, and measures of effectiveness to counter international instability caused by the lack of legitimate governance.

Sixth, the formulation of foreign policy and military management must take place within a conceptual framework. A paradigm, or theory of engagement, is either developed and implemented by policymakers in a relatively rational way and for well-accepted ends or is thrust upon them by a variety of internal and external forces in an ad hoc crisis reaction manner and for questionable short term ends. In the past, the United States worked hard to develop coherent theories of engagement. A great deal of intellectual energy, national debate and writing, to say nothing of war gaming, went into the question of how and under what circumstances the United States could contain the Soviet Union. Now, the United States must seek to understand a new central strategic problem and be able to deal with more than television images and the symptoms of international instability.

Finally, this discussion leads us back to where we began—to the core strategic problem of legitimate governance in the post–Cold War world that foreign policy and military management must address. To be sure, nuclear proliferation, Russia, Germany, China, ethnic and irredentist conflicts, human starvation, refugee flows, and trade wars are all serious problems and potential threats. Underlying all these issues, however, is the core problem of failed or failing states and "wars of national debilitation, a steady run of uncivil wars sundering fragile but functioning nation-states and gnawing at the well-being of stable nations."[5]

The implacable challenge in pursuing a legitimate governance theory of engagement is one of "accepting the responsibilities of moral and political leadership that history plainly intended (the American people) to bear."[6] The general task is to apply the theory on the basis of a realistic calculation of threats, interests, and resources.

The Threat(s)

The first step in developing an appropriate response to the threats inherent in the current unstable international security environment is to recognize the basic elements that define the basic threat and dictate the response. An examination of these defining characteristics provides a beginning point from which to examine the threat. The second step is to recognize that there is no longer a single monolithic threat, such as Soviet expansion, to contain. The contemporary threat situation is complex and multidimensional. The third step is to elaborate the task required to meet the threat and the challenge associated with it. The strategic vision that results from implementing these three steps provides the basis for success in dealing with the contemporary uncomfortable international security situation.

The Basic Elements That Define the Threat and Dictate Response

The first defining element that dictates response is the relationship of legitimate governance to stability and instability. Legitimate governance is based on the moral right of a government to govern—and the ability of a government to govern morally. Popular perceptions of corruption, disenfranchisement, poverty, and lack of upward social mobility tend to limit the right, and ability, of a regime to conduct the business of state. Until and unless the major institutions and a substantial proportion of the population feel that their government deals with these and other issues of political, economic, and social injustice fairly and effectively, the potential for nascent or established internal or external enemies to destabilize and subvert the government is considerable.

The second element involves the role that economic development plays in ensuring security and stability. In the present international dialogue, security is largely defined in terms of ensuring stability through political, economic, and social development. The reality of the security requirement also includes modernizing and professionalizing for multidimensional conflict on a number of fronts ranging from physical combat with an "enemy" military or paramilitary force, to the building and protection of infrastructure, to the implementation of an all-out reform program. Thus, economic development alone is not sufficient for stability and security. The economic development requirement equates to a holistic national capability-building program that can meet society's perceived needs. Finally, these policies and programs must be accomplished at a pace and in a manner that is culturally acceptable. Integrated policies and programs that further the security and stability goal provide the bases for internal order and progress.

The third element that helps define the threat and appropriate response to it is the relationship between legitimacy and the political competence. Political competence generates the capability to effectively manage, coordinate, and sustain political, economic, and social development. This capability enables leaders to strengthen national institutions and create a purpose and will the citizenry can support. The degree to which this political objective is achieved is dependent on the development of a foundation of legitimacy. Political competence, based on a foundation of legitimacy, will determine the level of influence that a nation can exert abroad and will define, more than anything else, the ability to maintain and enhance its internal security and well-being.

In sum, legitimate governance or the lack of legitimate governance is the basis for stability or instability. Threats to a nation and to the international community grow out of instability. As a result, the contemporary threat is defined in three highly interrelated parts. The first concerns the inability of the state to guarantee internal order and progress. The second concerns the inability of the state to protect and enhance its interests in an increasingly aggressive world. National development provides the only effective counter to both of these types of threat. There is a third part as well. Experience indicates that the inability of the state to develop the political competence and will to recognize and deal effectively with the first two types of threat is a threat in itself.

There are two additional threat elements that U.S. policymakers must address when considering the possibility of intervention or involvement to help other countries achieve security and stability. First, experience shows that the long-term commitment of human, financial, and other resources can be staggering. The most important thing that decision makers must do in determining whether or not to help a vulnerable or failing state is to define the political end-state and calculate the long-term costs required to achieve it. Overextension in one situation, or in several, is as much a threat as any other that can be listed.

Second, experience also demonstrates that ignoring an instability problem or only providing short-term and cosmetic solutions to a related threat can be debilitating. Short-term and cosmetic solutions are just that—short-term and cosmetic. Because instability in one place can cause instabilities elsewhere, related threats can ultimately become directly menacing to the United States. Again, failure to recognize and deal with a threat in its early stages is a threat in itself.

The Complex and Multidimensional Threat Situation

Analysis of the problems of governance and stability in the current international security arena takes us beyond traditional international relations and the need to monitor bilateral agreements. It even carries us beyond the requirement to provide humanitarian or refugee assistance in cases of human misery and need; to protect a people from another group of people or from a government; to compel one or more parties to a conflict to cease human rights violations and other morally unacceptable activities; or to repel aggression. Clearly, these problems constitute possible or probable threats and must be dealt with immediately and effectively, but they are only manifestations or symptoms of something more fundamental.

Thus, threats must be understood and dealt with on three complex levels. Moreover, the logical conclusion of the analysis of the problems of governance and stability takes us to the underlying multidimensional causes of instability and the lack of governmental capacity. This takes us to the challenge of national capability-building. Finally, the unilateral or multilateral activities to strengthen weak or failing nation-states must be clarified.

Threat Levels. It is helpful to think of the consequences of instability—such as terrorism, insurgency, ethnic cleansing, criminal anarchy, international organized crime, militant environmentalism, warlordism, and regional "teacup" wars—as *third- level threats* to national and international security. Root causes—such as environmental degradation, underdevelopment, and poverty—must be recognized as *second-level threats* to security and stability. The inability or unwillingness of governments to develop long term, multidimensional, and morally acceptable means to maintain and enhance national well-being must be understood as the most fundamental *first-level threat.*

Strategic planners and decisionmakers must contemplate all three levels of threat in dealing with a national or international security matter. To the extent that all three levels are strongly present in any given stability strategy, they favor success. To the extent that they are generally weak, or only one or two are strongly present in a strategy implementation process, they do not favor success.

For example, once an illegal internal enemy—such as Peru's *Sendero Luminoso,* Sierra Leone's armed pillagers, or Southeast Asia's narcotics organizations—becomes firmly established, first-level reform and development efforts aimed at second-level root causes on the part of a targeted government may be insufficient to neutralize the organization that is generating a third-level threat. The illegal challenger organization will finally be defeated only by a superior organization and a political-economic-moral-military strategy designed to neutralize or eliminate it. The sum of the parts of a desired countereffort to deal with a third-level threat equals not only a certain capability to coordinate political, economic, psychological, and moral objectives on the first and second levels, but also to exert effective deadly force at the third level.

Capability-Building. The international security dialogue focuses on the problem of national development. The national development definition of national security is ultimately dependent on eradicating the root causes of instability. Underdevelopment and the resultant individual and collective poverty (i.e., root causes of instability) are being recognized as the world's most overwhelming threats. On the positive side of this issue, national capability-building implies long term multilevel and multilateral political, socioeconomic, and security activities that seek to legitimize and strengthen the institutions and infrastructure of a nation-state to preclude serious instability or to avoid a relapse into instability. On the negative side of this problem, the lack of a holistic national capability building program implies all of the instabilities and threats associated with the corrosion of the fabric of society.

Ultimately, however, the threat would come from the highest echelons of government failing to recognize and deal with the dangers that deficiencies in national political, economic, and security capabilities pose to a society and its neighbors. As a consequence, the lack of legitimate political competence is potentially the greatest single threat to national and international security, stability, and well-being.

For example, authoritarian governments insensitive to social and political change—such as those of the former Soviet Union, Eastern Europe, and elsewhere in Africa, Asia, and Latin America—have supported unidimensional economic growth policies and programs over the past 50 years. These policies and programs have produced environmental degradation, increased poverty, backwardness, and social violence. It appears that opinion leaders and decisionmakers have done little more than watch, pontificate, and improve their personal fortunes while ecosystems, infrastructure, and stability are slowly destroyed, and hundreds and tens of thousands of innocents are displaced or die.

Unilateral or Multilateral Activities to Strengthen Weak States. Unfortunately, a vulnerable or failing government is not likely to have the multilevel and multidimensional capabilities that are required for survival in the new world disorder. If it had the implied capabilities, it probably would not be threatened. If it is to survive, the threatened regime must ultimately develop the political competence to legitimize and strengthen itself and its security organizations.

In the short term, however, a vulnerable government will likely require outside help in developing these capabilities. Probably the best an outside power or coalition of powers—such as the United States or the United Nations—can do is to help establish a temporary level of security that might allow the *guided* development of the ethical and professional underpinnings necessary for the promulgation of a holistic strategy of governmental legitimization and strengthening.

In the long term, a threatened government cannot depend on an outside power or coalition of powers to do these things for it. No group or force can legislate or decree these qualities for itself, but it can develop, sustain, and enhance them by its actions over time. Legitimization and internal stability derive from popular and institutional perceptions that authority is genuine and effective and uses morally correct means for reasonable and fair purposes. The need for a foundation of legitimacy within the concept of governance and stability is a prime lesson for vulnerable regimes and their international allies in the coming decades.

Conclusion. Separately and together the complex and multidimensional threats resulting from a lack of legitimate and strong governmental institutions generate a vicious downward spiral that manifests itself in disparate activities in which the lowest common denominator is instability. Thus, national and international security will depend not so much on conventional military or police law enforcement activities as on international and domestic policies and strategies that provide for political competence, economic progress and social justice, and personal and national security (i.e., legitimate governance).

The Challenge and Tasks Required to Meet the Threat(s)

The challenge of the post–Cold War era is to come to terms with the fact that contemporary security—at whatever level—is a major political-economic-social-psychological-moral problem. In this connection, we postulate that the lack of legitimate governance constitutes the central strategic problem in the contemporary international security environment, and that the primary center of gravity is the people of a country. People are the basic source of physical, psychological, and moral strength that is the hub of all power and movement on which virtually everything in the contemporary international environment depends.

In short, the challenge is to change perspectives and adopt a populace-oriented model that relates as much to the root causes as to the consequences of instability.

The task, then, becomes one of focusing attention on the long term political as well as the short term military outcome of any given contemporary uncomfortable or ambiguous conflict situation. In every case, this task would be to ensure that every policy, program, and action (political, economic, opinion-making, and security) contribute directly to the maintenance, or enhancement, of legitimate governance. Experience clearly shows that if internal and externally supported defense, development, or other security efforts do not help to achieve that political end-state, they will be irrelevant or even counterproductive.

Summary

In those situations in which U.S. interests require involvement or intervention, it is necessary to understand that the essence of any given contemporary threat situation relies heavily on grievances such as political, economic, and social discrimination as the means through which a vulnerable or failing political actor or regime is attacked. This is the fundamental nature of the threat from virtually any illegal challenger, and it is there that any response must begin. In this connection, there is an urgent need to adopt a new political mentality capable of visualizing interrelated security, socioeconomic, and political competence and legitimacy factors and of generating new and flexible methods of national and international coordination and teamwork to achieve legitimate governance in threatened states.

A Legitimate Governance Theory of Engagement

In the post-cold war strategic environment, a legitimate governance theory of engagement should be a guide to U.S. and allied actions. The level of commitment, resources, and duration of involvement in applying the paradigm should, of course, be based on the type and persistence of the threat, the desired political end-state, and the ability to disengage if guidelines or milestones are not met.

Legitimate governance is more than de facto or de jure legitimacy. Legitimate governance concerns the manner of governing rather than the fact of governing or international recognition that a given legal entity represents a nation-state. Legitimate governance is defined as governance that generates a viable political competence that can and will effectively manage, coordinate, and sustain security, and political, economic, and social development.

A foundation of legitimacy and political competence are the key components of legitimate governance. The political competence component is derived from a foundation of moral legitimacy. Moral legitimacy is based on a political architecture in which that government derives its just powers from the governed, and it is absolutely essential to governmental cohesion, national development, security, and thus, stability. Thus, legitimate governance is the basis for peace, stability, and well-being for an individual country and for its neighbors. In these terms, legitimate governance is not a simple enlargement of American democracy; it is a pragmatic foundation for successful foreign policy and strategy in the current international security environment.

In this context, it is important that we do three things. First, we must sketch the stability equation—emphasizing the political competence component; second, outline the five key indicators constituting the essential architecture for a foundation of moral legitimacy; and third, make a final clarifying comment with regard to the application of the legitimate governance paradigm.

The Stability Equation

The fulfillment of a holistic legitimate governance and stability imperative consists of three principal elements that are necessary to strengthen government through substantive, coordinated improvement in the civil and military bureaucracies, the economy, and the society. These elements constitute a basis for understanding a holistic legitimate governance theory of engagement and a realistic and pragmatic approach to stability.

The three elements of a general legitimate governance-stability equation (i.e., S) that must be developed are: first, the military-police capability (i.e., M) to provide an acceptable level of internal and external security; second, the economic ability (i.e., E) to generate real security and socioeconomic development; and third, the political competence (i.e., PC) to develop a type of governance to which a people can relate and support. It is heuristically valuable to portray the relationships among these three elements in a mathematical formula: $S = (M + E) \times PC$.

The political competence component of the equation is so critical that it merits a multiplier in our proposed equation. The use of the multiplier means that the sum of the whole can be substantially altered by the elements that constitute national political competence. The ultimate value of the economic and security elements of the equation can be reduced to nothing or nearly nothing if the political competence component is absent or weak— for example, $100 \times 0 = 0$.

The security (i.e., M) and the socioeconomic (i.e., E) components of the legitimate governance-stability equation are generally well understood. As an example, the Brazilian security dialogue has been attempting to define national well-being in terms of stability and economic development since the early 1960s.[7] Clearly, however, in Brazil and elsewhere, the key political competence (PC) component is not as well understood, developed, and operationalized as the other two components.

Brazilians and many others, including U.S. decisionmakers, have emphasized economic development and military security under the assumption that social and political development would automatically follow. That has not happened. Two different trends appear to dominate the period since the ending of the Cold War. First, many countries—including every country east of the former iron curtain—were brought to the point of economic collapse by corrupt and incompetent political leadership. Second, economic development in many countries—such as China—has created a very disruptive political reform dynamic of its own. Governments that have not been responsive to that force find themselves in "a crisis of governance," growing social violence, anarchy, and even the process of being swept away. Thus, the development of political competence upon a foundation of moral legitimacy is a challenge that must be met—the sooner the better.

The Essential Architecture for a Foundation of Moral Legitimacy

For a fragile or vulnerable government, the highest priority must be legitimizing and strengthening the state. The data show that there are five salient conditional indicators (i.e., independent variables) of moral legitimacy that must be implemented by virtually any political actor facing the nontraditional and traditional threats and internal violence inherent in the current international disequilibrium. These variables are not new in discussions dealing with the idea of legitimacy. They reflect traditional theoretical concepts closely associated with the classical political-philosophical notion of legitimacy.[8]

What is new is, first, the specific combination of variables considered to be the most powerful indicators of legitimacy. Second, the interdependence of these variables has not often been stressed. Third, the interdependence of the legitimacy dimension with the other principal components of the general legitimate governance-stability paradigm outlined above has not been stressed. Fourth, these variables can be used as objective measures of effectiveness at the macro level for winning or losing in the contemporary conflict arena. Finally, and perhaps most importantly, this model was not conceived a priori. It was developed empirically and warrants some confidence that the findings are universal and explain much of the reality of the contemporary security environment.[9]

The five variables that define the legitimizing and strengthening of the state are: free, fair, and frequent *selection* of leaders; the level of participation in or acceptance of the political process; the level of corruption; the level of political, economic, and social development; and the level of regime acceptance by major social institutions.

The first indicator of legitimacy is associated with the philosophical concept of popular sovereignty. It is that of free, fair (e.g., open), and frequent selection of leaders. In this context, free election or selection of leaders means the absence of corruption in the process that is used. Free and fair selection of leaders also means that the process used must be culturally understood and acceptable to the people involved. This universal requirement for the selection of leaders is a strong indicator—and measure—of governmental moral legitimacy.

The second component and indicator of legitimacy is that of individual participation in the political process, or individual support of the political process. This variable is also associated with the concept of popular sovereignty. Although the periodic free and fair selection or election of leaders is an important element in defining moral legitimacy, it should not be considered by itself as a sufficient indicator. Uncoerced popular participation in or acceptance of the political process is another key to a foundation of moral legitimacy for any given method of governance. Participation or acceptance subsumes the subsequent manifest support of the results of that process— and the government—by a large majority of the governed. Thus, a high level of popular support for the political process is also a strong indicator—and measure—of government legitimacy.

Third, the level of corruption of the political, economic, social, and security organs of a nation-state is closely related to the degree of strength or weakness of the state governmental apparatus. Moreover, corruption can be a major agent for destabilization. The corruption phenomenon has a crucial impact on a regime's ability to perform its functions fairly and equitably. Experience demonstrates that the necessity of meeting a specific client's needs, and the intensity of the client's expectations and demands, mitigates against legitimate governance—and against any allegiance to the notion of the public good or consent of the governed. As such, the level of corruption is another important indicator—and measure—of stability and moral legitimacy.

The fourth significant component of moral legitimacy is that of security and political, economic, and social development. The reasons are straightforward. These elements are the bases for the internal strengthening of the state and for developing the capability to protect and enhance national interests in an aggressive and disorderly world. A perceived high level of these elements reflects a political system that is responsive to the needs of the governed. Such a system is inherently "just" and stable. Experience shows that the level of a regime's ability to fairly and effectively provide resources for personal security and national development is another indicator—and measure—of stability and legitimacy.

The fifth and last component of moral legitimacy is that of regime acceptance by major social institutions. History illustrates that the problems of a society in transition and becoming more and more complex (i.e., modern) cannot be solved by a central government acting alone. This effort requires the cooperation of business and industry; urban and rural labor unions; educational, religious, and cultural institutions; local, regional, and national bureaucracies; and the security forces. As a consequence, active acceptance or support of the existing and nascent societal institutions of a nation-state is a reinforcing requirement for legitimacy. A high level of such acceptance is the final indicator—and measure—of moral legitimacy.

All these five indicators of legitimacy in the past and in the present focus on the moral right of a regime to govern. That moral right can be perceived as having been originally derived from the governed in the form of a "social contract." The social contract as described in traditional political theory is maintained through the continuing consent of the governed, and through the continuing acceptance of a nation's social institutions. That consent and acceptance are dependent on governments providing or creating propitious conditions for the general well-being in a morally acceptable manner. If a regime—for any reason—breaks that contract, internal and external instability is the likely result.

These key indicators and measures of moral legitimacy are not exhaustive, but they provide the basic architecture for the common actions necessary to assist embattled governments (e.g., fragile democracies) constructively in their struggle to survive and develop. As such, these indicators constitute a strong coherent conceptual framework, or paradigm, from which policy, strategy, and operational efforts might flow. The paradigm is equally valid for policymakers of threatened states as well as policymakers of major powers supporting vulnerable states. The degree to which a political actor effectively manages a balanced mix of these five variables enables political competence. At the same time, these variables provide the basic foundation for the long term, holistic application of proactive political, economic, moral, informational, and security actions necessary for legitimizing, strengthening, and stabilizing a governing regime.

Final Comment on the Legitimate Governance Theory of Engagement

The legitimate governance-stability equation is important to the foreign policy maker for at least three reasons. First, the foundation of moral legitimacy is the engine that generates political competence. Political competence is the most salient factor within the paradigm. Second, the stability equation or paradigm consists of two other factors—a military-security component and a socioeconomic component. Third, to the extent that all three strategic-level factors are strongly present in any given instability scenario and governance problem, they favor success in controlling it. To the extent that they are generally weak, or only one or two are strongly present in any situation, they do not favor success. Thus, the degree to which an international political actor effectively strengthens and skillfully manages a balanced mix of these three factors—security, socioeconomic, and political competence—the better the actor can implement a holistic strategy for sustainable development and security.

The difficult political problem of creating a foundation of legitimacy upon which to build the political competence for legitimate governance cannot be wished away. It is a problem that ultimately must be resolved internally by indigenous leaders. Nevertheless, that effort will often require some outside help. Unless international and national leadership recognizes what is happening at the macro level and reorients its thinking and actions to deal with the legitimacy issue, the problems of stability and security will resolve themselves—there won't be any. Thus, when U.S. interests are threatened by events in a weak and menaced state, the main element of U.S. policy and strategy must go beyond promoting simple "democracy" (i.e., the election of civilian leaders) to guiding supported leaders in a long-term, patient, but firm and vigilant pursuit of moral legitimacy.

Conclusions

The general threat to the international community in the contemporary security environment is the widespread challenge to incumbent governments' moral right to govern. It can be direct, as in the case of the highly organized and politicized *Sendero Luminoso* in Peru, or it can be indirect, as in the case of roving bands of generally apolitical rebels in Sierra Leone. In any case, the basis for this challenge is the growing perception that many governing regimes are not providing or cannot provide the necessary balance among political freedom, economic and social development, and physical security that results in peace, stability, and well-being for the populations of a given societies. In that context, a challenger's proposed explicit or implicit alternative political structure—even if it is that of warlordism or tribalism—represents a different (and to it, a better) way of attaining that balance. Thus, an incumbent government must protect and enhance its own moral legitimacy because that is the primary means by which it might survive. Sun Tzu reminds us that "Those who excel in war first cultivate their own humanity and justice and maintain their laws and institutions. By these (moral) means they make their governments invincible."[10]

Within this context, the main element of policy and strategy for governments not facing massive challenges to legitimacy, such as the United States, must be that of a legitimate governance theory of engagement to deal with general and specific threats outside their frontiers. At the same time, such relatively unchallenged governments would probably do well to assess their own situations in terms of Sun Tzu's advice. This political strategy can be pursued by the careful application of two sets of related variables. The first set provides the basic architecture for a foundation of moral legitimacy upon which political competence rests. The second set of variables centers on the general multidimensional legitimate governance-stability paradigm within which the political competence component is absolutely key. A theory of engagement encompassing these two sets of variables can be applied to confront specific political reform problems, socioeconomic problems, and security problems at specific strategic points when they show signs of encroaching on the interests of a peaceful and stable world.

There is a problem in dealing too literally with the proposed legitimate governance theory of engagement, however. It cannot be applied in every case where television coverage, academic rhetoric, or lobbying activities evoke calls for compassionate action on the part of the United States to alleviate a clearly unhappy or dangerous concern, challenge, or threat. Compassion should underscore but not dictate U.S. foreign policy and military management.

The general rule would be that responsible U.S. policymakers and decisionmakers must carefully calculate gains and losses, and when the case warrants, intervene earlier rather than later. If done earlier, this normally implies the initial and intense use of low-cost diplomatic and civilian resources and military support units to ensure legitimacy and stability. If done later, this normally implies the initial and intense use of high-cost military combat units to respond to a losing situation. Ultimately, however, the only test for involvement—whatever its form and level—is that of self-interest. That is the only morality within the anarchy of world disorder.[11]

In this era of geopolitical change, the United States has the opportunity and responsibility to redirect policy from one that is essentially ad hoc crisis management, and too subject to the whim of television coverage and domestic polling, to one that is basically proactive and positive, and to which the American people can relate. By emphasizing the foundation of legitimacy, along with socioeconomic, security, and political competence factors, this theory of engagement draws on the major currents of U.S. foreign policy making to provide a new paradigm.

The paradigm does two things. First, it provides a conceptual framework by which to cope successfully with the changed and transitional international environment. Second, the adroit application of this paradigm can help make the world—and the United States—a better place in the long term. This theory of engagement is the quintessence of American pragmatism—a marriage of Wilsonian idealism and *realpolitik*.

If the United States is to fulfill the promise that the end of the Cold War offers, there is no choice but to meet the legitimate governance challenge of the new world disorder.

Notes

1. X (George F. Kennan), "The Sources of Soviet Conduct," *Foreign Affairs* (July 1947), pp. 566-82.

2. Ibid., p. 582.

3. This theory of engagement is based on more than 200 interviews conducted by Dr. Max G. Manwaring and Col. Alfred W. Baker, USA. Those interviewed were civilian and military experts directly involved in more than 60 low-intensity conflict situations since World War II. The interviews were conducted in the United States, Europe, the Middle East, and Latin America over the period 1984-1987. More than 150 additional interviews have been conducted by Max G. Manwaring and Ambassador Edwin G. Corr over the period 1987-1995. The basic research was reported in Max G. Manwaring and John T. Fishel, "Insurgency and Counterinsurgency: Toward a New Analytical Approach," *Small Wars and Insurgencies* (Winter 1992), pp. 272-310. The model as a whole is statistically significant at the .001 level, and predicted an impressive 88 percent of the win/loss results of the 69 cases examined. The most salient independent variables defining the legitimacy dimension of the model are derived from a Probit Analysis of the data. The probit coefficient for the legitimacy dimension of the model = 2.56 and is statistically significant at the .025 level.

4. Eugene V. Rostow, *Toward Managed Peace: The National Security Interests of the United States, 1759 to the Present* (New Haven: Yale University Press, 1993), p. 4.

5. Leslie H. Gelb, "Quelling the Teacup Wars," *Foreign Affairs* (November-December 1994), p. 5.

6. Kennan, "Sources of Soviet Conduct."

7. Brazilian national security doctrine provides the basic architecture and the rationale for governmental allocation of values and resources for national well-being. It is a result of work done over the years at the Superior War College (ESG) and synthesized principally by General Golbery da Couta e Silva, General Carlos de Meira Mattos, and others. See as examples: General Golbery da Couta e Silva, *Aspectos Geopoliticos do Brasil* (Rio: Biblioteca do Exercito, 1957); *Planejamento Estrategico* (Rio: Biblioteca do Exercito, 1955); and Carlos de Meira Mattos, "O Pensamento Revolucionario Brasileiro," *Journal do Brasil*, 15 nov 1964, Caderno Especial. More recent work would include: Vice-Almirante Armando Amorim Ferreira Vidigal, "Uma Nova Concepcao Estrategico par o Brasil—Um Debate Necessario," *Revista Maritima Brasileira* (jul-set 1989), pp. 49-71; "Reflexoes Adicionais sobre 'Uma Nova

Concepcao Estrategico para o Brasil—Um Debate Necessario,'" *Revista Maritima Brasileira* (jul-set 1990), pp. 49-61; and Juacy da Silva, "Doutrina e Metodos da ESG: Uma Visao Global," *Revista da Escola Superior da Guerra* (No. 8, 1987), pp. 91-120.

8. As an example, see Larry Diamond, Juan J. Linz, and Seymour Martin Lipset, *Politics in Developing Countries: Comparing Experiences with Democracy* (Boulder, CO: Lynne Rienner Publishers, 1990). Also see: John Locke, *Of Civil Government* (Chicago: Gateway, n.d.); John Stuart Mill, *Considerations on Representative Government* (Chicago: Gateway, 1962); Jean-Jacques Rousseau, *The Social Contract*, trans. by Charles Frankel (New York: Hafner Publishing Company, 1951); George H. Sabine and Thomas L. Thorson, *A History of Political Theory*, 4th ed. (Hinsdale, IL: Dryden Press, 1973); Sheldon S. Wolin, *Politics and Vision: Continuity and Innovation in Western Political Thought* (Boston, MA: Little, Brown and Company, 1960); Leo Strauss and Joseph Cropsey, *History of Political Philosophy*, 2d ed. (Chicago IL: The University of Chicago Press, 1972); and J.L. Talmon, *The Origins of Totalitarian Democracy* (New York: Frederick A. Praeger Publishers, 1960).

9. Manwaring and Fishel, "Insurgency and Counterinsurgency."

10. Sun Tzu, *The Art of War*, trans. Samuel B. Griffith, 1st ed., (London: Oxford University Press, 1963), p. 88.

11. George F. Kennan, "Morality and Foreign Policy," *Foreign Affairs* (Winter 1985/86), pp. 205-218.

4

End-State Planning: The Somalia Case

Bruce B.G. Clarke

War plans cover every aspect of a war, and weave them all into a single operation that must have a single, ultimate objective in which all particular aims are reconciled. No one starts a war—or rather, no one in his right senses ought to do so—without first being clear in his mind what he intends to achieve by that war . . .

—Carl von Clausewitz

U.S. strategies in past Third World conflicts and crises have evolved largely ad hoc and from a set of cumulative constraints. Various U.S. administrations have tended to base their strategies more on what they believed the United States should not or dare not do than on what the situation of a particular conflict or crisis might optimally require.[1] Moreover, in many cases the United States was incapable of attacking the opponent's center of gravity (i.e., the hub of all power and movement upon which everything depends) because of an incorrect understanding of the intensity of the opponent's objectives, or because of the fear of escalating the conflict beyond the limits of political constraints. This problem underlies the broad decision that the United States must make before deciding whether or not to intervene in a given hostile activity related to a dispute between two or more opponents or in a humanitarian situation.

The solution, in part, to this problem is end state planning (ESP). ESP starts from Clausewitz's statement that war is a continuation of politics by other means but with two qualifying arguments that Clausewitz would make. First, military violence is required only when the conditions or changes sought cannot be achieved through political/diplomatic, economic, or informational/ psychological means.[2] Second, ESP advocates the synchronization of all national civil and military tools of power so as to gain the most synergism from the interaction of the variables selected for action.[3] The ESP argument concludes that, if the United States is going to succeed in the future conflicts in which it may become involved, civil and military forces must be structured and employed in ways that are primarily a function of the center of gravity of both sides to the conflict, and there must a clear definition of what success looks like.[4]

There is a calculus suggested by this logic. The idea is to conduct a formal strategic assessment before one engages in a hostile or humanitarian situation and starts down a "slippery slope" that may perhaps lead to some form of disaster. In the end state planning process, considerations such as national interests, the management structure needed to guarantee a unity of effort, primary and secondary objectives, resultant "milestones," and the criticality of timing to the entire process will become apparent. ESP provides the vehicle to address these issues early on and thus to try to preclude problems.

ESP allows one to think logically, in synchronized small phases, about the conditions that one seeks to create. It also allows one to consider opportunities that may arise and obstacles that must be overcome. It is critical to realize which is which and what the implications for ultimate success might be. This chapter will provide a brief discussion of the principal considerations in the ESP assessment process and a detailed hypothetical illustration of end state planning. In conclusion, it touches on concepts that one must consider when thinking about winning and, in turn, what "winning" really is.

Principal Considerations in the ESP Process

End state planning is a logical process that highlights critical interrelationships between the basic political and military guidance about objectives in a particular conflict situation and the various centers of gravity. Each of these pieces of guidance has its own utility but does not go far enough. ESP is a refinement of the strategic planning process that seeks to explain a desired outcome—the end state—in terms of the ultimate strategic political objective of the proposed effort. Decision makers and planners should never lose sight of this bigger picture.

Political and Military Guidance

At the strategic level of planning there are three critical pieces of guidance that need to be developed for any contemporary civil-military endeavor:

- A clear statement by the political authorities of the desired political situation in the post-hostility and settlement phases of a conflict or crisis—a vision of what the area should "look like" following involvement;

- A clear set of secondary diplomatic, economic, and informational objectives that, when achieved, will allow the above primary strategic political vision to become reality; and
- A set of military objectives that will, when achieved, allow the above to happen. [5]

If such guidance is not forthcoming, the planner will have to assume the guidance. Given the criticality of the end state to the process, any leader who fails to provide a vision has made it possible that he or she will lose control of both the process and the end state. In this case, the dispute frequently cycles back to the beginning of the hostility process, and the seeds of the next conflict are sown in the present one.

The vision of the post-hostility environment is critical. "Victory" is achieved when the primary strategic political objective is accomplished. The key is to be able to clearly define both the political conditions and the situation that one envisions existing when both the conflict and the root problem that spawned it are over. The next task is to translate them into a set of national political-military objectives. This is not as easy as it sounds.

One must be able to envision what is necessary to cause an opponent to change political and military objectives. This requires understanding the environment in which the conflict/dispute is occurring, knowing the opponent and his allies, and understanding the opponent's objectives. With such understanding, one may develop a clear idea of what is necessary and what is possible—thus avoiding "mission creep" and "making the conflict into something that it is not," and ensuring success.[6]

If the first two elements of guidance are forthcoming, the end state planner can use that guidance and the variables it introduces as a starting point for determining the various diplomatic, economic, social, psychological, and security objectives and starting the end state planning process. It may become obvious from the guidance what the variables are, or at least some of them. Conversely, as the planner fleshes out the details of the end state, it should become obvious what the operational variables are. In this situation the planner can then start working from where he is toward the end state and simultaneously work backward from the end state to the present. Additionally, if, during the war gaming that occurs during the planning process, the planner discovers a "new" variable, he or she can add it to the ESP matrix and revise the plan.

While working from the two ends (i.e., the desired end state and the present), the planner should see what possible critical events will preclude progress if nothing is done. These critical nodes then become items of focus. In some cases they may in fact be one's own center(s) of gravity.[7] They also may define decision points. The difference will be a function of their criticality. At these points ESP branches and sequels can be developed that seek to attack successfully the opponent's center of gravity and/or defend one's own. Such branches and sequels must eventually return to the end state. Throughout the plan and each of its branches and sequels, there is a critical set of actions that must be taken or must occur to allow the end state to be achieved. It is critical that these actions be recognized and dealt with.

Centers of Gravity

Clausewitz suggests that by attacking what he calls the center of gravity, one can more quickly overcome the opponent's will to resist. He counsels that:

> . . . one must keep the dominant characteristics of both belligerents in mind. Out of these characteristics a certain center of gravity develops, the hub of all power and movement, upon which everything depends. That is the point against which all our energies should be directed....For Alexander, Gustavus Adolphus, Charles XII, and Frederick the Great, the center of gravity was their army....Among alliances, it lies in the community of interest, and in popular uprisings it is the personalities of the leaders and public opinion. It is against these that our energies should be directed. [8]

The one glaring omission from most strategic planning processes is any discussion of protecting one's own center of gravity. War, or any other type of activity related to a dispute over end states between two or more sophisticated opponents, will have both sides attempting to defend their own center(s) of gravity while attacking the opponent's. It is in this dialectic of will that a victor will emerge. The side that has correctly analyzed itself and its opponent, determined the center of gravity of both, and successfully attacked the opponent's center of gravity while defending its own will come out ahead. This side will achieve its political objectives; the other side will be forced to change its objectives to accommodate the winner. That is what "winning" is—getting the losing side to change its political objectives to accommodate the winner's.

When discussing centers of gravity one should also discuss culminating points, quit points, and the synchronization process. There should be a direct link between the center of gravity and the culminating point—the point beyond which success is not likely.[9] Therefore, one should try to anticipate both an opponent's culminating point and one's own so that one is rapidly forcing the opponent toward the opponent's culminating point while not moving toward one's own. In many cases a belligerent may not even realize that he has reached the culminating point or may not believe it. This scenario suggests a need to force realization by having all political, informational, and psychological means available brought to bear on that center of gravity. For example, in retrospect, the United States reached its culminating point in Vietnam in the spring of 1968 following the Tet

Offensive and the "Agony of Khe Sanh," but continued to fight until December 1972. It was then that the political utility of the conflict was deemed to be less than the potential benefit. Henry Kissinger and Richard Nixon understood that fact in 1969 and thus began the efforts to quit the war—Vietnamization, the peace talks, and so forth—to salvage some credibility while disengaging. The North Vietnamese facilitated public understanding of these realities by their Easter offensives and the creation of the public perception that a U.S. victory was not possible. This is a classic case of the "quit point," or actual time that hostilities end, being far beyond the culminating point.

The "quit point" follows the self-realization of approaching, having reached, or having passed the culminating point.[10] If the opposition has an ability to escalate the conflict, it may choose to escalate if it is reaching its culminating point and realizes it. The U.S. escalation of the bombing of Hanoi in December 1972 may be a case in point. This possibly in turn suggests a need for escalation dominance or the elimination of the opposition's escalation capability. If the opposition escalates, there is also the possibility that both sides miscalculated the criticality of the issue being fought over and the center of gravity. If this development occurs, the conflict takes on a completely new character. The multiple changes of the war in Korea may be a case in point.

Synchronization is the technique that one uses to bring the elements of national power together to most effectively attack an (opponent's centers of gravity while defending own's own.[11] In the synchronization planning process, one seeks to anticipate the opponent's responses to the actions taken to reduce the effectiveness of the response and enhance the utility of the use of power. The key to synchronization is to ensure that the actions undertaken are mutually supportive and occur in a logical sequence. For example, one cannot impose an embargo or blockade until the military forces are in place to enforce it. Before putting military forces into place, one must gain international support for the effort. The key is to lay all of this action out beforehand to know what the critical path is, where the decision points are, and what the options are in terms of each of the elements of power at each of the decision points. The idea is to bring the requisite political, diplomatic, economic informational, moral, and military power to bear at the decisive time and place. If done properly it also reduces the complex into a series of small executable parts. Synchronization relates ends, ways, and means to each other and points all efforts toward the central purpose of the effort—to achieve a clearly defined strategic political objective.

The concept of synchronization of the total effort brings us back to where we began—the need for a clear vision of the situation following U.S. involvement in a given hostility or humanitarian situation. What will the situation be when the "mission" is completed? What do we want it to be? Is there a gap between the two visions? How might the gap be closed? Is it worth the effort?

Summary

There is a 10-step analytical process in end state planning. The steps are as follows:

Step 1. Define the problem. What is the nature of the dispute/problem? How important is the issue to the United States? What are the objectives of the parties to the dispute? What is success/"victory?" What are the victory criteria? What are the various parties' centers of gravity?

Step 2. Define "settlement" or strategic vision. What do we want the situation to look like after the conflict is completed? What is the nature of the settlement that we seek? What are the political, military, and other objectives?

Step 3. Analyze courses of action. Lay out options in terms of the elements of national power and relate them to the centers of gravity. Conduct a cost-benefit analysis for each element of power—consider second and third-order implications. Establish the upper limits on the power to be used.

Step 4. Select a course of action that will achieve the "victory criteria" within the upper limits of power that have been decided upon. If there is no course of action that will achieve success under the constraints imposed, stop the process. Do not go the next step. Go back to Step 1, or exit the problem. If there is a course of action that will achieve success within the upper limits of power that have been established, go to Step 5.

Step 5. Synchronize the political, military and other actions required for the course of action selected.

Step 6. Execute the plan/strategy.

Step 7 Evaluate to determine if the plan is unfolding as envisioned.

Step 8. Based on the evaluation, return to Step 1 or Step 2, or if "victory" has been achieved then proceed to:

Step 9. Execute the post-intervention political process planned for in Steps 4 and 5. As a result of this process one will either proceed to the last step, start over again, or exit the situation.

Step 10. Move to formal or informal settlement.

The process presented here is not a cure-all or the only method of approaching end state planning. The key is understanding the interrelated parts of a problem and the thought process that allow one to develop strategies that have a high probability of success.

In these terms, it will be heuristically useful to posit a hypothetical end state planning process that might have been logical at the time when the United States began its consideration of the Somalia problem.

A Hypothetical Example of End State Planning

As a way of demonstrating the concept of end state planning, let us assume that it is mid-December 1992. The decision has not been made by the president to deploy troops to Somalia to protect the food distribution system, and a National Security Council officer has been tasked to brief the present and incoming assistants to the president for national security affairs on how to disengage from Somalia, if we were to choose to intervene. The briefer will use the end state planning technique to build a strategy that will allow the United States to disengage, while still seeking to achieve the end state objectives. The briefer is trying to develop for the decision makers both the near- and long-term costs to such an intervention and the complexity of the interactions that must occur for the United States to achieve its objectives and be able to disengage.

Ladies and Gentlemen. In analyzing the situation in Somalia in December 1992 one sees rival warlords competing for power; widespread looting, disease, and famine; and a total breakdown in domestic decisive authority. To plan for the restoration of Somalia as a viable nation-state as an end state, one must establish phases and variables and then interrelate specific activities by variable, as shown in the following chart or matrix.

Concept							
Variables	Phase I	Phase II	Phase III	Phase IV	Phase V	Phase VI	End State
Security							
Support							
Economic							
C^2							
$ = Funding							
Diplomatic = US/UN							
Somali Political							
PSYOP							
INTEL							

For the purpose of planning the U.S. intervention and subsequent disengagement from Somalia we have planned on eight phases and selected 10 variables based upon the internal and external requirements that we see as being necessary to bring Somalia to a developing nation status. These variable were then considered over the eight phases, which ranged from the existing looting and famine that we find in Somalia today to a Somalia that is an independent, self-ruling country that enjoys a developing nation status.

<table>
<tr><td colspan="2">The eight Phases used for this analysis were:</td></tr>
</table>

0	- Famine and Looting
I	- U.S. Intervention
II	- U.S. Provided Security
III	- U.S. to UN Transition
IV	- UN Peacekeeping
V	- UN Disengagement
VI	- UN Transition
End State	- Stable, Growing, Somalia

The end state of a Somalia as a developing nation exercising decisive authority over its population in terms of the variables selected, is shown below.

End State	
Security:	Provided by Somalia, active police and court system
Support:	None required; security assistance
Economic:	Developing nation status
C^2:	Normal national functions
$ = Funding:	Foreign aid; domestic banking and financial system
Diplomatic = UN:	Self government(s) - 1, 2, 3 parts deterrence
Somali Political:	Centralized decisive authority; "war crimes?"
PSYOP:	Deterrent themes
Media:	Success story; discredited clan violence
INTEL:	Provided by Somalia

For most of the U.S. forces to disengage we need to achieve these results or success criteria. The efforts in early phases are designed to do this. If, however, we do not achieve the end state, we risk having to return.

Success Criteria
PVOs Functioning
Mass starvation averted
UNOSOM II effective

Phase I

In our synchronization matrix, phase I looks like the following:

Phase I: U.S. Intervention	
Security:	USMC
Support:	USMC; Open port
Economic:	
C²:	CJTF, U.S. Mission, UN High Command, AID, PVOS, UN Elements OPCON to U.S. Forces
$ = Funding:	DOD; AID, PVOS
Diplomatic = UN:	UNOSOM II—15K; police training; Northern Somalia; OAU presence expanded; U.S. Ambassador at large; increased PKS; 607 contract
Somali Political:	"Ceasefire"; PVOs; empower/focus on elders
PSYOP:	Coming ashore; move weapons
Media:	One the beach; "bleeding hearts"
INTEL:	Identify local leaders; identify arms caches monitor: local alliances, regional reactions, coalition building

A Somalia that is exercising decisive authority over the population and has discredited the warlords and even tried some of them for their crimes against the population is a long way from where the country is at the end of 1992. The key is to plan the incremental solutions over time to the problems that might preclude achieving the above end state. Additionally, one must determine which are the critical variables in each phase, to allow the situation to evolve/transition to the next phase.

Our matrix highlights the tasks to be accomplished as and before the marines come ashore. The local population has to be advised in the psychological operations (psyop) campaign that the marines are coming ashore and that their heavy weapons should be moved or that they will be destroyed. Intelligence has to monitor the population to determine the effectiveness of the psyop effort. We need to seek a ceasefire to enhance the ability of the private voluntary organizations (PVOs) to get around because the PVOs are the only form of government in terms of service provided to the population.

Obviously in terms of support, the marines have to open the port to allow military and relief supplies to flow in. The economic situation it a difficult problem in that there is currently very little of the previous market activities. In terms of command and control, there are presently numerous independent actors in Somalia. One of the efforts through the process will be to seek to gain unity of effort. Funding is initially from the United States military, that is, the Department of Defense. Obviously, the Agency for International Development (AID) and the PVOs also are providing help. We need to rapidly move form U.S. funding to UN funding.

In the diplomatic arena, we need to now refine the rules of engagement and the organization of UN Operations in Somalia (UNOSOM) II, so that we can stand it up in a subsequent phase. We also need to make plans for police training. The Germans trained the Somali police force before, and we hope they will be willing to do that again. We would also suggest that we might want to stand UNOSOM II up in the northern part of Somalia and then gradually extend its scope and command authority to the south, thus allowing it to gain operational experience in a more tranquil environment. Finally, in the diplomatic arena, we want to seek Organization of African Unity (OAU) support for the peacekeeping operations so that they can help replace either the United States or UN forces at some time downstream. We may want to consider creating a U.S. ambassador-at-large to run interference for the combined joint task force (CJTF) commander so that we can work the political problems with the allies and ensure that the military commander is free to do his job without political interference. We also need to negotiate for increased peacekeepers for subsequent phases and, as mentioned earlier, execute an agreement with the UN, called a 607 Contract, to gain UN funding for the operation.

Initially, obviously, we want to see some formal ceasefire, as noted, and we want to secure and make credible the PVO effort. More importantly, we want to empower the elders: to take the power away from the warlords and give it to the elders, who are the traditional course of power in Somali society. The warlords will be the center of gravity in Somalia, just as public support at home will be our center of gravity. If we can undermine the warlords' popular support while maintaining our own, we will have successfully "attacked" the opponents' center of gravity while protecting our own.

As for the media, they are going to be on the beach, and they are going to be playing the roles of advising the American people of where we haven't been and of the destitution and hunger that exist there. We need to understand that they are going to play this message and to the extent possible get them to highlight the themes and messages that we want to see get public attention.

Finally, we want to identify local leaders and identify where the arms caches are to monitor them. At some time in the future we may need to destroy those caches. We also want to be sensitive to the formation of local alliances that could create downstream problems and change the mission from one of humanitarian assistance to peace enforcement, as we seek to separate the warlords. We need to be sensitive as to how U.S. forces expand from Mogadishu to ensure that no single warlord is given an advantage as a result of our actions. (Unless, of course, we decide to abandon the elders and empower a warlord.)

The diplomatic variable is key to this and subsequent phases. Unless we can accomplish these diplomatic tasks we will be unable to transition to subsequent phases and thus not proceed toward achieving the end state.

Phase II

Phase II: U.S. Provided Security	
Security:	Balanced disarament/demobilization
	Buy weapons
	USA and USMC (relief centers & airfields secure)
	UNOSOM II to North = PK
	Police training, court development
Support:	USA—maximum contract/maximum offshore/local hire
	UNOSOM II- building/supporting UN Forces (North)
	U.S. builds mission essential infrastructure
Economic:	Monetization in secure areas
	Market reopen
	Planting begins
	PVOs
$ = Funding:	UN-DOD; AID
	PVOs
Diplomatic = UN	UNCRAO approved and beginning
	Allied $
	ROE redefined
Somali Political:	Local political activities/structure
	Reestablished-legal system
	UNCRAO support coordinating committees
	Minimal U.S. military effort

In Phase II, we have to worry about disarming the warlords in a balanced disarmament or demobilization. We do not want to make any of the warlords perceive that they are being put at risk vis-à-vis another warlord, until the effort has proceeded sufficiently to prevent them form being a threat. The warlords' culminating point will have passed when they are incapable of significant opposition. It should be noted that if they sense that they are approaching their culminating point, they may escalate by attacking the security forces to undermine popular support in the United States. Both the United States and UN must guard against this possibility. Obviously, the army and marines will provide security and the relief centers and airfields will be secured.

If we form UNOSOM II, as discussed in the diplomatic portion of the previous phase, we will now stand it up in the northern part of Somalia to assume control over the peacekeepers there, primarily Canadians. We will then gradually expand their control of the south, giving them an opportunity to learn to function as a combined staff without any significant threats.

The eventual relief-in-place should be both functional and geographic, when things are ready. We obviously will also start police training to eventually hand over the security mission to the newly formed local police. Accompanying this must be the establishment of a court and legal system.

Support will be done primarily by the United States Army, but we will seek a maximum contract of effort and keep a maximum amount of our logistical support "over the horizon,' or offshore, because it could become one of the sticking points that will preclude us from getting out. Our logistical tail will require security; thus, if we are to minimize the forces in country we must minimize the logistical infrastructure. We also want to hire as many local people as possible, going through the local elders and letting them select the people. This will both empower the elders and allow them to start to put money into the economy. As UNOSOM II becomes operational in the north, it is going to have to start building its own supporting logistical forces out of UN-provided forces. This may, in fact, become one of the critical variables. Finding sufficient logistical support elements for UNOSOM II may be a problem. It may be in this area at phase IV or V that we will find the United States having forces remaining in the country.

The United States' forces will also have to build the essential infrastructure in terms of roads, bridges, and port and airport facilities to allow us to accomplish our mission. As we begin to secure areas and return them to some form of stability, we will also have to introduce money so that we can get beyond a barter economy. We want to reopen markets so that we can have people out there working. In March the planting season will begin and they need to make preparations for it during this phase. Obviously, the PVOs will continue to do their share toward helping the economy along. At this point we hope that the UN and AID are doing the funding for these efforts—not the Department of Defense.

On the diplomatic front, we want to create the United Nations Civil Reconstruction and Assistance Organization, UNCRAO, which will require a significant diplomatic effort. In essence, we are creating something similar to a high commissioner and a government-like organization. UNCRAO should function as a unified government, providing goods and services to the Somali people. It will eventually be taken over by Somalis.

UNCRAO will perform the nation-building functions, thus freeing the U.S. military from most of those roles and facilitating its withdrawal. Should UNCRAO be incapable of coordinating the affecting the nation-building mission, there will be a point at which other activities become useless. In this regard, we will, of course, require allied funding. We also need to redefine the rules of engagement (ROE) for subsequent UN phases.

We should focus our political activities at the local village level. This should be done through UNCRAO, not the United States military. If the United States military becomes involved in nation building, then we will be embedded in the country for a long time, precisely what we are seeking to avoid. We also need to get UNCRAO's support and have it form coordinating committees to coordinate the transportation and provision of relief supplies. Again, minimal U.S. military effort should be devoted here.

The psyop theme throughout all of this should be "help you help yourself." In other words, we will give the people a reason to be involved in the process. If we decide to buy weapons, then we need to play that as a psyop theme. We also could consider jobs for weapons as a way of inducing people to turn in their weapons. And finally, we need to deal with qat abuse.

The overall goal, of course, throughout, and particularly at this point, is to isolate and discredit the warlords so that they are not seen as heroes but rather as the bandits that they are. Continually, we want to identify cache locations, threat forces, and war criminals for subsequent action.

The critical event during this phase will again be the accomplishment of the diplomatic tasks. Additionally, if starvation has been averted by the end of this phase, we have achieved our objective and can begin the transition to UN-provided peacekeepers.

Phase III

Phase III: U.S. to UN Transition	
Security:	CBMs
	UNPK = UNOSOM II
	U.S. Relief in place
	Some local police/paramilitary
	Disarmament/demobilization
Support:	Mass starvation averted
	USA downsizing - UNOSOM increasing
	Back haul U.S.
Economic:	U.S. sustains minimal mission essential
	Infrastructure
	UNCRAO becomes operational
C^2:	UNPKS to UNOSOM II as U.S. departs
	UNH to UNOSOM II + UNCRAO
	CJTF to Ambassador
$ = Funding:	UN-DOD; AID;POVS
Diplomatic = UN:	UNCRAO funding
	Sanction enforcement
	U.S. relations with Kenya—security assistance
Somali Political:	Return of middle class/resettlement
	Expanding local control - maintain
	Clan balance - legal system
PSYOP:	Local government success

Because Phase III is when the United States starts to withdraw and the UN starts to build up, we want to put confidence-building measures (CBMs) in place such as reaction force exercises to demonstrate to the warlords that a return to their old habits is unacceptable. We also want to introduce the increased number of UN peacekeepers working under UNOSOM II's control. They should conduct a relief in place with U.S. forces. We should have some of the local police and paramilitary organizations that were formed in previous phases who can begin to take over, with the allied peacekeeping forces, some of the security missions. They should have a direct link to the developing legal system. Obviously, the disarmament or demobilization of local Somali gangs will continue.

At this point, we should have averted maximum starvation, achieved the success criteria, and the United States should be downsizing its support effort while the UN support command (UNSCOM) is increasing its share of the load. Obviously, we would also begin back hauling equipment to the United States or selling or giving it to UNSCOM.

The United Nations peacekeepers will revert to UNOSOM II's control as the United States departs. The UN high commissioner will have a command relationship, a political command relationship, over UNOSOM II and UNCRAO. In other words, the United Nations high commissioner will have a military arm and a civilian reconstruction arm. The commander of the U.S. Joint Task Force will answer to the U.S. ambassador.

Funding, of course, will remain to be a UN responsibility with DOD's costs being minimized. Obviously, AID and the PVOs will continue their efforts. At the UN and in other diplomatic arenas, we need to continue to focus on getting different countries to fund UNCRAO. We also need to enforce the existing sanctions, specifically arms sanctions, which will be difficult. There are numerous arms in both Kenya and Ethiopia that could be flowing over the borders. U.S. relations with Kenya in the past have been somewhat strained, and it may be necessary for the United States to provide security assistance to gain Kenyan help in closing that border.

On the political side, we hope to attract the middle class who have migrated away from the country and get them to resettle and begin to work. We seek to expand local control and maintain the planned balance among the warlords or ideally among the elder clan leaders, so that we have created a balance of power between the clans, as peaceful politics and the rule of law begin to take root.

We want to point out the successes of local government so that self-government can build a momentum of its own and the effectiveness of the balanced disarmament and demobilization will be apparent. Additionally, we want people to think of ways other than the force of arms to resolve their differences.

We need to media, of course, to reflect the success that we have had. The press is going to define the criteria of the victory; therefore, we want to make sure that what they are defining is what we are interested in.

We want to continue to identify groups who might resist and monitor movement toward any arms caches that we know about. We are also going to have to build, at some point, a United Nations information or intelligence system, so that UNOSOM II cannot be surprised.

Phase IV

Phase IV: UN Peacekeeping	
Security:	UNOSOM II = UNPKS
	Local courts/police gaining confidence
	Related forces—U.S.
Support:	UNOSOM II/UNSCOM—minimal U.S. military
	UN contract by function - type/local
Economic:	UNCRAO - takes over trans, asset maintenance
	Centralized system bing rebuilt/crops growing
	UNOSOM II continues building
C²:	UNH/U.S. country team
	U.S. commo team
$ = Funding:	UN; USAID; PVOS
Diplomatic = UN	More allied $; mandate; = reaction force
	ROE expansion over UNOSOM I
Somali Political:	PVOS work with UNCRAO/local authorities
	"Balance of power"
PSYOP:	Rebuild media; UNCRAO; U.S.
Media:	UN effectiveness
INTEL:	Movement to caches
	Development of UN info system

During Phase IV, the United Nations is providing the key peacekeeping force and U.S. forces are minimized. UNOSOM II has assumed control over all of the peacekeepers. UNOSOM II should also be growing as a professional military organization. Local courts and police are operating and gaining the public's confidence. We would have to have reaction forces, probably U.S., ideally offshore, but possibly in country.

UNOSOM II and its support command (UNSCOM) are providing the support. This may require minimal U.S. military services because other nations just don't have the capability to provide some of the logistical services that the United States does. The United Nations should be contracting by function, type, and locale.

In the Somali economy, UNCRAO should take over the transportation and road maintenance to reduce the UNSCOM requirement in this area. This could also be contracted to local entrepreneurs. We need to rebuild the centralized economy, specifically a market economy.

The UN high commissioner should work with the U.S. country team headed by the U.S. ambassador. U.S. communication teams around the country may be required to maintain contact with the relief force. We would hope that this could be done through local police forces, but the requirement for communications will be there.

Obviously, the United States, except for AID, will be out of the funding business. We will have to continually push in the diplomatic arena for more dollars, and we will have to have a mandate and very specific rules of engagement for the reaction force. The rules of engagement must be much broader than UNOSOM I had.

We also want to encourage the PVOs to work with UNCRAO and the local authorities. At this point, we should be rebuilding a local media through UNCRAO and/or U.S. efforts. We want to be able to play the theme of UN effectiveness in the media so as to preclude similar types of requirements elsewhere in the world.

Again, we want to continue to monitor for movement to caches and the movement of arms overall as this will signify the possibility of renewed hostilities. A working economy, effective police forces, and some rudimentary political/legal activity will be required to allow us to transition to the next phase.

Phase V

Phase V: UN Disengagement	
Security:	UNOSOM reduces—constabulary
	CBMS; reaction force (MEU)
Support:	Backhaul of UNOSOM II
	Increase local contract
Economic:	UN continues infrastructure development, especially
	for internal security
C^2:	U.S. country team - commo to village for security
$ = Funding:	UN; AID; IMF
Diplomatic = UN:	None
Somali Political:	Clan/regional gov't functioning
PSYOP:	Support government, discredit factions
Media:	Local functioning
INTEL:	Phase info support to Somalia

In phase V, the UN has been successful and UNOSOM II starts to phase itself out. We have established a local constabulary, which is having success in maintaining the peace or trying in the courts the offenders. A series of confidence-building measures (CBMs) including a reaction force drill where we actually demonstrate out ability to come back in significant force would assure the population that, if necessary, we will be back. An ideal reaction force would be a marine amphibious unit offshore, out of sight.

We will continue to backhaul all U.S. and UNOSOM II equipment and to increase local hire. The economy of the country should continue to grow with its infrastructure continually improved through UNCRAO. We especially want to look at the road system to that lightly armored reaction forces could react to any banditry and thus provide internal security.

In command and control, the U.S. country team will be fully up and operating. We will need to ensure that some form of communications down to the villages exists, so as to be able to react and provide security to the villages.

The UN and AID will be providing funding, but also it is at this point that the International Monetary Fund or similar such resources should be brought to bear to further enhance the economic development of the country.

At this point, diplomatically, the mission can be declared a success and there should be minimal further diplomatic efforts required. We want to play up in our psychological and media operations that the regional government is in fact up and functioning and that everything is going fine. We also want to transfer the information system that we built to support UNOSOM II to the follow-on Somali government.

Phase VI

Phase VI: UN Transition	
Security:	Local police; reaction forces = MEU/other
Support:	Security assistance
Economic:	Market system
C^2:	UNCRAO departs
$ = Funding:	IMF; World Bank
Diplomatic = UN	
Somali Political:	Continued centralization
PSYOP:	
Media:	Success story
INTEL:	Continue to monitor

In phase VI the UN is almost out and local police are up and operating. There are still reaction forces available to reinforce them. Security assistance is the only form of support required.

A market system is working. UNCRAO is going to depart at this point, and the International Monetary Fund and the World Bank will be assisting in building a Somali economic system.

Diplomatically, the Somali government may rejoin the community of nations and reestablish normal relations with its neighbors and other countries. We want to continue to move toward centralization of the Somalis political system, and we want to continue to play the message of what a success Somalia has been.

At the end of this phase, we will have the end state of a Somalia that is self-government, that is a developing nation, and that is up and growing.

End State

End State	
Security:	Provided by Somalia, legal system
Support:	None required; security assistance
Economic:	Developing nation status
C^2:	Normal national functions
$ = Funding:	Foreign aid; domestic banking and financial system
Diplomatic = UN	Self government(s)—1, 2, 3 parts deterrence
Somali Political:	Centralized decisive authority; "war crimes?"
PSYOP:	Deterrent themes
Media:	Success sotry - discredited clan violence
INTEL:	Provided by Somalia

Under diplomatic activity I have not recommended whether there should be one, two, or three Somalias. There are tendencies for separatism in the country. We really don't want to choose sides at this point because should we do so, we will be caught in the middle no matter how it falls out.

We may want to consider war crime tribunals to deter similar warlords in places like the Sudan from thinking that they can get away with what the Somali warlords tried. This is why we are talking about deterrent themes, a legal system, and the discreditation of clan violence.

Critical Events
$ Money—Allies; US; UN; PVOS
Diplomacy—UN & UNOSOM II/UNSCOM
Public Opinion

The key event that may inhibit this whole operation is funding. If the nations of the world don't come to the U.S. or the UN's support and if the public doesn't support the private voluntary organizations, this could become a very expensive operation.

Diplomatically, it is critical that we get UNOSOM II stood up and create the United Nations Support Command (UNSCOM) and the United Nations Civil Reconstruction and Assistance Organization (UNCRAO).

The ability of the United States to conduct this operation to a successful conclusion will depend on continued public support.

Key Themes

Key Themes
U.S. as Honest Impartial Broker
Elder Empowerment & Warlord Isolation
Support Privitization = Contract
Disarmament/Demobilization
Resource Allocation: U.S.; Coalition; Somalia
UNSCOM
UNCRAO
Over the Horizon Logistics
Functional Phased Relief: Security and Support
Success Criteria: Elusive
Maintain Public Suppport

Some key themes throughout the process are the importance of the diplomatic initiatives. Success in creating the required organizations and giving the police training and things of this nature that our diplomatic initiatives create will drive the transition from one phase to another. The U.S. military will not control this transition process. Additionally, the other key theme throughout is our ability to maintain a balance of power between the different warlords (the centers of gravity) as we slowly eliminate their power. Should one of them feel threatened or see his position being significantly eroded, compared with one of his competitors, he could react in a very negative fashion and put U.S. forces at risk. We must avoid creating a situation where a warlord perceives that there is a window of opportunity to discredit U.S. or UN efforts or gain a marked advantage over his competitors.

Additionally, we need to streamline the entire support requirement to minimize U.S. costs in terms of people and funds by creating the UN organizations noted, using private contracting to the maximum extent possible, and utilizing over-the-horizon logistics. The relief-in-place must be phased and functional in terms of both security and support.

Finally, the success criterion of averting mass starvation is a transitory and elusive criterion that will be defined mostly by the media.

Throughout this process it is critical that we protect our own center of gravity by maintaining public support.

Ladies and gentlemen, this concludes my briefing. Do you have any questions?

Conclusion

End state planning suggests that victory is achieved when the primary strategic political objective for a given situation is accomplished. The key is to correctly analyze the situation, correctly understand the parties to the dispute/problem and their objectives, and successfully defend one's own center of gravity while attacking the opposition's center of gravity.

The analytical model proposed here provides decision makers and planning staffs a unique process to guide thinking and planning by focusing on the principal concepts that one must consider when thinking about success in foreign policy and military management. These concepts may be summarized as:

- The need for a clear and achievable strategic vision—an end state.
- The need for clear supporting political-military objectives.
- An understanding of both the opponent and oneself that fosters an accurate determination of the centers of gravity.
- The ability to attack the opposition's center of gravity while defending one's own.
- The ability to synchronize the appropriate national civil-military tools of power for attacking/defending the various centers of gravity.
- The ability to predict culmination and quit points and know whether the opponent is approaching one so that an appropriate response can be anticipated.
- The criticality of winning—accomplishing the ultimate political objective.

ESP is a methodology suggested by Clausewitz's admonition to understand the political nature of conflict and to become involved only when one is clear about what one intends to achieve by entering into a conflict situation and how one intends to conduct it. End state planning is key to any such endeavor, and it depends upon having a clear strategic vision from which to start.

Notes

1. The analysis presented here is a summary of an exhaustive study by Stephen T. Hosmer, "Constraints on U.S. Military Strategies in Past Third World Conflicts," (Santa Monica, CA: RAND, N-2180-AF), July 1984.

2. Carl von Clausewitz, *On War*, trans. and ed. by Michael Howard and Peter Paret (Princeton, NJ Princeton University Press, 1976), pp. 92–93.

3. Ibid., p. 92–93, 95

4. Ambassador David C. Miller, Jr., "Beyond the Cold War: An Overview and Lessons," in Max G. Manwaring, ed., *Gray Area Phenomena: Confronting the New World Disorder* (Boulder, CO: Westview Press, 1993), pp. 165–166.

5. Bruce B.G. Clarke, "Conflict Termination: A Rational Model," *Terrorism* (vol. 16, 1993), pp. 35–50.

6. Clausewitz, *On War*, pp. 88–89.

7. Ibid., pp. 595–596.

8. Ibid.

9. Ibid., p. 528

10. Bruce B.G. Clarke, "A Primer on Joint Warfare," (Carlisle, Bks., PA: US. Army War College, 1995), unpublished manuscript, pp. 6–7.

11. Clarke, "Conflict Termination," pp. 45–47.

5

Application of Theory and Principle: The Case of El Salvador

Ambassador Edwin G. Corr

On March 20, 1994, Salvadoran citizens went to the polls for the ninth time in 12 years to participate in what they billed as the "elections of the century."[1] The elections symbolized reconciliation and the end of 11 years of destructive civil war. The peace agreement of January 16, 1992 between the Government of El Salvador (GOES) and the Farabundo Martí National Liberation Front (FMLN) ended armed conflict that had claimed as many as 75,000 lives.[2] El Salvador is markedly different in the mid-1990s from what it was in the violent, chaotic days of 1980. The society is more open, there is greater freedom, political and public institutions are improving, the economy is growing, and the peace for which Salvadorans yearned so long has been achieved.

El Salvador's internal transformation during the civil war distinguishes that country's experience with small war from that of many others. The thesis of this chapter is that significant political, economic, and social changes within Salvadoran society created a more legitimate political system and together with changes in the world arena permitted reconciliation between the GOES and the FMLN. The negotiated peace was based on perceptions of the various contending parties that society had been sufficiently transformed to permit peace and an acceptable future.

Rebel commander Fermán Cienfuegos stated that El Salvador's was the first revolution in Latin America won through negotiations.[3] For the government's part, the existing constitutional order had been maintained, all major power contenders were incorporated into the political process, and institutions were in place for an increasingly legitimate and viable democracy. Without continued progress, however, El Salvador could return to violence and conflict.

Dr. Armando Calderon Sol, the presidential candidate of the right-of-center National Republican Alliance (ARENA) party, won a runoff election on April 24, 1994 over Dr. Ruben Zamora. Zamora was the candidate of a coalition constituted by the FMLN (now a legal political party) and former opposition parties allied with the FMLN during the civil war. The former guerrillas clearly established themselves, at least for the time being, as the second most powerful political force in the country.

In retrospect, the path by which Salvadoran democrats—with U.S. support—reached a satisfactory resolution to their conflict reflects the tenets of the Manwaring paradigm and the legitimacy theory of engagement set forth in chapter 2. Research for the paradigm was based on 43 low-intensity conflict cases. The underlying premise of the Manwaring paradigm is that "the ultimate outcome of any counterinsurgency effort is not primarily determined by the skillful manipulation of violence in...many military battles." Rather, the outcome will be determined by (1) the legitimacy of the government, (2) organization for unity of effort, (3) the type and consistency of support for the targeted government, (4) the type and consistency of support for the insurgents, (5) intelligence (or action against subversion), and (6) the discipline and capabilities of a government's armed forces and civil institutions. Attention to all six factors can lead to a successful negotiation to end conflict or, if necessary, to defeat the opposing force. The most important factor in small wars is legitimacy, the moral right to govern.[4] Examination of the El Salvador small war reveals the validity of Manwaring and Corr legitimacy theory of engagement in at least this case.

Origins of the Conflict and the Internal Power Contenders

El Salvador's stability and progress were increasingly threatened over the years by the growing number of people, especially landless farmers, excluded from sharing equitably in the nation's economy and participating meaningfully in the political system. The conflict grew out of a history of social, economic, and political inequities. As in many other Latin American societies, there were great disparities in income, land tenure, and social justice in El Salvador. In the years before the revolution began, these tensions intensified, and political forces of the Right and Left began to coalesce more clearly around specific issues. The result was a growing environment of confrontation and violence that eventually erupted into civil war.

Military governments that ruled El Salvador from 1948 until 1972, in keeping with the concept of tutelary democracy popular among the Latin American military at the time, had gradually opened the political system. The pace of political liberalization and the extraordinary economic growth of the 1960s and early 1970s did not stay ahead of the growing demands of the populace, however. Population growth, the political awakening of the lower classes through transistor radios and social change, and the emergence of opposition political leaders put pressure on the military-dominated political structure. This pressure intensified in the aftermath of the Salvadoran-Honduran war of 1969. José Napoleón Duarte and his Christian Democratic Party (PDC), in coalition with small parties of social democrats and communists, threatened the dominance of the El Salvador armed forces (ESAF) in the 1972 elections. The officer corps was not willing to give up the emoluments of power and blatantly used fraud to deny Duarte the presidency. Military repression after 1972 created an increasingly revolutionary situation.

Beginning in 1970, armed movements claiming to seek justice and correction of their society's ills emerged. They received inspiration and training from Fidel Castro's Cuba. Insurgents robbed banks and held the wealthy for ransom to build war chests. Guerrillas committed acts of sabotage and terrorism. By the end of the 1970s anarchy prevailed. Mobs of the Popular Revolutionary Bloc (BPR) numbering 50,000 to 100,000 people owned the streets. Ministries, factories, and large businesses were under siege; management was held hostage. Bombings began at dusk and continued through the night.

Young, reform-minded officers carried out a coup d'état on October 15, 1979 that was aimed at restoring order, restructuring society, and establishing democracy. The junta was immediately and violently rejected by a revolutionary Left that was intent on capturing power to create a Cuban- or Sandinista-style regime. The reactionary Right equally rejected the junta as a threat to its power and way of life. Killings by right-wing death squads were rampant. The Right was financed by the wealthy oligarchy and allied with elements of the public security forces. They were committed to preserving or returning to the status quo ante.

In the chaos, violence, and near-anarchy that characterized El Salvador in the late 1970s and early 1980s, a major part of Salvadoran society was polarized between extremists of the Left and the Right. Both groups had grown and were armed. Radical and violent leftist demonstrators obtained their desired quota of martyrs from the repressive security forces. Fidel Castro helped the five different guerrilla armies unite in 1980 as the FMLN. Supported by Cuba, Nicaragua, and the Soviet Union, the FMLN planned to defeat the armed forces of El Salvador, rally the people to support a new social order the FMLN would impose, and install a Marxist-Leninist government. Popular leftist organizations allied with the guerrillas made orderly rule by the government impossible. Between the radical Right and Left was an emerging moderate, democratic group initially dominated by the PDC. Democratic advocates were also found in political parties to the right and left of the PDC and in business and labor groups. The democratic center constituted the third of the three major Salvadoran power contenders from 1979 to 1992. This moderate group waged a continuing struggle to be the legitimate government of the country. They tried to expand and to gain unity of effort against the insurgency. The lack of support from the Right and the Left and the outside aid to the guerrillas made the center's efforts difficult. The two extremes set themselves above any semblance of the law and the constitutional order that might have once imperfectly existed. They were wed to violence as the means to defend and advance their visions of society. Salvadoran democrats were confronted with building democracy in an environment of internal chaos and civil war.

External Actors and El Salvador

Although Salvadorans' decisions and actions were the determining elements in the evolution and direction of their society and politics, external events, interventions, and support were sometimes as important to specific outcomes in El Salvador as internal developments. Four developments in the world arena affected Central America and El Salvador during the 1979-1994 period—two negatively and two positively from the U.S. point of view.

First, Americans were concerned that the USSR had become more aggressive and was seeking military superiority, while the relative power of the United States was declining. Dramatic events in 1979 heightened Americans' sense of threat and insecurity. The fall of the shah of Iran, the subsequent 444-day ordeal of U.S. diplomats being held hostage, oil short-ages, the Soviet brigade in Cuba, the Sandinistas' victory in Nicaragua, and their threat, with Soviet and Cuban backing, to spread their Marxist-Leninist revolution throughout the region affected the psyche of U.S. leaders and people. It seemed to many that the USSR was menacing the United States' soft underbelly, and that Central America and even Mexico could eventually fall under the dominance of the then major adversary of the United States.

Second, there were historical concerns of Latin American governments about U.S. intervention. These were based especially on Mexican resent-ments since the Mexican-American War and on South American reactions to U.S. support for the British instead of the Argentines in the Falklands War. These resentments caused Latin American governments outside Central America to oppose more strongly U.S. policy in Central America. The Contadora Group of negotiators (consisting of Mexico, Colombia, Venezuela, and Panama as mediators, and Brazil, Argentina, Uruguay, and Peru as supporters) showed this influence as they tilted toward Sandinista interests versus those of other Central American governments and the United States while attempting to promote a Central American peace agreement during the mid-1980s.

Third, the worldwide expansion of democracy, especially in Latin America, from the mid-1970s increasingly made the Marxist Sandinista regime and the FMLN less attractive and the programs and goals of Central American democrats more supportable. Salvadoran President Duarte and Costa Rican President Oscar Arias influenced this shift of world opinion on Central America.

Finally, the decline of the Cold War in the late 1980s and its end in the early 1990s further discredited the Sandinistas and the FMLN. Their Marxist-based goals and programs became more anachronistic and less popular. Equally important were the reduction and cessation of their foreign economic, military, and diplomatic support. The decline of such support contributed to the FMLN's change of emphasis in ideology toward social democracy and its willingness to negotiate in the late 1980s and early 1990s.

Leftist insurgent leaders and movements were inspired, trained, and materially supported by foreign communist governments and supported by Latin American and West European governments who found in the conflict a way to vent their anti-United States and anti-Reagan feelings. Substantial numbers of the Salvadoran oligarchy financed the extreme Right. Support for the Salvadoran center came principally from the United States and other Central American governments. U.S. government interests and objectives for Central America throughout the 1979 to 1992 period under Presidents Jimmy Carter, Ronald Reagan, and George Bush were enunciated in the *Report of the National Bipartisan Commission on Central America*, published in January 1984:

> Central America is both vital and vulnerable. . . .
>
> The use of Nicaragua as a base for Soviet and Cuban efforts to penetrate the rest of the Central American isthmus . . . makes it a challenge to the security interests of the United States. . . .
>
> Our task . . . is to help our neighbors not only to secure their freedom from aggression and violence, but also to set in place the policies, processes and institutions that will make them both prosperous and free. . . . [5]

United States Government Policy Implementation

Increasing attention has been given among American security strategists to what has been termed "end state planning" as an essential element for successful conduct within conflict and for successful termination of conflict. There is also repeated recognition (usually citing Clausewitz, Sun Tzu, Liddell Hart, and Harry Summers) that conflict strategy should be related to political goals, that victory can come by focusing on nonmilitary aspects of conflict, and that policymakers should protect their own "centers of gravity" while attacking or working to change the adversaries' centers of gravity. Nevertheless, in their efforts to prescribe and analyze, current military strategists—while paying lip service to the importance of nonmilitary factors as a means to avoid disputes and conflicts or gain victory in them—invariably return to disproportionate emphasis on the military component of conflict.

Bruce B. G. Clarke argues there are three pieces of critical guidance that need to be developed during a dispute that may result in hostilities:

- "a clear statement by the political authorities of the desired situation in the post-hostility and settlement phases; a vision of what the area should 'look like' following hostilities;
- a clear set of political objectives that when achieved will allow the above to become a reality; and,
- a set of military [and civilian?] objectives that will, when achieved, allow/cause the above to happen."[6]

Political authorities of the U.S. government in the 1980s, after an initial period of confusion and some vacillation, consciously and deliberately set out the desired outcome of the Salvadoran conflict and defined objectives to help Salvadoran democrats transform their society in the direction of the desired end-state. When I became chief of mission to El Salvador in August 1985, President Reagan's instructions to me were clear and simple: "Go down there and help Salvadoran leaders consolidate constitutional democracy, attain peace, and improve the standard of living for their people." Secretary of State George Shultz's orders to me were similar, although more elaborate. My instructions differed little from those given to all U.S. chiefs of mission of the 1979-1994 period. We were to help democrats of all political parties and groups consolidate democracy.

After my arrival in El Salvador, I called a meeting of the country team of the embassy and set forth the overall goal (the end state) of the U.S. government as described to me by the president and secretary of state. In pursuit of this goal, I said, the United States would use its resources and influence only in support of Salvadoran programs. The country belonged to the Salvadorans, and the Salvadoran government could become legitimate and democratic only if it were sovereign and responsive to Salvadorans. In keeping with the overall goal of helping the Salvadoran democrats to establish a legitimate Salvadoran democratic political system, although I continuously mentioned publicly U.S. support for democracy and human rights, in contrast to my predecessors I gave no substantive public political speeches and analysis. I knew that for Salvadoran legitimacy to grow, the U.S. government's public profile had to diminish.[7]

As I told the country team, the support of the U.S. government for Salvadoran efforts to establish a viable constitutional democracy fell into five major interrelated, and at times incompatible, areas. The United States objectives were to support Salvadoran efforts to (a) create the political institutions and attitudes necessary for a lasting constitutional democracy (democratization); (b) reduce human rights abuses and improve the justice system; (c) foster economic growth and development, generate employment, and distribute more fairly the nation's wealth; (d) seek peace through effective efforts at dialogue, negotiations, and national conciliation while successfully conducting the war; and, (e) help establish peace and democracy in all of Central America. These areas were reviewed continuously, and at times formally, to ensure their continuing validity, alternative courses of action to achieve them, and their consequence in terms of successes and failures of Salvadorans advancing toward the overall goal as laid down by the president and the secretary of state.

Failure by Salvadoran democrats to make progress in these areas would ensure that those elements of society long excluded from power and not receiving a just share of the nation's wealth would remain excluded, and thus maintain the revolutionary situation that had evolved. The primary security interests (i.e., preventing the spread of Marxist-Leninist governments favorable to the USSR in Central America) and ideals of the United States (democracy and human rights) in El Salvador were best served by helping Salvadorans to consolidate and expand a functioning constitutional democracy and to create a more just and prosperous society.

The Course of the Conflict and Societal Change

Following is a brief examination of the conflict and the degree to which Salvadorans transformed their society in three of the five areas that the U.S. government selected as priorities for its support: democracy; human rights and justice; and economic growth and development. Negotiations and conduct of the war, which constitute the fourth supported area, are treated in two following separate sections. This chapter does not examine specifically Salvadoran efforts to establish peace and democracy in the region.

It is important to emphasize that the military aspect of the conflict was, of course, critical, but overall the military struggle was only one of several interrelated and critical fronts in which success was necessary. The principal factors in the El Salvador case mirrored the major elements of the Manwaring paradigm for low-intensity conflict. The government and the FMLN were locked in a struggle over which of the two legitimately reflected the will of the people and had the right to govern. Both depended heavily on support from foreign governments. Both, and especially the GOES, were plagued by problems of unity and coherence, lack of good intelligence, and the lack of discipline and capacity of their armed forces.

Democratization

In El Salvador, as in Latin America as a whole, democracy became the principal source of legitimate government in the 1970s and 1980s. The history of El Salvador from 1979 to 1994 was the center's struggle to gain legitimacy by reincorporating the democratic Left while withstanding the armed attack of the FMLN and to win from the Right a commitment to extended democracy while trying to curtail the violence of the undemocratic Right. The democrats also confronted the difficult task of establishing civil authority over the ESAF.

The junta under Duarte implemented measures, including agrarian reform, that began to take away from the Marxist Left the banners of social improvement and concern for the popular sectors. Political parties were vitalized, and workers and peasant leaders strengthened their organizations. The first free elections in 50 years were held in 1982 for a constitutional assembly, which, after drafting a constitution, served as an interim legislature. The FMLN and its civilian ally, the Democratic Revolutionary Front (FDR), refused to participate, despite concerted efforts to include them.

Provisional President Alvaro Magaña held things together from 1982 to 1984 by preventing either the undemocratic Right or the Left from grabbing power. He unified the fragmented armed forces and held presidential elections. Duarte defeated the rightist ARENA candidate Roberto D'Aubuisson in 1984. Subsequent national elections were held in 1985, 1988, 1989, 1991, and 1994, with run-off elections in 1984 and 1994. The litmus test of democracy was passed when in 1988 President Duarte ceded control of the legislature to ARENA and in 1989 yielded the presidency to the ARENA victor, the moderate and competent Alfredo Cristiani.

Throughout the 1980s the power contenders within the Salvadoran political system learned to live and work together against the FMLN; and, by the end of the decade the GOES and FMLN-FDR, although at war, began to seek areas for accommodation. The FDR ran candidates in 1989. In the 1990s dialogue and negotiations were increasingly sincere. Following the 1992 peace accord, the FMLN became a political party; and in the 1994 municipal, legislative, and presidential elections, it became the second political force in the country. By 1994 all political groups were at last included in the political process and could seek their aims peacefully.

Attitudinal change necessary for a functioning democracy is more difficult, takes more time, and is more important than institutional/bureaucratic change. There is a symbiotic and reinforcing relationship between institutional and attitudinal change. Altering attitudes about human rights, the submission of security forces to civil authority, and creating a dialogue among contending power groups to find solutions to national problems within a spirit of give-and-take and compromise are essential. Salvadoran progress in these key attitudinal areas was significant, and underlay the broadening and deepening commitment of Salvadorans to the democratic process.

Human Rights and Justice

El Salvador had long had a reputation for violent repression. The U.S. embassy began keeping records in 1980 and calculated 750 noncombatants killed per month by political violence. A number of these senseless killings were highly publicized, such as the assassination of Bishop Oscar Romero, the American church women, and later the Jesuit priests. Progress on human rights was slower than desired, and at times was marked by dramatic setbacks, but was, overall, steady. The average number of deaths of noncombatants clearly attributable to political violence dropped to two per month in 1991, when the embassy ceased collecting such statistics.[8] There were also many other forms of human rights abuse, including torture, disappearances, displacement of peoples, and a very inefficient and corrupt judicial system.

The ESAF and elements of the undemocratic Right, especially through paramilitary groups and "death squads," were responsible for the bulk of human rights violations in the 1970s and early 1980s. By the mid-1980s, because of growing ESAF and GOES political strength (in part because of U.S. assistance), the FMLN was forced to change its military strategy to rely more on sabotage, assassination, and terrorism, making it increasingly responsible for human rights violations. In the case of both the government and the guerrillas, human rights abuses undermined their legitimacy. Growing public disgust with FMLN abuses from 1985 onward was a major factor in the shift to public acceptance of the Salvadoran government. The extent and horror of FMLN crimes have not been adequately studied or recognized.

Human rights abuse was curbed also by the Salvadoran justice system, although it was and remains inadequate. Duarte's initial project for judicial reform was approved by the Salvadoran National Assembly in 1985 and supported by U.S. aid. A revisory commission carried out analytical studies and developed draft legislation. By 1990 11 major reform laws had been enacted. During negotiations with the FMLN, further major changes were adopted, nearly all of which had already been proposed but not yet adequately enacted. During the 1985 to 1994 period the judiciary became more independent and received greater resources. Higher standards and better training for judges were required. The police was placed under civil rather than military authority. Much remains to be accomplished, but much has been achieved. A key question remains the degree to which members of the ESAF and public security organizations and upper class and politically prominent Salvadorans are subject to the law and civil authority.

Economic Growth and Development

Near-anarchy, insurgency, and military-PDC junta reforms caused El Salvador's gross domestic product (GDP) to fall by 22.2 percent and real per capita GDP by 26.5 percent between 1978 and 1982.[9] The reforms redistributed wealth and political power to previously ignored sectors of society but also caused readjustments. On top of war damage, a catastrophic earth-

quake in 1986 was followed by two years of drought and then flooding from
a hurricane. By 1984, the Duarte government, with U.S. support, had
stabilized the economy and, despite the difficulties of redistribution and
nature, by 1987 had achieved a 2.6 percent growth rate, but the economy
was still in very bad shape when President Alfredo Cristiani assumed office
in June 1989.

President Cristiani implemented comprehensive macroeconomic and
structural reforms based on the free-market model. The ARENA government dismantled the state marketing monopolies, privatized the banking
system, and made clear its preference for individual ownership of agricul-
tural lands as opposed to large production cooperatives, although it did not
dismantle the latter. Macroeconomic indicators in nearly all areas improved
dramatically and have remained high. Annual growth in gross national
product has been around 4 percent or higher throughout the 1990s.[10] In 1994
growth was 6 percent, with 9 percent inflation. The major question today is
to what extent the improvements are being shared by all sectors of Salvadoran society.

Conduct of the War

In 1981 the ESAF consisted of 14,000 firemen, policemen, and soldiers
who were neither equipped nor trained for counterinsurgency. The ESAF
valiantly repelled the FMLN's January 10, 1981 so-called final offensive at
a time when resumption of U.S. military assistance and training had been
announced but had not commenced. The ESAF's often brutal and repressive actions alienated people and created more guerrillas than they eliminated, however. Full-time FMLN combatants at the time of the 1981 final
offensive probably numbered less than 5,000. After FMLN withdrawal
from the cities to concentrate on a rural-based insurgency, the number of
full-time combatants grew to 12,000 in 1983. They received support of arms,
ideology, and training from Nicaragua, Cuba, and the Soviet bloc. The ESAF
initially was tied down in the static defense of towns and economic
infrastructure. The FMLN occupied territory, could move rather freely
about the country, and could choose the time and location of its attacks so
as to field superior numbers in major attacks.

The fighting spirit of Salvadoran soldiers and U.S. military training and
equipment (especially helicopters)[11] were key to FFAA military successes.
The GOES improved its capacity in intelligence, especially after 1985, and
strengthened the discipline of the FFAA and public security forces. For the
most part the armed forces' treatment of the populace after 1983 was more
humane than it had been. U.S. assistance, although erratic in its levels and
flow, enhanced GOES progress. The advantage tilted to the ESAF because
of the government's will to implement social and economic reforms, coor-

dinate better activities between civilians and the military, improve performance in human rights, and move the nation toward democracy. By 1984 the ESAF had taken the offensive. It forced the FMLN to disperse into small units to avoid total defeat. By 1985 the FMLN had shifted to a strategy of sabotage of the economy, terrorism, and intimidation. The aim was to make the country ungovernable and undermine governmental legitimacy. The resulting violence and FMLN brutality actually diminished the FMLN's own legitimacy.

The 1986 earthquake seriously interrupted the military momentum of the GOES and ESAF. In 1987, the FMLN returned warfare to San Salvador through bombings, terrorism, and popular demonstrations. On November 11, 1989, guerrillas boldly launched their largest offensive since January 1981 in an effort to reverse the correlation of internal and external forces working against them. Despite demonstrating notable military capability, the FMLN was again defeated when the people did not rise up. This military defeat was offset, however, by an army unit's senseless murder of six Jesuit priests, which tipped international opinion, especially within the U.S. Congress, against the Salvadoran armed forces and government. There were perceptions of a military stalemate, at least for the short term. This provided a basis for the negotiations under United Nations (UN) auspices from 1990 to 1992 that ended the conflict.

The role of the armed forces was critical throughout the conflict. At the same time, overall, it probably constituted about 20 percent of the total Salvadoran effort. (This is the monetary proportion of total U.S. assistance: 20 percent military and 80 percent economic.) Of course, at crucial junctures the military effort consumed 90 to 95 percent of the national effort, for example, during the guerrillas so-called final offensives in January 1981 and November 1989. The military and civil efforts, when implemented correctly, were mutually reinforcing, and not separate. A continuing major effort was to achieve a national campaign plan that incorporated both military and civil programs and military offensives so as to gain maximum advantage over the guerrillas and simultaneously increase governmental acceptance (legitimacy).

Beginning with a Salvadoran campaign plan devoted almost exclusively to military efforts, U.S. embassy officers and military advisers helped the Salvadoran government and FFAA develop a comprehensive plan to conduct the war. Especially important were U.S. Southern Command military strategy assistance teams under Gen. Fred Woerner in 1981 and under Gen. Marc Cisneros in 1988 that stressed an integrated effort. Understanding the complementary roles of military and civilians is necessary to assessing one's own centers of gravity as well as those of the adversary. Salvadorans, with U.S. help, finally achieved a sufficient level of coordination of civil and military efforts.

Negotiations

The first time I defined for the country team the U.S. government's overall goal (end state) in its support of the Salvadoran government and the five areas (objectives) in which the U.S. government would concentrate its influence and resources in support of Salvadoran efforts and programs, I mistakenly did not specifically include negotiations as a distinct part of the quest for peace objective. Within a week I clarified this objective to the country team. In the first presentation I had termed the fourth area of U.S. support merely as "conduct of the war." In the second discussion a week later, I explained my perception that war was an instrument of policy aimed at achieving a political settlement by forcing the adversary to negotiate acceptably. A full-court press to negotiate an acceptable solution (one likely to result in a democracy at peace) not only made sense in bringing to an end as rapidly as possible the bloodshed and carnage, it was also key to building legitimacy for the Salvadoran government. The desperation of the Salvadoran people for an end to the war was so great that no government could have increased its legitimacy without sincere negotiations. Presidents Duarte and Cristiani both fully realized this, and, finally, by January 1989 so did the FMLN.[12]

Efforts to negotiate a solution began with the junta in 1980, when President Duarte reached out through the Catholic Church to the FMLN and the radical Left.[13] Joaquín Villalobos of the FMLN told reporters in Mexico City in September 1989 that the guerrillas had made a mistake by not negotiating a peace agreement in 1980.[14] What a tragic confession after a decade of destruction and bloodshed! Just as the junta tried to convince the FMLN-FDR to participate in the 1982 elections, the Magaña provisional government futilely invited FMLN participation in the 1984 elections.

Duarte, following his 1984 election victory and as the tide of battle and public opinion turned favorably toward the GOES, used a UN General Assembly address to force the FMLN to the negotiating table. Hopes for peace were high after the initial sessions in La Palma but were dashed by FMLN demands at the follow-up meetings in Ayagualo. The FMLN-FDR rejected the 1983 constitution and took the position that little in El Salvador had changed after the coup, that there still existed an unjust political and economic system at the service of a rightist oligarchy. The goals of the FMLN-FDR in the early 1980s were aimed at establishing social justice through a Cuban or Sandinista-style regime. They regularly called for an end to all U.S. military aid, for guerrilla imposition of a "democratic revolutionary government," for a cease-fire in which the FMLN-FDR would occupy territory, and, finally, for the maintenance of guerrilla armies. At some unspecified date after society had been restructured, elections would be held.

President Duarte in his 1986 state of the union address invited the FMLN-FDR to talks. They agreed to meet in the small Salvadoran town of Sesori but the FMLN-FDR chose at the last minute not to attend. Formal negotiations were again held pursuant to the August 7, 1987 Esquipulas II Agreement (often referred to as the Arias Plan) at the residence of the papal nuncio. The FMLN-FDR did not budge, although the two sides agreed to create joint commissions to work toward accords. The FMLN suspended these talks after the second round.

The FDR decided to participate in the 1989 presidential elections. FMLN leaders surprisingly announced in January 1989 that they would abide by the election results *if* elections were postponed until September 1989. This postponement would have contravened the 1983 constitution, which the FMLN had long sought to discredit. Duarte offered to meet the guerrilla demands through a joint executive-legislative-judicial decree or a national plebiscite, but ARENA would not agree, because its leaders feared delay might threaten their expected victory in the March elections. A top FMLN leader told me in 1994 that the FMLN had worried that Duarte would succeed in meeting the FMLN demand. The FMLN proposal had been merely a tactical ploy, not a sincere offer. The Duarte government met at least 17 times with the FMLN in efforts to negotiate peace during its five years in office.

Newly elected ARENA President Cristiani immediately made clear his intention to continue negotiating with the FMLN. He personally persuaded the UN secretary general to mediate. The FMLN entered into talks in 1989 but suspended them just before launching its November 1989 "final offensive." Negotiations resumed in 1990. Agreements were reached incrementally on a number of important reforms to continue progress toward democracy. Further structural changes were agreed upon to improve human rights and the justice system, to separate the military and police, to reduce the military, to put the police under a civilian ministry, to legalize the FMLN as a political party, and to reincorporate FMLN members into Salvadoran society. Final agreement was reached on December 31, 1991, just before expiration of Secretary General Javier Perez de Cuellar's mandate.

Prospects for El Salvador

A look at El Salvador today reveals many who are still excluded from a just share of the material and social wealth of the nation. Critics allege that movement toward restructuring the economy to ensure greater economic equity and with it a further redistribution of political power has ended. They argue that peasant and working class advancements toward political empowerment, land, and a bigger share of the economic pie have come to a halt. In their view, the economic oligarchy, middle class entrepreneurs, and the military are again dominant at the expense of lower class workers and peasants.

Any new political system that negates the steadily increasing inclusion of the excluded since 1979 would probably approximate the oligarchically dominated and limited democracy of El Salvador in the first decades of the twentieth century. In this power pattern the oligarchy and the middle class, now much larger in numbers, would dominate the armed forces. Should this pattern be reemerging, the prospects for development and democracy are diminished. It will probably be impossible to declare definitively that Salvadorans have successfully established democracy and a minimally acceptable level of justice for at least another decade.

Evaluations and Lessons Learned

The thesis of this book is that the elements necessary for success in the conduct of U.S. foreign policy and the protection of American national security interests include, as they did during the cold war, a theory of engagement, a functional management and implementation structure, and an effective military and civil bureaucracy with appropriate weaponry and resources. Max Manwaring and this author propose in Chapter 2 a legitimacy theory of engagement for the post–Cold War period. At the beginning of this chapter, the six elements of the Manwaring paradigm are outlined as the most critical factors for successful outcomes in low-intensity conflicts. These are the heart of Manwaring's and my legitimacy theory of engagement. Finally, I have also emphasized the need for clear vision in terms of the desired and possible end state of disputes and conflict, which is necessary for the formulation of proper policy and actions in Third World conflicts.

The El Salvador case has many lessons to offer for students of small wars. The conflict was born at the height of the Cold War and came to an end after it was clear that the cold war was over. The insurgency had its roots in social, economic, and political problems that had evolved for decades, but it was greatly exacerbated and lengthened by foreign encouragement and support.

In the Salvadoran case, the U.S. government consciously and clearly tried to formulate its policies and programs in a manner that would enhance the legitimacy of the Salvadoran government and lead to a democratic outcome. These actions were in keeping with the Manwaring paradigm and the legitimacy theory of engagement. The Salvadoran case lends credence to these two conceptual approaches. The highest level U.S. political leadership clearly articulated the desired end state in El Salvador, which provided an overall goal and direction to U.S. policies and actions.

With respect to conflict management, as will be noted in chapter 9, several U.S. ambassadors to El Salvador during the 1980s complained about inadequate Washington management and coordination, although in the end it proved sufficient. Nonetheless, the erratic manner in which the U.S. government provided military and economic support to the Salvadoran government and armed forces detracted from more effective implementation. Moreover, the description provided on El Salvador particularly reinforces the argument that organization of effort must be related to the concept of political legitimacy.

U.S. foreign policy toward Central America and the goals and programs of Salvadoran democrats were vindicated, but, as in every human endeavor, there are areas where the Salvadorans and their U.S. supporters could have done better. In addition to the five priority areas (objectives) for which the U.S. government used its resources and influence in support of Salvadoran programs, there are at least two other areas that should have been given greater emphasis.

The FMLN-FDR, both by design and by the nature of their supporters, was able to gain a public relations and a diplomatic advantage in Europe and among the U.S. public that the GOES even to this day has not overcome. U.S. foreign affairs and assistance bureaucracies had neither the capability nor the legal authority to support GOES public information programs to explain and clarify the record, even though top foreign affairs officials were aware of the need. Congress, in fact, curtailed executive branch efforts in this area. Perception is more important than reality in the struggle over legitimacy.

Second, El Salvador's civilian bureaucratic capacity to plan, implement, and coordinate programs was very weak. This weakness not only prevented the effective extension of GOES programs to earn the support of the Salvadoran people, especially in conflict zones, but also greatly impeded the assertion of civil authority over the military. The Salvadoran armed forces had the guns and generally were bureaucratically superior to civilian agencies. The U.S. foreign assistance bureaucracy lacked the ability to help strengthen capacity and unity of effort of Third World civil bureaucracies. The growth of legitimacy is intricately linked to performance. The U.S. government still needs greater capabilities in these two areas for future small wars.

In most small wars, the attainment or strengthening of legitimacy and progress on Manwaring's other critical factors require a basic transformation of the society in question. Unless there are greater vital interests, such as U.S. security, the U.S. interest is for a democratic outcome. By giving priority to democratization, human rights and justice, a growing and more equitable economy, defense and negotiations, and peace in the region, the United States contained a threat to its security; and Salvadoran democrats, with our help, transformed El Salvador to achieve peace and constitutional democracy.

The world will continue for decades to be characterized by great power rivalries, regional conflicts, and internal as well as external small wars. In coping with small wars, attention to all six factors of the Manwaring paradigm can lead to successful negotiating to end conflict or, if necessary, to defeating the opposing force. The most important factor in small wars is legitimacy, the moral right to govern. The United States should be guided in its foreign policy in the post–Cold War era by a legitimate governance theory of engagement. The U.S. government must ensure that every policy, program, and action (political, economic, security, and opinion-making) contribute directly or indirectly to the maintenance, or enhancement, of legitimacy for the force the United States supports, be it a regime or an insurgency.

Notes

1.   Jack Spence and George Vickers, *El Salvador Elections 1994: Toward a Level Playing Field?* (Cambridge, MA: Hemisphere Initiatives, Inc., 1994), p. 1.

2.   In Salvadoran official statistics the number of deaths caused by the war between January 1981 and July 1991 was 30,907. "Todo lo que ha hecho el FMLN en 11 años fue enumerado por Ponce," *El Mundo* (San Salvador), July 24, 1991, p. 3.

3.   Thomas Long and Frank Smyth, "How the FMLN Won the Peace," *Voice*, February 18, 1992, p. 19.

4.   See Max G. Manwaring and John T. Fishel, "Insurgency and Counter-Insurgency: Toward a New Analytical Approach," *Small Wars & Insurgencies*, 3 (3): 272–310 (Winter 1992); Max Manwaring, ed., *Uncomfortable Wars: Toward a New Paradigm of Low-Intensity Conflict* (Boulder, CO: Westview Press, 1991); Stephen Sloan, "Introduction," in Edwin G. Corr and Stephen Sloan, eds., *Low-Intensity Conflict: Old Threats in a New World* (Boulder, CO: Westview Press, 1992), pp. 3–16.

5.   National Bipartisan Commission on Central America, *Report of the National Bipartisan Commission on Central America*, January 1984, pp. 126–127.

6.   Bruce B.G. Clarke, "Conflict Termination: A Rational Model," *Terrorism*, vol. 16, pp. 25–50. For further thinking and writing in this area, see Carl von Clausewitz, *On War*, ed. and transl. Michael Howard and Peter Paret (Princeton: Princeton University Press, 1976); Sun Tzu, *The Art of War*, transl. Samuel B. Griffith (New York: Oxford University Press, 1963); B.H. Liddell Hart, *Strategy* (New York: Praeger, 1967); Harry Summers, *On Strategy: The Vietnam War in Context* (Carlisle Barracks, Penn.: Strategic Studies Institute, 1981).

7.   I say this not in criticism of the very able Ambassadors White, Hinton, and Pickering. During their stewardships in El Salvador the situation ranged from anarchy to chaotic. By the time of my arrival the form, although not the content of democratic institutions, had been established.

8. *Report on the Situation in El Salvador*, April 1, 1990, United States Department of State, p. 21; Corr telephone conversation with the State Department El Salvador desk officer, 5 November 1993.

9. Edwin G. Corr, "Including the Excluded in El Salvador: Prospects for Democracy and Development," in Peter L. Berger, ed., *Institutions of Democracy and Development*, Sequoia Seminar Publication (San Francisco, CA: ICS Press, 1993), p. 184.

10. Oscar Alfredo Santamariá, "Investing in El Salvador," *North-South* 4, no. 1 (July/August, 1994): 43–46.

11. Salvadoran effectiveness in the deployment of helicopters owes much to retired Central Intelligence Agency operative Felix Rodriguez who taught pilots helicopter attack tactics while preventing civilian casualties.

12. Edwin G. Corr, "José Napoleón Duarte: Architect of Peace and Father of Salvadoran Democracy," *Extensions* (A Journal of the Carl Albert Research and Studies Center, Summer 1992), pp. 11–14.

13. José Napoleón Duarte with Diana Page, *Duarte: My Story* (New York: G.P. Putnam's Sons, 1986), p. 169.

14. "El Salvador: Conversations With Two Foes," *Time*, October 2, 1989, p. 26. The FMLN launched its November 1989 offensive less than six weeks later.

PART TWO

The Second Pillar of Success: Tools of Power and Appropriate Weapons Systems to Support the Theory

6

New National Security Challenges

General Wayne A. Downing

The fall of the Berlin Wall and the subsequent dissolution of the Soviet Union signaled the end of the Cold War and the superpower nuclear confrontation. These two major events, and the resulting peaceful reunification of Germany and withdrawal of Soviet troops from Eastern Europe, heralded what many hoped would be an era of peace and cooperation in the international political environment. Even the Gulf War seemed to presage a revitalization of international cooperation in solving the world's problems. Unfortunately, events have not borne out the positive hopes of many of the world's leaders and peoples. Instead, the United States, and much of the rest of the world, finds itself confronted with a much more complex, dynamic international environment, with many new or renewed challenges that require innovative and creative solutions. Many of these hold the potential for conflict below the level of full scale war.

Those who follow low intensity conflict, peacetime engagement, peacetime competition, operations short of war, and now operations other than war (OOTW) have generally felt that the mainstream military paid too little attention to the conflict environment which lies below full scale war. The term or acronym used is not important. What is important is that this environment will continue to be a very important focus of U.S. foreign policy in a still unstable world.

The purpose of this chapter is to give the author's views on the application of joint and multinational military force in the new international environment. I will look at trends in the areas of national security, future military challenges for the U.S., a view of OOTW and its leadership and technological implications, and conclude with operational criteria for the use of military force. This last area is designed to provide general guidelines

---

This paper reflects the views of the author and not the views of the U.S. government, the Department of State, or the Special Operations Command.

for determining when and how to commit the military in the pursuit of national interests in a practical, effective, and justified manner.

Trends

National security in a dynamic, changing world is complicated by two divergent trends. The first is toward democratic states and free markets. It is coupled to rapidly accelerating technological change promising new solutions to many previously intractable problems and a much improved future for many of the world's peoples. This trend is manifest in the growth of democracy in Latin America and parts of the former Soviet Union, and in the vibrant economies of the Pacific Rim.

The other trend is toward the disintegration of sovereign and mutually respectful nation-states. It is characterized by a breakdown of the authority of nation-states and international bodies, widening social and economic disparities, and a degeneration of traditional societal mores. This trend is exacerbated by the emergence of long-repressed ethnic, religious, and cultural hatreds, increased acceptance of violence or the threat of violence to resolve disagreements, and the rise of non-national and transnational groups that threaten traditional nation-states. This trend is exemplified by the collapse of central governmental authority in several states (Somalia and Rwanda being two recent examples), the rise of Islamic fascism, the increased activity of criminal cartels, and the outbreak of insurrection in many parts of the former Soviet Union, the Balkans, sub-Saharan Africa, the Caribbean Basin region, and Asia.

Global disintegration had been masked for several generations by the relative political stability imposed on the world by the Cold War superpower rivalry of the Soviet Union and the United States. The evaporation of Soviet power and influence, in particular, has exposed a myriad of frustrated, unhappy, and impatient peoples who find it increasingly difficult to achieve social, political, and economic self-expression within the New World Order. This alienation is not limited to areas of the former Soviet Union. It has economic, religious, cultural, and political manifestations as diverse as the renegade capitalism of the Golden Triangle drug traders on the China-Burma border and the worldwide Islamic struggle.

There are a number of destabilizing factors at work in the world today that contribute to a pessimistic view of an unstable world. The United States will have to deal with many of these factors, to include:

- Continued fragmentation of the former Soviet Union;
- Weapons proliferation, especially the proliferation of weapons of mass destruction (WMD);
- Ethnic strife;
- Virulent, xenophobic nationalism;

- Religious extremism;
- Narco-trafficking and the related activities of narco-terrorists.
- International criminal activity
- International terrorism; and
- Population growth in poor and underdeveloped areas creating demands that outstrip infrastructure capacities and result in shortages of food, medical care, and other necessities with the consequent spread of disease and famine.

In some regions, such as the Balkans and parts of Africa, such as the Horn, southern Sudan, Liberia, and Rwanda, these problems are exacerbated by a social climate in which violence has become a part of the cultural landscape. In these hotbeds of anarchy, conflict is often the norm and not the exception, and Western values of tolerance and respect for the rights of others are incomprehensible.

Amidst these challenges, the United States seeks to preserve a stable global environment in which its national interests can be served through the development of democratic states and peaceful access to free markets and resources. These objectives are presently challenged directly and indirectly by:

- Renegade totalitarian states such as Cuba, North Korea, Iraq, Iran, and Libya;
- National secessionists such as the Bosnian Serbs, the Spanish Basques, and the Chechens; and
- Transnational groups such as Hizballah and the criminal drug cartels of the former Soviet Union, Asia, and South America.

The Future Military Challenge

The basic mission of U.S. military forces is to fight our nation's wars. In the post–Cold War era, they have been charged with an ever expanding range of peacetime responsibilities. Part of the reason the military is being called upon to meet these peacetime challenges is that the military has unique capabilities not found in other government agencies and organizations. The military has a versatile command structure, rapid high-volume global mobility, organic worldwide communications, regional expertise (e.g., in language, culture, economics, and medicine), and the ability to protect and defend itself and those organizations and individuals with whom it works.

Often, the resolution of these emerging challenges requires a mix of government, non-government, private for-profit, and private non-profit organizations. Add to that international organizations, and you have the environment which is known as the interagency world. Operating as one element in an interagency environment, the military component can help create an effective and efficient synergism within the interagency process.

However, the interagency process is an extremely frustrating and cumbersome mechanism. It often comes across as broken — with excessive layering and requiring time-consuming coordination. Many of the participants are bureaucratic organizations. This can cause them to focus, not on the operation's overall goal or objective, but on their own sub-goals and objectives and the effect the operation will have on their organization. In many cases, there is either no clearly defined lead agency or the lead agency lacks authority is reluctant to take charge and make the difficult decisions required for action.

This lack of unified direction clearly hampers progress and success. It often results in excessive negotiation, bickering, and inaction. Another phenomena observed is that the military's high visibility, task orientation, and aggressive closure with challenges, often puts the soldier in roles disproportionate to their proper contribution. The interagency arena is the forum we can expect to operate in, but it is far from an ideal playing field.

Conceptually, the operational environment for all military challenges may be grouped into *war* and *operations other than war* (OOTW). These two areas cover the full range of military operations from peacetime to global war, and the U.S. military must be competent in all of them.

While the U.S. will likely remain the unchallenged military superpower well into the next century, the manner in which American military power is exercised will have to accommodate dramatic changes taking place in the political, economic, and technological landscape of the world. To bound the problem, I will make several assumptions about the future in which the United States will apply its military power:

- The U.S. will continue to have vital national interests beyond its shores, particularly in the production, supply, and transportation of strategic minerals and petroleum supplies.
- The U.S. will continue to maintain military force as an option for dealing with threats to national interests.
- The military capabilities of the U.S. will be centered on a relatively small, professional armed force emphasizing power projection from the continental U.S., rather than maintaining large overseas garrisons.
- A low public tolerance for casualties coupled with mass access to battlefield information via the news media will trigger traditional Congressional awareness and oversight of the role of military.
- When appropriate, the U.S. will intervene, as directed by the National Command Authority (NCA), in concert with multinational task forces following request for U.S. forces from international organizations such as the UN and the Organization of American States.

- U.S. domestic support will be required for all large and protracted overseas commitments.

OOTW, Maneuver Warfare in the Information Age, and Fourth Generation Warfare

OOTW comprises military activity conducted below the level of open warfare, and is further subdivided into operations that either *do* or *do not* involve the use of force. Such operations encompass a wide range of activities where the military instrument of national power is used for purposes other than large-scale combat operations. Some examples are arms control, combating terrorism, counterdrug operations, security assistance, noncombatant evacuation, humanitarian and civil support operations, peace operations, and support to insurgencies and counterinsurgencies. OOTW may involve a combination of air, land, sea, space, and special operations forces as well as the integrated and complementary efforts of other government agencies and nongovernmental organizations. Although these operations are often conducted outside the United States, they also include military support to U.S. civil authorities. OOTW can occur before, during, or after a war. The dividing line between war and OOTW is not always clear-cut.

Both war and OOTW may take place in high technology industrial states or in less advanced areas of the world. At one end is the threat from modern high-technology nation-state, operations I term as Third Generation Warfare, or Maneuver Warfare in the Information Age. At the other end are operations against non-nation state actors of terrorists, ethnic factions, religious radicals, and crime/drug cartels, who engage in what I call Fourth Generation Warfare, or "Niche" Warfare. Examples of the later abound in the ongoing strife in Bosnia, Somalia, Columbia, Peru, Rwanda, and the former Soviet Union. The challenge for the U.S. military is to create a force that can fight and win against a wide range of threats.

In a high-technology environment characterized by nation-states in conflict, the relevant military weapons, forces, and doctrine will emphasize smaller size and weight, greater speed and precision, "knowledge dominance" of the enemy and the operational environment, fewer casualties, and less collateral damage. Success here will require the military to maximize and integrate the effects of knowledge, speed, violence, and precision. Intelligence—or more appropriately, *knowledge*—will be employed to pierce the fog of war, minimize uncertainty, and reduce risk. The rapid and accurate acquisition of relevant and useful *information* for friendly purposes and the concomitant denial of such to the enemy, cumulatively termed "information warfare," may become the most important facet of combat. In this arena, information should rise to coequal status with the traditional elements of national power—political, economic, and military. Information warfare may ultimately shape battles and campaigns in the other elements, and in some cases will preclude significant struggle altogether. The next battlefield may take place in cyber-space, with power supplies and information nets being threatened by techno-terrorists from within the information superhighway.

The military understands the centers of gravity in nation states which are vulnerable to our third generation precision forces. Finding these centers of gravity in fourth generation challenges will require an entirely different approach, if we can find them at all. The enemy here may have its origins and sustenance, not in the infrastructure of a highly developed centralized industrial nation-state, but rather in the deep-seated social, economic, and political concerns of angry and alienated populations in unstable social, political, and economic environments. Third generation warfare forces may be ineffective where the roots of the problems are transnational, varied and diffuse, and combat is against widely dispersed, fleeting and often unorthodox threats such as subversion, extortion, kidnapping, assassination, bombing, and psychological operations. High-technology equipment and forces may be inapplicable or counterproductive in regions where the threats are less traditional. In this environment opponents may be singularly unafraid to sacrifice their lives for their beliefs, and leaders and organizations by virtue of their overt or clandestine distribution among "noncombatants" may not be subject to swift surgical strikes.

Leadership

Effectiveness in these diverse and contradictory environments requires a flexible and versatile force that can employ a complete complement of direct and indirect means across the full range of military operations. The U.S. military will need operational and tactical leaders with a keen sense of the political implications of their actions, who understand the underlying causes and motivations of conflict and the paths to its resolution, who can adapt quickly to changing rules of engagement, and who can act decisively and appropriately in all circumstances. These leaders must be imaginative and innovative, capable of thinking effectively under immense pressure and inspiring their subordinates to do the same. They must be able to integrate widely varying capabilities into a sound overall plan attuned to the specific environment in which they are operating.

Above all, in fourth generation warfare, leaders at the national level must recognize that the military is most often not the solution to these challenges. It is only a means, and not necessarily the most important means, within an integrated and coordinated interagency response to a combination of social, economic, political conditions that threaten national interests. Our future leaders must be able to operate with skill, knowledge, and adroitness in the cumbersome interagency arena.

National leaders must also recognize how increasing economic interdependence will influence military operations in situations short of overt warfare. With rising economic and social interdependencies, nations will be more than ever concerned with preserving their sovereign prerogatives. Nations and regional and cultural combinations of states will be more sensitive to foreign military intervention, either in their own territories or in the territories of neighboring states, even if that intervention is nominally in their best interests. At the same time, however, competition among nations for natural resources will intensify, and security interests tied to the uninterrupted supply of such resources will expand.

Military success in the future will thus depend on the ability of national and military leaders to recognize the form of operations to be engaged in and to understand the desired military and political end-state to be achieved. Prior to employment of military forces, conditions must be identified that will facilitate successful military operations. There should always be a clear mission statement, which lays out the desired end state. The environment must be evaluated to set appropriate rules of engagement, such as in successful U.S. operations in Haiti in 1994-95. This allows our forces to establish moral and physical dominance appropriate to the situation and political goals. Interagency participation will be required. Finally, clear orders must be transmitted to commanders in the field so they in turn can issue orders consistent with national policy objectives.

With the desired end-state in mind, our national leadership must consider four things:

- Bringing to bear the full power of the U.S. government on a situation through the interagency process.
- Selecting the appropriate military forces to address the situation.
- Training the force on the environment, simulating reality to the maximum extent possible, with due emphasis on political, cultural, and military considerations.
- Employing the force with initiative, perseverance, and mastery of the complex environment.

A warning on applying military force: Every situation is unique and must be analyzed independently as a unique situation. Beware of applying lessons from Somalia 1993 blindly to Haiti 1994, for example.

Technological Implications

Technological advances will significantly alter military operations in several fundamental ways. First, the role of the military as the primary driver of technological innovation has probably already ended and been replaced by the private sector. This will force changes in military acquisition processes, and could in some instances place the military in a technologically inferior position when facing unorthodox nonmilitary threats. Those threats will have access to the same or better off the shelf commercial technology, and will have easier access than a military encumbered by military acquisition law guidelines.

Even though no other superpower may emerge as a threat to U.S. interests, the research and development community must continue to explore new ways to stay ahead of potential hostile actors and monitor their capabilities so as not to fall prey to a technological breakthrough that would threaten our forces. As noted above, even without their own active R&D programs, hostile actors can take advantage of "off-the-shelf" technologies available on the world arms bazaars, and gain the advantage on U.S. forces called upon to resolve a crisis.

The goods news here, however, is that even when the technological capabilities of potential threats may appear to be similar to those of U.S. forces, the U.S. military has demonstrated an unparalleled ability to successfully integrate diverse technologies with proven tactics, techniques, and procedures. This is key. The bottom line is that hostile actors may have state-of-the-art technology, but they probably will not have the ability to pull it all together and make it work synergistically.

Technological advance may also mean significant limits on the ability of one nation-state to surprise another. With the proliferation of satellite and battlefield surveillance technology, the skies are open to anyone who can use them. As a result, it may be less possible to achieve operational-strategic surprise such as was attained by the Japanese at Pearl Harbor, the Allies at Normandy, or United Nations forces at Inchon.

Future battlefield weapons systems will also become increasingly lethal (in terms of range and yield), mobile, agile, concealable, and available. Many systems will become smaller, more diffuse and redundant. As newer weapons systems are produced, older systems will be handed down to other nations. By the middle of the next century, for example, a large number of unstable, unpredictable belligerent actors can possess fixed and mobile intermediate-range ballistic missiles (IRBM) capable of carrying domestically-produced nuclear, biological, or chemical warheads thousands of miles from their launch sites. These systems and their components will become harder to find and fix by standard technical means, and their threatened use will entail more compressed response times.

Additionally, non-nation state actors will be able to conduct their operations more easily, with less chance of detection by not using highly sophisticated delivery systems. For example, the World Trade Center bombers used a 1976 Econoline van and the Oklahoma City terrorists used a rented truck.

Tailored data collection and applications of interactive artificial intelligence in planning and execution military operations will allow the military to literally and figuratively "see" their targets with greater precision, significantly reducing uncertainty and risk at all stages of operations. Enhanced mobility, sustainment, and communications systems will give the military unprecedented reach, staying power, survivability, and responsiveness. The military will be able to move against objectives on shorter notice, and will provide and be provided with greater quantity and higher quality of real-time information during operations through the use of secure miniature video cameras interfaced with VHF/satellite communications. At the same time, we must not lose sight of the fact that hostile countermeasures are likely to be enhanced in parallel ways.

The intelligence community must monitor the latest technological advancements and how potential threats are exploiting them. More than simply watching CNN and reviewing the latest satellite photos, quality intelligence requires *reliability and confidence* in the intelligence gathered. This often mandates having human eyes and ears on target. Furthermore, target information has to be transmitted quickly and transformed into usable intelligence relevant to the operator on the ground.

Technological advances will also be critical to the previously mentioned discussion of information, specifically in dealing with the psychological element of *information warfare*. The U.S. must be able to fight and orchestrate the war of images and influence the perception of U.S. government involvement in war and OOTW.

Moreover, information warfare must include a formidable defensive capability that can deal with renegade "cyber-terrorists" and more traditional nation-state threats to U.S. information systems. We have entered the age where society's technological-based infrastructure (e.g., electrical power, water supply) can be disrupted or even destroyed by hostile actors or hackers with a personal computer on the INTERNET. Defensive systems and procedures will continue to be critical in this evolving area.

Finally, future technologies can assist the U.S. military focus on regional and cultural orientation. The language and cultural training which have been a benchmark of special operations forces, are growing in importance for a greater cross-section of the U.S. military. Possibilities exist for information systems which can provide virtual reality simulation for any location and situation on this earth. Such virtual realities could include cross-cultural interactions and either require or develop language proficiency to navigate the program.

Operational Criteria

In an increasingly complex world, threats to vital national interests are no longer the single criterion for the employment of force. Moreover, many of the problems that do require military force require much more than just military force to solve problems. In this environment, those charged with making the decision to employ U.S. military forces need a set of simplified guidelines that provide a reasonable means to evaluate the efficacy of sending American men and women into harms way. The following criteria is a suggested way to look at some of the key issues that should be evaluated any time the use of force is contemplated.

What combination of national power is applicable? The national leadership should carefully consider the use of political, economic, psychological, and informational elements of power prior to commitment of U.S. military forces. National power is a dynamic formula in which each element plays a role relative to the others. Circumstances dictate the relative prominence of each in combination with others, and different elements of power predominate at different times. When applying military power, it is not enough to identify the military as the lead or supporting agent. A successful interagency effort must take into account the relationship the military will have with other elements of the U.S. government within the interagency process.

Who is to be in charge? We cannot afford to forget to put someone in charge. Whoever it is must have the power to make decisions, even contentious ones, and make them stick. This may be the most difficult issue to come to grips with, as it will go against many long established operating procedures for many different agencies. But no single issue has the potential to make a greater impact on the interagency process than that of appointing a single, responsible individual to ensure a coordinated, synchronized operation that directs all efforts towards the goal set by the nation's leaders.

Is the military role an appropriate one? The question is not whether military power *can* be exercised, but whether it *ought* to be exercised. The military should not, and cannot afford to, do missions which other organizations train for and which do not make use of the military's unique skills. Many examples exist of appropriate military roles. The military can provide immediate and timely air and sea lift of bulk and outsize cargo in support of other government agencies and non-government agencies. Regionally-oriented special operations civil affairs units can provide a bridge to a nation's civilian population by establishing public safety, health and welfare; handling dislocated civilians (refugees); and coordinating disaster and humanitarian relief. Special Forces, augmented in psychological operations and civil affairs units, can provide many skills required to restore order in troubled areas.

Does the national will support the commitment of forces? Lack of national will undermines military morale, cohesiveness, recruitment, retention, and operational effectiveness. Premature termination may undermine U. S. national objectives and may place lives in danger.

Does the international community support the commitment of forces? The United States retains the capability to engage in unilateral military intervention in many parts of the world. However, the reality is that in most cases the use of military force outside clear-cut situations of self-defense requires the consent of relevant portions of the international community through whose land, air and sea space American forces must traverse. Without consent secured through the diplomatic process, the application of American military force can be cast by opponents as naked aggression. *However, this is not to say that the United States should not pursue unilateral operations necessary to protect and defend vital national interests.*

Is the employment of military force operationally feasible? The military cannot afford to waste precious resources on missions that are beyond its capabilities. This doesn't mean that the military cannot take on difficult missions. The U.S. military should continue to look for innovative ways to accomplish the difficult; but at the same time, it should recognize the limitations of military force. Perhaps an interagency effort in conjunction with other international governmental and non-governmental organizations could satisfy a situation, and would be better received in the international arena.

Are required resources available to execute the application of military force? Even if the use of force meets all of the above criteria, the actual operation may be beyond the capabilities of the resources available. Or, the requirements of a military operation may expand far beyond what was originally estimated. In these cases, the application of military force may just be unaffordable and counterproductive to overall national interests because it requires too many resources to support it.

Does the expected outcome of the application of military force justify the risk? This criterion is crucial and eliminates many proposed military operations. The military should not conduct operations because they are possible. Some operations are possible, but make only a marginal contribution to the national interest. The risk must justify the expenditure of resources, especially lives. Resources and lives should not be wasted on high-risk/low-payoff operations. When U.S. military forces are employed, they are under the constant scrutiny of the U.S. Congress and the world media. A small number of casualties in an isolated corner of the world can result in a national furor, with enormous potential to influence the course of U.S. policy. Is the risk worth the goal?

These seven questions provide a clear set of tests to determine the feasibility and utility of military operations. They ensure that the military are pursuing meaningful operations that contribute to the national interest and that resources are applied wisely. These questions, applied as criteria, could assist national leaders objectively evaluate potential operations and should ensure a realistic perception of military capabilities. The military's role is to provide its civilian leadership with clear advice on capabilities and potential options for use of the military instrument of national power.

Conclusion

In the past, we have often prepared for the last battle—not the next one. There is no way to know with certainty what future conflicts or OOTW will involve the employment of U.S. forces. Nor is there a formula for apportioning the defense budget in preparing land, air, maritime, space, and special operations forces to best face such contingencies. U.S. policy makers, legislators, and military leaders must be intimately familiar with America's national interests, the elements of power used to pursue these interests, the dynamic global environment in which these interests are pursued, and the significant threats to such interests. Premised on this knowledge and understanding, the future role of the military element of power within the conduct of the national security and foreign policies will be flexible, capable, relevant, and appropriate.

7

Confronting the "Hard Decisions" of Redefined Sovereignty and the Tools of Intervention in the New Security Environment

Dennis F. Caffrey

Even the most casual observer is astonished at how much the international landscape has changed recently. It is not an exaggeration to state that the world has changed more profoundly in the past five years than in the preceding fifty. Admiral Paul David Miller, Supreme Allied Commander, Atlantic, has compared today's multi-polar world security environment to the "aftermath of a hurricane . . . where the guideposts for action are missing."[1] Perhaps an even more accurate description of today's turbulent situation would be the aftermath of a major earthquake, with its continuous, and often jolting, after-shocks.

Unfortunately, although the major threat to peace and stability has been eliminated with the end of the Cold War, dozens of other threats now replace it. These "new" threats are less conventional in nature but are certainly not new to the world scene. In fact, some have been around for many years. Having been overshadowed and repressed by the more menacing and resource-consuming aspects of the cold war, these threats are now clearly visible and highly volatile. We find that not only has the game of world political order and stability changed, but the rules and players have as well. Instead of now living in a safer world, we are faced with an increasing *world disorder* that forces us to reevaluate traditional concepts such as threat identification, sovereignty, and intervention.[2] Multilateral preventive diplomacy, peacemaking, peacekeeping and postconflict peace building may now be the new watchwords on the world scene, but unilateral actions have far from disappeared. The road map to guide us through this landscape of turbulent change and discontinuity has yet to be fully developed.

International organizations and individual nations, particularly the United States, are being forced to confront what United Nations Secretary General Boutros Boutros-Ghali has termed "hard decisions" as they reexamine the traditional definition of sovereignty and intervention in their struggle to resolve intrastate conflicts and salvage failed or faltering states.[3]

Sovereignty Through a New Looking Glass

The modern world's legal and political structure originated with the Treaty of Westphalia in 1648. This "watershed" event provided legal recognition for states and a state system independent of the papacy. Since then, sovereignty has been viewed in terms of protecting the physical and political integrity of states from external forces. John Herz has pointed out that the strength and resilience of the state have traditionally resided in its capacity to perform two major functions: defending those citizens who lie within its physical borders and promoting their economic well-being.[4] The end of the cold war transformed the existing imperatives concerning international security and the concept of sovereignty. No longer do the dominant considerations in defense planning revolve around the possibilities of a massive Soviet ground assault through Germany's Fulda Gap to the heart of the North Atlantic Treaty Organization (NATO) alliance, with the associated possibility of using nuclear or other weapons of mass destruction. Security issues appear to have slipped down in the policy agenda of many nations, having been replaced by more mundane "low policy" problems dealing with trade, welfare, and economics.

The majority of the problems that beset us today (insurgencies, organized crime and terrorism, ethnic strife, illicit drug trafficking and the transnational consequences of instability visibly reflected in mass refugee migrations, epidemic diseases, and environmental devastation) have little to do with the "high policy" issues of peace and war, conquest and domination. One term being used to describe these new challenges is the "gray area phenomena" (GAP), which Peter Lupsha has defined as "threats to the stability of nation-states by non-state actors and non-governmental processes and organizations."[5] Almost daily our television news shows and newspaper headlines describe crisis situations in different parts of the world (Rwanda, Somalia, Bosnia, Haiti Algeria, etc.) in which established governments either have lost their ability and legitimacy to govern or are in immediate danger of so doing.

The seeming inability of many modern states to satisfy the security requirements of their citizens and the diminished significance of international security issues in general are matched by many states' growing inability to provide economic prosperity for those within their borders. The decline in national self-sufficiency produced by a complex world economic order has meant that the prosperity and, in some cases, the very survival of particular states is now increasingly being determined by events and developments beyond their borders rather than any decisions taken by their governments.

There are two clear signs of our changing times. The first manifestation is the increasing number of instances in which the international community attempts to come to the rescue of these failed or faltering states, not to protect them from foreign aggression, as in Kuwait, but rather to save them from their own inability or unwillingness to resolve internal, domestic situations. Images of Bosnia-Herzegovina, Somalia, and Rwanda immediately come to mind. Other domestic situations, such as a miscalculation in fiscal or monetary policies, may also give rise to more subtle forms of intervention. Mexico's devaluation of its national currency, the peso, in late 1994 is a case in point. This action triggered not only a domestic but also an international economic and political crisis. Within days, the so-called tequila effect was being felt throughout the financial markets in the United States, Argentina, Brazil, and Chile, as the value of the peso plummeted and foreign investors scurried to protect their investments throughout the Western Hemisphere. The unilateral $20 billion bailout in loan guarantees approved by President Bill Clinton averted a far more serious crisis but was viewed by many, both within and outside of Mexico, as an example of economic intervention that violated Mexico's national sovereignty.[6]

The second and most significant sign of change is the concomitant willingness of the world community to redefine the traditional concept of sovereignty. Frequently, the United Nations (UN) is being called upon to "intervene" physically in what for generations were considered the sacrosanct internal affairs of sovereign states.[7] The once heretical concept of "intervention" appears to be losing many of its worst connotations and is expanding in acceptance, especially when undertaken for "the best of humanitarian reasons." Meanwhile, the legal norm of "sovereignty" is contracting and undergoing substantial transformation, and the concept of security is being expanded to include the notion of social and economic "well-being."[8]

In April 1991, then UN Secretary General Javier Perez de Cuellar stated that the traditional prerogatives of state sovereignty needed to be reassessed in light of "the shift in public attitudes toward the belief that the defense of the oppressed in the name of morality should prevail over frontiers and legal documents."[9] His successor, Boutros Boutros Ghali, clearly supports the need for redefining sovereignty. He believes the time of absolute and exclusive sovereignty has passed and has called upon world leaders to understand this dramatic change and to find a balance between their needs for good internal governance and the requirements of an ever more interactive and interdependent world.[10] Alex Rondos argues that when a government can no longer guarantee food, shelter, clothing, and a modicum of health to its population, it abdicates the right to sovereignty. When a government permits or even perpetuates acts that are a brazen contravention of these most elementary human rights, often in the name of the state, it in effect has eliminated the legitimacy of its security and sovereignty and, in today's environment, openly invites intervention.[11]

This "need" for greater international security cooperation has not emerged as the result of any apparent conscious deliberation, but rather from the pressure of dynamic, ongoing events. Many of these situations that clamor for outside help are due in part to the fact that the cold war did not end by strategic design or formally negotiated process. As Janne E. Nolan et al. describe: "It was terminated by diffuse, spontaneous historical forces powerful enough to override the prescriptions of established policies, powerful enough also to induce massive social transformations."[12] The UN is increasingly acting to fill a power void created by the combination of faltering states that are either incapable of dealing with their own deep-rooted problems, or unwilling to do so, and major powers that are increasingly reluctant to become involved in such problems unilaterally.

This new view of the world postulates that the overriding threat we must face is one of "global chaos" or a "virus of disorder." Timothy Wirth, Undersecretary of State for Global Affairs, has cited environmental degradation, poverty, disease and conflict driven migration as "the primary threats to human society."[13] Robert Kaplan added considerable weight to this argument in his sobering *Atlantic Monthly* article, "The Coming Anarchy," in which he describes firsthand the destruction wrought on West African states by poverty, corruption, crime, AIDS, and malaria. He argues that "West Africa's future, eventually, will also be that of the rest of the world." Kaplan is convinced that this environmentally-driven anarchy will be "the national-security issue of the early twenty-first century" and should replace George Kennan's strategy of containment of communism as the driving concern of American foreign policy.[14] The Clinton administration's efforts to develop a replacement strategy based on "enlargement of democracies" are still in their formative stages. In the meantime, we are seeing more and more cases of justifiable intervention in an effort to resolve the problems of the gray area phenomena. Unfortunately, these efforts often have been belated, ill-defined and incomplete.

Choosing Sides and Practicing Triage

Over the years, the United Nations has based its peacekeeping operations on three fundamental principles: the consent of the parties involved in the dispute (usually sovereign states), impartiality, and the non-use of force except for self-defense of UN personnel. Recent events and the evolving nature of intrastate conflicts in the post–Cold War era cause us to reexamine these principles. The role of the UN in northern Iraq and Somalia as peacemakers was vastly different from that of the more familiar peacekeepers on Cypress and in the Sinai.

The first glimpse of this new reality of UN peace operations took place in northern Iraq after Kuwait had been liberated from Saddam Hussein's forces. Responding to public pressure generated by media broadcasts of starving, freezing Kurds, and not wishing to have the Gulf War victory offset by massive human suffering, the UN Security Council approved Resolution 688 condemning Iraqi repression of their Kurdish minority. It further asserted that the wave of refugees pouring into Turkey and Iran represented a threat to "international peace and security."[15] The United States led a multilateral operation to protect the rebellious Kurdish ethnic minority from a vengeful Saddam Hussein. In a truly precedent-setting decision, the United Nations had intervened in the internal affairs of Iraq *without its consent, while at the same time abandoning any semblance of neutrality as to how the dispute should be resolved.*[16]

Shortly thereafter, the United Nations and the United States became engrossed in Somalia and the fragmented remains of the former Yugoslavia, especially the newly formed republic of Bosnia-Herzegovina. These missions, which had been approved by the Security Council, were described by some as "humanitarian interventions," but it soon became apparent that the desire to alleviate human suffering inevitably leads to political tasks. This is especially true when the basic conflict is still raging and there is very little peace to be kept. As Michael Mandelbaum points out, the noble gesture of attempting to relieve hunger invariably led to the 'poisonous tangle of local politics."[17] The United States and United Nations soon found themselves maintaining a de facto Kurdish autonomous zone in northern Iraq, attempting to simultaneously carry out counter insurgency and nation-building operations in Somalia, and seeking to devise a political settlement and then convincing the warring factions to accept it in Bosnia. Their success in each of these cases has been marginal at best, while their actions, or at times inactions, have given rise to a chorus of dissidents. In Bosnia especially, the UN tried to be both forceful and neutral, but often appeared weak and hesitant, and in many instances may have only "abetted slow-motion savagery."[18]

Although there was ample justification for helping the Kurds, Bosnians, Somalis, and, later on, the Rwandans on moral and humanitarian grounds, it is unreasonable to expect that these generally incomplete international interventions and selective disregard for traditional state sovereignty will continue much longer without serious consequences. In Somalia, UN efforts were initially highly successful in alleviating the mass starvation and in reestablishing a functioning food distribution network. Unfortunately, little progress was achieved in resolving the fundamental political and socio-economic causes that had given rise to the chaos in the first place. Initial attempts to address the underlying problems were unsuccessful and finally led to the withdrawal of the UN peacekeeping mission. The cost of intervention in Somalia reflects two years of international effort, an expenditure of $3 billion, and more than 300 UN casualties in dead and wounded, in addition to the thousands of Somalis who perished before and during the intervention. The harsh reality of this intervention was summed up by a U.S. Army officer who observed as the last UN forces were withdrawing from Mogadishu in March 1995, "I guess they've got to work it out themselves."[19]

That is the crux of the matter. So long as the parties to the dispute do not wish it to be resolved, it will continue. If neither side is capable of defeating the other on the battlefield, or if both refuse mediation, there is little real prospect for meaningful resolution. In Bosnia for example, Richard Betts argues quite forcibly that, by insisting on impartial intervention, the United Nations has succeeded in keeping either belligerent from achieving victory, but not in making them stop trying. The rationale behind the policy of evenhandedness was that it would encourage a negotiated settlement. Unfortunately, the result was not a peaceful solution and an end to the killing, but rather "years of military stalemate, slow bleeding, and delusionary diplomatic haggling."[20]

Once civil order has broken down to the extent that it cannot be internally reconstituted, the only viable choice for the international community is either to tolerate the violence, under the guise of impartiality, until it produces some self-limiting outcome or to intervene with sufficient strength to impose a solution and the return of civil order. It would appear that impartiality functions best when intervention is needed least: for example, where conflict has played itself out and the belligerents need only the good offices of a mediator to supervise the end to hostilities (Cypress and the Sinai). To date, tolerance has been the dominant choice, but this has been more by default than conscious decision. In Bosnia, armed international intervention to force a peace has been excluded as a practical matter, not because the UN and NATO lack the appropriate means, but because no coalition of countries has been willing or able to construct the necessary political consensus domestically or internationally to carry it out. Simultaneously, each belligerent still clings to notions of a military victory, and the killings continue on all sides.

Political disintegration is now becoming so widespread that civil violence could lead to a general conflagration if tolerance remains the only realistic international option.[21] As noble as the concept of impartiality may be, it is not always realistic to apply it. As was pointed out earlier, the United Nations removed the veil of impartiality in regard to the Kurds of northern Iraq against Saddam Hussein. There was no doubt about the UN position favoring ousted President Jean-Bertrand Aristide over the Haitian military junta. Only eleventh-hour negotiations precluded a potentially bloody invasion to restore Aristide to power.

For the immediate future, there will undoubtedly be more instances of UN interventions. Richard Betts offers sage advice to both the United States and the United Nations in their future interventions. He reminds them that "to make peace is to decide who rules." If these outside forces cannot decide on who should be in charge after the fighting has ceased in a given conflict, then intervention should not be undertaken. Betts also urges that half-measures, or the middle-of-the-road approach so often favored by politicians and bureaucrats, be avoided. They often fail to resolve a situation and usually only heighten the suffering.[22] Once again, this is a manifestation of the UN wanting to do good, but often only doing "too little, too late."

The UN must be willing to react to crises sooner and in a more determined manner. This could well result in the UN abandoning its impartiality in selected circumstances and choosing to back one side over the other. The humiliating failure of the UN to protect the declared "safe haven" of Srebrenica is the most glaring example of the ineffectiveness of impartiality. Once the determination to intervene and back one side over the other is made however, then the United Nations must be fully prepared to employ the appropriate level of force to end the hostilities quickly. The intervening international force must above all be militarily credible, with sufficient "teeth" to ensure success. The UN and the participating nations should be prepared to face the unpleasant but inevitable fact of having to deal politically with casualties among their own forces and some civilians as well.

Betts points to such cases as Bosnia and Somalia in which the imperative to halt the slaughter and starvation is too much to be ignored by even the most hard-boiled realists. He argues that intervention can be warranted even if it does not aim to produce peace, but rather to end human suffering. I disagree. Although such humanitarian intervention is perceived as "the right thing to do" and can be beneficial in easing the public conscience, it may not always be the most appropriate course of action in the long run for either the victims or the world community. I believe however, the hazards of such "unfocused" humanitarian intervention can only lead to greater tragedies than those it is trying to resolve.

As much as health care providers would like to save everyone in a mass casualty situation, they are trained in and prepared to perform triage procedures. Triage allows them to balance the condition of the patients or victims with the resources available to assist them. The harsh reality is that not everyone can be saved every time. The United States and the United Nations need to reflect on the prospect of someday having to perform international triage. If they are not willing politically to address crises early on and in a decisive manner, they may eventually be faced with a situation that is so complex and brutal, with the belligerents so unwilling to compromise, that the projected costs of intervention would be so staggering in terms of human and material resources, that they would outweigh the potential benefits. In such an extreme case, they would simply opt to *not intervene*. They would refrain from any direct actions, essentially allowing the "fire to burn itself out." They would isolate the "infection" and ensure appropriate steps to prevent the contagion from spreading. Once the crisis has subsided, they would proceed to 'pick up the pieces" and reestablish a functioning infrastructure, while caring for the survivors.

Rwanda offers a partial preview of what this might be like, even though it did not represent a deliberate case of international triage. Rather, it was more indicative of political and bureaucratic indecision and half-hearted measures. While the Security Council laboriously debated what course of action to take, and then was extremely slow to implement corrective actions, hundreds of thousands of Rwandans were brutally slaughtered and more than one million of their countrymen fled as refugees into neighboring nations. As cruel as it may sound, Rwanda is closer to reaching a solution today than is Bosnia!

What must be done to effectively confront the challenges of the gray area phenomena, while at the same time preparing for what I believe will be the hard decisions of occasionally abandoning impartiality and conducting triage?

Opportunities for Enhancing International Cooperation

The present international system is in a state of uncertain transition whose outcome is highly unpredictable. Despite the recent flare-up of the border dispute between Ecuador and Peru, the risk of traditional interstate confrontation, especially among the industrialized nations, is steadily declining. Exactly the reverse is true of the prospects for intrastate conflict, however. Throughout what has been referred to as the "zone of conflict," which includes the former communist states in Eastern Europe, most of Sub Saharan Africa, portions of Latin America, and Southern Asia, a marked downward spiral of economic decline, exacerbated by official mismanagement and corruption, has given rise to governments that are on the verge of collapse. The legitimacy of these governments is being challenged, often violently, by their own citizens. The combination of economic decline and national disintegration gives rise to a "failed state syndrome,"[23] of which Somalia and Rwanda are but two of the clearest and most painful recent examples. It is becoming more apparent that the underlying causes of these conflicts cannot be cured by force of arms. Only multifaceted, comprehensive economic, political, and social actions, undertaken over the long term, will have any prospect for meaningful success.

Much of the world's political attention and resources are now focused on reacting to the most volatile manifestations of gray area phenomena. The world community must fashion an appropriate form of cooperation through which it can address these post-cold war threats and challenges. Peace and development must be the twin themes for international cooperation. Few would argue that sustainable development is the most important challenge facing humanity today and that it provides a secure basis upon which peace can be established. Development is however, being overshadowed by the growth of intrastate conflicts and what Boutros-Ghali has termed "the urgency of peace-keeping."[24] Let us now look at some of the major areas where cooperation for peace operations *and* development might be enhanced.

Intellectual Reevaluation

In order to respond fully to the challenges of the new world reality there must be an adequate understanding of just what is taking place. A great deal of intellectual energy, writing, and debate took place over many years and directly led to the development and refining of the policies and theories of engagement during the Cold War. A similar intellectual undertaking is urgently required in both the public and private sectors to address the multiple aspects of the gray area phenomena. How should the new security policy and strategies be defined? What should be the new theories of engagement? How and when do we apply the various civilian and military instruments of power to achieve the desired endstate? Just as the Goldwater-Nichols Department of Defense Reorganization Act of 1986 was the impetus for making "jointness" (operations involving the forces of at least two services) a reality, some external intellectual stimulus may be required to foster "combinedness" (operations involving the forces of two or more countries). These and many other questions will only be answered as the result of a deliberate refocusing of intellectual capacity in this direction. One such attempt is made in this book. The essay by Manwaring and Corr offers the foundation for a clear policy and strategy.

Terminology and Definition

A significant subset of this intellectual reevaluation will of necessity have to come to grips with the terms and definitions now evolving. Perhaps the clearest example of this need relates to the myriad of terms associated with UN peace operations. Some are new, others are not, but they are being interpreted differently, without a general consensus as to their exact meaning and acceptance. In June 1992 Secretary General Boutros-Ghali presented his *Agenda for Peace*, which separated peace support operations into four categories: preventive diplomacy, peacemaking, peacekeeping, and peace-building. Without entering into a detailed analysis of these items here, suffice it to say that they do not match the contents of the United States Joint Chiefs of Staff publications.[25] Before any meaningful policy can be developed, these terms and definitions should be agreed to by all agencies involved in peace support missions. Additionally, all terms and definitions must be carefully analyzed for their full legal financial, political, and doctrinal implications.

Organizational Structure

Once it has been determined what needs to be done, how should we organize to maximize unity of effort and increase probability of success? Is the current governmental structure adequate? Do additional responsibilities need to be assigned, or must new departments, branches, or institutions be established? What should be the relationship and responsibilities between and among agencies? Which agency should exercise overall coordination authority? Should the lead agency role shift if the nature of the activity is primarily diplomatic, law enforcement, or military?

Interaction with Non-State Actors

Governments will no longer be able to avoid dealing with the existence and potential influence of these groups. They fall into a variety of categories. First, there are the international or inter-state governmental organizations (IGOs) as they are sometimes called. NATO and the European Economic Community (EEC) fall into this category. Second, there are interstate non-governmental organizations (NGOs) that reside within sovereign states but are independent of their governments. This group of non-state actors is very diverse in character and purpose and includes religious movements, multinational companies, terrorist organizations, the Red Cross, criminal groups, and so forth. Some of these organizations are known as private voluntary Organizations (PVOs). The third category consists of, are those individual citizens who, for one reason or another, are sufficiently important to be regarded as actors on the world stage. For example, in late 1994 former President Jimmy Carter achieved an agreement for a truce in Bosnia Herzegovina, following up his highly publicized earlier negotiation successes in North Korea and Haiti. More direct dialogue and partnerships between constructive NGOs, PVOs, selected prominent individuals, and certain government agencies are needed to formulate well coordinated and realistic solutions.

Planning Procedures

The United States and other countries will have to decide if their present strategic and situation-based planning procedures are adequate to meet UN peace operations or other post-cold war requirements such as counter-narcotics. Can these new requirements be incorporated into existing military planning structures and procedures, or do their interagency aspects require modification or expansion of the present system, or perhaps the creation of a parallel system? Should the military be the lead agency in such a process? How can national planning be harmonized with UN headquarters, regional organizations, and various multilateral forces for peace operations? How can the planning process be flexible yet prevent "mission creep" or "mission shrink"? What is the proper role for interacting with the media and influencing public opinion?

Command and Control

What are the lines of command and control that need to be established? Are they direct or convoluted, as in the early stages between NATO and the United Nations in Bosnia-Herzegovina? Will all national contingents be willing to subordinate themselves to a coalition force commander? What are the legal ramifications of such a command structure? How can the strong points of various contingent forces be best utilized? As was learned in Somalia, there must be one clear command structure, with no second guessing by subordinates who, before acting, call their own national capitals for final confirmation.

Training

What impact will these nonconventional combat roles have on a nation's combat readiness? Do all units receive training for these missions, or only selected units? Will the training be carried out in accordance with some internationally agreed-upon standard? It would seem fairly obvious that the majority of required training must be done in advance and on a recurring basis, rather than on the eve of a deployment in support of peace operations or some other gray area phenomenon situation. As appropriate, individual countries could offer their experience and expertise in specific functional areas, as well as combined simulations and exercises to other interested nations. Norway, Finland, Sweden, and Denmark are doing just that. Also, a permanent peace support operations and/or gray area phenomena curriculum could be incorporated into appropriate military and civilian leadership courses.[26]

Equipment Challenge

What are the appropriate types of equipment for these new confrontational situations in which the adversary may not always be armed, at least in the conventional sense? New weapons and their tactics, along with rules of engagement, will need to be developed. For example, the U.S. Marines redeploying to Somalia in February 1995 to protect the withdrawal of the remainder of UN personnel were equipped with a variety of nonlethal weapons ranging from "bee-sting" hand grenades, to shotguns that fire wooden and rubber pellets, to machines that spray a sticky foam barrier for crowd control.

Intelligence

The timely gathering, analysis, and dissemination of intelligence is essential to enable national and world leaders to anticipate and be proactive rather than reactive in crisis situations. Increased emphasis must be placed on predictive intelligence to formulate better policy and more timely and realistic responses. What information will need to be shared with other agencies, friendly countries, regional organizations, and the United Nations to meet the new world challenges effectively and in a timely manner? What is the needed balance between national level intelligence assets (satellite imagery and signal intercepts) and human assets (HUMINT)? How will the world intelligence communities restructure in light of this new situation and mounting pressures to reduce their often large and secretive budgets? How, with whom, and under what circumstances will intelligence data be shared? What are the practical and legal restrictions and prohibitions for so doing? What measures must be in place to safeguard the civil and human rights of citizens? How will sources and methods be adequately protected?

Conflict Resolution and Indicators of Success

Although certainly not new areas, these two aspects become even more critical in today's world. When the objectives are clear and attainable, the execution of specific operations tends to be more successful. Conversely, the absence of well defined, realistic objectives will only exacerbate military missions and often necessitate ad hoc adjustments which result in a clouded vision of the desired political endstate or definition of success.

Conflict Avoidance

First and foremost, greater efforts must be expended on avoiding conflict situations or defusing them before they reach crisis proportions. This will require more emphasis on preventive actions than on reactive ones. Decisive political and economic pressures must be applied much earlier than in the past to prevent situations from deteriorating to the point that armed intervention appears to be the only viable course of action. This coincides with Boutros-Ghali's concept of "preventive diplomacy."

Restructuring the Security Council

Sooner rather than later, the permanent membership of the United Nations Security Council must be adjusted. Its membership will have to be enlarged by including certain key regional countries with increasing global importance. This will be very difficult for the original five permanent members to accept because it will be seen as diluting their powers and further exacerbating the decision-making process. Nevertheless, I believe it is inevitable if the Security Council is to address the world's problems adequately in a more representative fashion. India, Egypt, and Brazil would be three of the countries that might be considered for this enhanced membership.

New or Enhanced Partnerships

Regional organizations and major regional powers will also have to play an increased role in addressing potential or actual crisis situations. They have a vested interest in resolving conflict situations involving their neighbor states as soon as feasible. The same will be true for the non-governmental agencies. One of the most common criticisms of the "state-centric" approach to international politics is that it seriously undervalues the significance of the numerous non-state actors that have emerged on the international state.

The Media Factor

One of the most difficult aspects will center on the media and how its reporting can affect or even dictate the formulation of difficult foreign policy decisions. We have already seen the important service provided by the international media in reporting the plight of the Kurds, the starvation in Somalia, and the continued atrocities in Bosnia. This reporting contributed directly to the world community's decision to intervene. Nevertheless, we must not overlook the fact that the very advantages of the news media, often lumped together generically as "CNN," have some drawbacks. Top leaders are able to view breaking events immediately and directly from anywhere in the world. They often receive emotionally charged information before their foreign policy and intelligence experts are able to brief them on those events. Impressions and attitudes can be formed on the basis of "raw" information that is visually sensitive, emotionally charged, and of uncertain reliability. Time becomes compressed, and leaders find themselves in situations where emotions compete with reason. A decision to intervene on behalf of one of the belligerents or to practice triage by not intervening in a given situation will undoubtedly bring a storm of media reaction for which leaders must be trained to respond without appearing heartless.

Rebuilding a Failed-State

The decision to choose sides in a conflict must be implemented rapidly and carried out by an international military force that is adequately organized, trained, equipped, staffed, and informed on the local situation. Once hostilities are controlled, a second, more complex 'package" of actions must be initiated. This involves policing of civil order combined with the restoration of a legal system, the establishment of economic activity and regulations, the re-establishment of the press and electronic media, and the fostering of political parties. Military forces can only do certain portions of these functions and should not become involved in others. A wide variety of governmental and non governmental agencies must work hand in glove from the outset with the military to plan and implement these activities. Shifting from pacification to the fostering of a functioning civil society will be the greatest challenge of all. It requires a clear strategy for withdrawal and a blueprint for post-conflict, reconstruction which might include involvement in a long-term form of UN administration of a trusteeship for the affected country.

The almost inevitability of the requirements for additional UN "intervention" demand a full review of the various options for utilizing international armed force.

Options for the Use of International Force

The unprecedented stature currently being accorded international organizations and regimes, especially the UN, could not have been anticipated even five years ago. Today, multilateral action is the apparent policy instrument of choice. It enables the participating countries to share both costs and responsibilities. It further provides a cloak of legitimacy for intervening in areas that heretofore were well outside the bounds of acceptable international behavior. As we have seen, this multilateral intervention is often too little, too late, rather than "too much, too soon." Michael Mandelbaum describes the present situation as "agreement in principle, paralysis in practice."[27]

Any future interventions will have to adequately address two principal issues: What are the appropriate criteria for intervention and how can we deliver an effective response? Specifically, the international community has not been able to clearly and coherently respond to the following questions:

- At what point does an internal conflict or crisis constitute a threat to regional or international peace and security?
- At what point can the principle of international solidarity and collective action, especially when motivated by humanitarian concerns, replace or override the principle of state sovereignty?
- What mechanism should be utilized to determine that intervention is necessary?

While the international community continues to struggle with finding acceptable answers to the above questions, the issue of how to intervene also needs to be looked at. There are several possible alternatives relating to the use of international force.

Unilateral Intervention

This option will continue to be available to the United States and, to a lesser degree, Russia and a handful of other regional powers. When vital national interests are involved, these powers will resort to force as the situation warrants. Russia has repeatedly stated its willingness to intervene in its "near abroad" whenever the well-being of ethnic Russians is seriously threatened. The recent actions against a breakaway Muslim minority in Chechnya are clear evidence of the capability and determination to use force. The United States acted unilaterally to remove the Noriega regime in Panama and would have done the same in Haiti if it had not obtained United Nations support for a multilateral military operation. As of this writing, Turkey is in the process of carrying out a major incursion into northern Iraq against what it calls "Kurdish separatist guerrillas."[28]

For very practical reasons the United States (and several other nations) will insist on retaining this unilateral military option. Not only is the United States the world's only superpower, but it cannot realistically plan its force structure on the vague assumption that other nations might be willing and able to bear the burdens of major military undertakings, especially if they require mass deployments of forces over considerable distances. Secretary of State Warren Christopher has stated: "When it is necessary, we will act unilaterally to protect our interests." He subsequently offered a caveat concerning the nature and extent to which U.S. military force would be employed, stipulating four criteria: the goal must be stated clearly to the American people; there must be a strong likelihood of success; the United States must have an "exit strategy," and the involvement of the U.S. military must have "sustained public support."[29]

Ad Hoc Coalitions

This approach involves a major power assuming a key leadership role and enlisting other countries to participate in varying degrees to achieve a specific outcome. This arrangement was used in confronting Saddam Hussein following his misadventure into Kuwait in the first major post–Cold War confrontation. The Gulf War was essentially a classic case of defending a state's sovereignty against external aggression, while seeking to restore and maintain the status quo ante. Rather than being a harbinger of the future nature of conflict, the Gulf War has been described as the "last gasp of a morally and politically clearer age . . . a replay of World War II, on a far smaller and less costly scale."[30] On the other hand, Richard Haass has labeled this as the "sheriff-and-posse" approach.[31] It offers clearly defined leadership roles and avoids standing bureaucracies, but it can be cumbersome and very time consuming in getting organized. Its principal weakness lies in defining the ties that bind the members of the "posse" and that could constrain their participation. It places considerable burdens on the "sheriff," who will frequently end up being the United States. This approach however, would tend to complement rather than constrain the United States' perceived superpower leadership role.

Regional Organizations

A number of geographically based security organizations have undertaken mediation, conciliation, and intervention in regard to security issues. The most well known of these are the North Atlantic Treaty Organization (NATO), the Organization of American States (OAS), the Organization of African Unity (OAU), the Arab League, and the Association of South East Asian Nations (ASEAN).[32] In spite of some historic weaknesses (rivalries among key members or fixation on single issues), regional organizations now appear more willing than ever to consider peacekeeping, selective peacemaking, and nation-building operations. (France's President Francois Mitterand offered to provide training, equipment, and logistical support for the creation of an "Inter-African Intervention Force.")[33] They offer the obvious advantages of physical proximity to the area in question, political legitimacy for any intervention, increased familiarity with the linguistic and cultural aspects of the crisis, and a vested interest in a successful resolution. Their member states generally will be the ones most directly affected by mass refugee movements and any widening of the conflict. On the negative side, these regional organizations have generally proven to be undependable. Most lack both military capabilities and political consensus to act in an effective, timely manner. In the case of NATO, which obviously has sufficient military wherewithal, it has repeatedly demonstrated a lack of political resolve in Bosnia-Herzegovina.

UN Designated Contingency Forces

In the above mentioned "sheriff-and-posse" approach, the UN role is essentially political, with the military leadership left in the hands of the "sheriff." Under this third approach, member nations would make specific forces available to the United Nations, which would then assume their operational control. The UN itself would become the "sheriff." The advantage of such an approach would be the predesignation of specific units for assignment to the UN under a wide range of possible scenarios. Although these units would remain under the day-to-day control of the member state, they could be equipped and trained in advance to certain international standards. This would significantly enhance their interoperability with counterpart forces from other member states, thereby reducing one of the major shortfalls of current multilateral operations. From a sovereignty perspective, the designation of these units would not mean their automatic availability and commitment to a specific United Nations mission. Some states would be eager to support a peacekeeping mission, but reluctant to become involved in risky peace enforcement or protracted and costly actions such as nation-building. The UN is still attempting to develop the organizational wherewithal to sustain 70,000–80,000 troops worldwide. Money is short, integrated training for multinational forces is scant, and contingents thrown together are uneven militarily and sometimes problematic in their attitudes toward local populations and each other. The operational procedures associated with an international chain of command will have to be carefully defined and refined to preclude some of the major problems seen to date in such endeavors.

Standing UN Force

This approach envisions a permanent standing force whose size would have to be determined through considerable debate. To have any credibility, this UN "army" would have to be sufficiently large to handle multiple crises simultaneously. It would consist of international volunteers, and its operational control would be directly in the hands of the UN Secretary General. It would provide a dedicated, immediately available force that could be deployed as soon as the Security Council so directed and would have more of a deterrent effect than the current procedure. Nevertheless, there are serious drawbacks. The expenses to organize, train, equip, and pay for such a force would be considerable and could even compete with scarce resources from member states who would prefer to utilize them for their own forces rather than for these "international mercenaries or UN legionnaires." There are obviously several sovereignty-related issues involved with the creation of a standing force of this nature. The existence of such a UN force could delay or preclude unilateral or regional interventions. One cannot discount, under certain scenarios, the real possibility of a confrontation between such a UN force and units of a major power whose interests are not in harmony with those of the United Nations.

The Role for the U.S. in These Approaches

One of the most remarkable post–Cold War phenomena has been the absence of vetoes in the UN Security Council. Before 1990, UN attempts at collective actions were often hobbled by a total of 279 vetoes cast by the permanent members of the Security Council (China, Great Britain, France, the Soviet Union, and the United States). From May 1990 until late 1994, there have been no such vetoes.[34] In this new found cooperative environment the Security Council has been able to undertake almost a score of peace operations, but it has also delayed certain actions or reached less confrontational compromises in several situations, mainly pertaining to Bosnia. Many of the organization's decisions have reflected a consensus, albeit at times a watered down and delayed one, in an effort to preserve its united front.

On several occasions we have seen Russia almost placed in an "either or" situation with respect to proposed actions against the Serbs, her traditional and ethnic allies. China has consistently voiced reservations regarding intervention, which could be related to her experience with pro-democracy protesters in Tienanmen Square. Sooner or later however, there will arise a substantial disagreement among the major member nations of the Security Council as to the course of action to follow. Then what will happen? What mechanisms will be employed to resolve that situation?

Finding the right role for the United States in these various approaches to the use of force will not be easy. U.S. interests will not lend themselves to a single choice but rather favor letting circumstances determine what the U.S. role should be in a given situation. Thus far, the United States seems reluctant to endorse the creation of a supranational force, while at the same time less than enthusiastic about devoting the time, the financial resources, or the forces to ensure that UN operations are carried out more to our liking.

The lessons learned in Lebanon, Somalia, and Rwanda suggest that U.S. participation in peacemaking and nation-building operations can be highly risky and even counterproductive. Undoubtedly, the placing of American soldiers on foreign soil is the strongest possible signal of United States resolve and leadership. Yet, the physical presence of U.S. military units can stimulate opposition and aggressive action against the operation that otherwise might not have existed. The prospect of killing or capturing U.S. military personnel is highly attractive in many parts of the world.

Certainly, the absence of U.S. combat units does not necessarily condemn a UN mission to failure. On the contrary, Australian General John Sanderson, who commanded the UN peacekeeping operation in Cambodia, maintains that a key to the success of his mission was the absence of U.S. combat troops.[35] Nevertheless, the United States will undoubtedly be called upon in the future to provide significant support to UN missions in those areas where it enjoys a comparative advantage: funding, intelligence collection and analysis, transportation, particularly airlift, and logistical support in general. Moreover, there should be no doubt that the first time the United States fails to protect its interests in a conflict involving commitment of large force, it will cease to be a military superpower.[36]

There is also the crucial and ever-present variable of potential U.S. casualties that policymakers dare not overlook. "Winning," in the eyes of the American public, is generally considered to be quick and decisive, with few casualties. Operation Desert Storm may have provided us with a distorted legacy in the sense that successful military action was achieved with minimal cost to the United States in terms of both immediate casualties and lost resources. This could give rise to increased public expectations for "quick-fix/low-cost" solutions at precisely the time that emerging new problems do not lend themselves to easy or painless resolution.

The prospect of seeing the flag-draped coffins of our young servicemen and women being returned from foreign shores touches a highly emotional and politically sensitive nerve. No administration in Washington can ignore for very long the plaintive cries to "bring the boys home" without adjusting its foreign policy. French General Philippe Morillon has commented publicly on what he describes as America's desire for "zero-dead wars."[37] We have only to recall the ignominious withdrawal of the *USS Harlon County* in the face of a Port-au-Prince mob immediately following the killing of 18 American soldiers in Somalia and the public desecration of some of their bodies in the streets of Mogadishu to establish the direct linkage between casualties and their impact on foreign policy.

If our military forces were to suffer significant casualties overseas, public confidence could erode to the point that the American people would not support further interventions, unless it were unequivocally clear that vital national interests are at stake.[38] Samuel Huntington believes that the American public will support intervention for clearly humanitarian reasons such as stopping genocide and mass starvation. He argues however, that the United States has no vital interest in "which clan dominates Somalia or where the boundary lines are drawn in the former Yugoslavia." Huntington further states, "It is morally unjustifiable and politically indefensible that Americans should be killed in order to prevent Serbs and Bosnians from killing each other."[39] Given this century's sad history in the Balkans, I would argue that stability in that region is of concern to the United States and its European allies. However, Huntington appears to have captured the prevalent feeling of the American public concerning involvement of U.S. combat troops in this foreign conflict.

Conclusion

The world must now come to terms with its own growing inability to cope effectively with all manner of disorders, from immediate crises to chronic problems. The post–Cold War era will continue to be characterized by the need for greater cooperation with legitimate partners, both domestically and internationally. Max Manwaring refers to this as "vertical and horizontal actions."[40] This cooperation must take place between the military services, between law enforcement agencies, between the armed forces and nonmilitary agencies, between government and non-governmental organizations, and among nations. Although one might argue that such cooperation will not guarantee success in meeting the challenges of the gray area phenomena in a specific situation, its absence is virtually a prescription for failure. The UN has begun to take the leading role, but is often criticized for being too slow. It will have to do more and much sooner in order to achieve the right balance of diplomatic, economic, and military actions to compel or coerce parties to seek peaceful solutions to their problems.

Renewed efforts must be focused upon nations resolving their own internal problems as the first and admittedly ideal course of action. Realistically, dispute resolution will often require some external, third party help. That outside assistance does not necessarily mean however, that the United Nations must be the source of the help or the arbiter of each solution. It is unrealistic to expect that the United Nations serve as the court of first, last, and only resort for all major internal conflicts involving failed or faltering states. We must rationally comprehend and emotionally accept that all threats to international peace and security *do not warrant the use of force* by the United Nations (or the United States). We must further recognize that not all changes to the status quo are undesirable.

Intractable disputes should be mediated by neighboring states or others with a vested interest to do so. Naturally, these states should possess the resources and credibility for an effective resolution. Regional organizations or under certain conditions, the collective community may opt to choose sides, intervening decidedly with military force on behalf of one of the disputing parties to bring the conflict to a timely solution. There may well be a small number of situations that are so complex or that would demand such an expenditure of resources, both human and material, over a protracted period of time, that the most prudent course of action will be to *not intervene*. These conflicts should be allowed to "burn themselves out." Once the fighting has subsided, the United Nations can arrive on the scene and begin to address the disintegration of internal political, judicial, and economic structures that lies at the core of the problem.

One hopes that there will be sufficient wisdom and courage to determine when and how to intervene, especially in those truly "hard decisions" of choosing sides and practicing international political triage. These decisions will undoubtedly be difficult in the face of heartrending media coverage of human suffering. Intervention in the internal affairs of states and the alteration of sovereignty will never be without potential hazards to all involved. Greater efforts must be expended on conflict avoidance than on conflict resolution. Dealing with the new world realities and the associated gray area phenomena will not be a quick or comfortable process. There will be the inevitable false starts, setbacks, and occasional failures. Nevertheless, there must be long-term resolve to meet these challenges, for world survival is at stake. The "urgency of peacekeeping" must be replaced by an "urgency of sustained development."

The present situation in Burundi presents an excellent opportunity for the world community to be proactive and apply the positive lessons learned from Somalia and Bosnia-Herzegovina. Burundi has all of the ingredients for a reenactment of the political and ethnic chaos that were found in its neighbor, Rwanda.[41] Let us hope that the world community will act before this failing state time bomb explodes.

Finally, we should recall what Dag Hammarskjold once observed: "The United Nations was not set up to bring humanity to heaven, but to save it from hell."[42]

Notes

1. Paul David Miller, "The Changing Security Environment: The Atlantic Command" in Dennis J. Quinn, ed., *Peace Support Operations and the U.S. Military* (Washington, D.C.: National Defense University Press, 1993), pp. 43–49.

2. For a detailed analysis of this concept see Wm. J. Olson, "The New World Disorder: Governability and Development," in Max G. Manwaring, ed., *Gray Area Phenomena: Confronting the New World Disorder* (Boulder, Colo.: Westview Press, 1993), pp. 3–32.

3. Boutros Boutros-Ghali, "An Agenda For Peace," report by the Secretary General, June 17, 1992, *in An Agenda For Peace* 1995(New York: United Nations, 1995),p. 40.

4. Herz's idea is contained in John C. Gamett, "States, State-Centric Perspectives, and Interdependence Theory," in John Baylis and N. J. Rengger, eds., *Dilemmas of World Politics: International Issues in a Changing World* (Oxford: Clarendon Press, 1992), p . 67.

5. Peter Lupsha, "Gray Area Phenomenon: New Threats and Policy Dilemmas," unpublished paper presented at the High Intensity Crime/Low Intensity Conflict Conference, Chicago, Illinois, September 27–30, 1992, pp. 22–23.

6. Bob Cohn and Bill Turque, "Peso Bill's Bailout," *Newsweek*, February 13, 1995, pp. 24–28.

7. The UN now has almost 80,000 troops deployed in 23 operations. See William H. Lewis, "Peacekeeping: Whither U.S. Policy?" in Quinn, ed., *Peace Support Operations*, pp. 113–114.

8. For more information on the redefinition of "security," see Amos Jordan, American National Security: Policy and Process (Baltimore: Johns Hopkins University, 1988), p.3, and Jessica Tuchman Mathews, "Redefining Security," in Robert J. Art and Robert Jervis, eds., *International Politics: Enduring Concepts and Contemporary Issues* (New York: Harper-Collins Publishers, 1992), pp. 546–557.

9. Olson, "New World Disorder," p.8.

10. Boutros-Ghali, "Agenda for Peace," p. 44.

11. Alex Rondos, "The Collapsing State and International Security" in Janne E. Nolan, ed., *Global Engagement: Cooperation and Security in the 21st Century* (Washington, D.C.: The Brookings Institution, 1994), p. 498.

12. Janne E. Nolan, John D. Steinbruner, Kenneth Flamm, Steven E. Miller, David Mussington, William J. Perry, and Ashton B. Carter, "The Imperatives for

Cooperation," in Janne E. Nolan, ed., *Global Engagement: Cooperation and Security in the 21st Century* (Washington, D.C.: The Brookings Institution, 1994), p. 19.

13. Jeremy D. Rosner, "Is Chaos America's Real Enemy?" *Washington Post,* August 14, 1994, p. C1 .

14. Robert D. Kaplan, "The Coming Anarchy," *Atlantic Monthly,* February 1994, pp. 48–58.

15. John Mackinlay, "Defining A Role Beyond Peacekeeping," in William H. Lewis, ed., *Military Implications of United Nations Peacekeeping Operations* (Washington, D.C.: National Defense University, 1993), p. 31.

16. Adam Roberts, "The Crisis in UN Peacekeeping," *Survival,* Autumn 1994, pp. 99–101, as reproduced in *Readings In Peacebuilding and Peacekeeping,* prepared in support of the OAS UNESCO Inter-American Symposium on Peacebuilding and Peacekeeping hosted by the Inter American Defense College, Fort McNair, Washington, D.C., April 3–4, 1995. Mandelbaum, "Reluctance to Intervene," pp. 4–5.

17. Michael Mandelbaum, "The Reluctance To Intervene," *Foreign Policy,* Summer 1994, pp . 4–5

18. Richard K. Betts, "The Delusion of Impartial Intervention," *Foreign Affairs,* November/December 1994, p. 24.

19. Joshua Hammer, "I Guess They've Got to Work It Out Themselves," *Newsweek,* March 13, 1995, p. 31.

20. Richard K. Betts, "The Delusion of Impartial Intervention," *Foreign Affairs,* November/December 1994, p. 24.

21. Nolan et al., *Global Engagement,* pp. 44–45.

22. Betts, "Delusion," pp. 30–33.

23. Gareth Evans, "Cooperative Security and Intrastate Conflict," *Foreign Policy,* Fall 1994, p. 4.

24. Boutros Boutros-Ghali, *An Agenda For Development 1995* (New York: United Nations Publication, 1995), pp . 17–21.

25. For a detailed discussion of these differences, see Dennis J. Quinn, "Peace Operations: Definitions and Implications," and John O. B. Sewell, "Peacekeeping Implications for the U.S. Military: Supporting the United Nations," in Quinn, ed., *Peace Support Operations,* pp . 17–26 and pp. 37–38.

26. Ibid., p. 21.

27. Mandelbaum, "Reluctance to Intervene," p . 17.

28. "Turks bomb rebel Kurds in camps inside Iraq," *Miami Herald,* March 22, 1995, p. 6A.

29. William H. Lewis, "'Assertive Multilateralism': Rhetoric vs. Reality", in William H. Lewis, ed., *Peacekeeping: The Way Ahead?* (Washington, D.C.: National Defense University, 1993), p. 15.

30. Mandelbaum, "Reluctance to Intervene," p. 3.

31. Richard N. Haass, "Military Force: A User's Guide," *Foreign Policy,* Fall 1994, p. 32.

32. For a more detailed review of the non-European regional organizations, see Leonard S. Spector and Jonathan Dean, "Assessing the Tools of the Trade," in Nolan, ed., *Global Engagement,* pp. 164–165.

33. *El Universal,* Caracas, Venezuela, November 9, 1994, p. 23. (An AFP report on the Pan African Summit held in Biarritz, France.)

34. Carl W. Hoffman, Jr., "The UN Secretary-General's Peacekeeping Proposals," in John N. Petrie, ed., *Essays On* Strategy XI (Washington, D.C.: National Defense University, 1994), p.50.

35. Michael Elliott, "The Neurotic Lion," *Newsweek,* September 26, 1994, p. 36.

36. General Frederick M. Franks, Jr., Commander, United States Army Training and Doctrine Command (TRADOC), in a paper titled "A Strategic Army for the 21st Century," presented to TRADOC's 20th Anniversary Seminar on Future Warfare, Fort Monroe, Virginia, June 30–July 1, 1993, p. 8.

37. Elliott, "Neurotic Lion," p. 36.

38. Franks, "Strategic Army," p. 8.

39. Samuel P. Huntington, "Non-traditional Roles for the U.S. Military," in James R. Graham, ed., *Non-combat Roles for the U.S. Military in the post–Cold War Era* (Washington, D.C.: National Defense University, 1993), p . 11.

40. Max G. Manwaring, "Beyond the Cold War: Toward a Theory of Engagement to Confront the Gray Area Phenomenon," in Max G. Manwaring, ed., *Gray Area Phenomena,* p. 70.

41. Chris McGreal, "Not another Rwanda: World keeps close tabs on abuses in Burundi," *Miami Herald,* March 23, 1995, p . 13 A.

42. Sir Brian Urquhart, "Peace Support: Implications for the U.S. Military," in William H. Lewis, ed., *Peacekeepers: The Way Ahead?*, p . 58.

8

The Search for Legitimate Partners in the New International Security Environment

Ambassador David Passage

For the first 40 years after the end of the Second World War, the world was divided—like Roman Gaul—into three camps: countries largely drawn, or pressured, or actually forced (by military invasion) into the ambit of the then-USSR; those attracted by shared interests toward the Western democracies led by the United States; and, beginning in the mid-50s, the so-called Third World of ostensibly nonaligned countries.

Those same years were also characterized by intense rivalry between the two principal centers of power, Washington, and Moscow, and, to lesser degrees, London, Paris, Beijing, and the capitals of the major members of the Non-Aligned Movement—New Delhi, Jakarta, Cairo, Accra, Dar es Salaam, Belgrade, and others. The USSR and People's Republic of China (PRC) lined up as many coreligionists as they could behind the red flag of communism; the United States and its allies devised a variety of stratagems in an effort to contain an expansionist Communist imperialism—principally by means of a series of mutual security alliances.

In this competition to sign up as many associates and other partners as possible, the West ended up—sometimes deliberately, sometimes inadvertently—in league with a number of otherwise disreputable regimes simply because they were willing to join our team, pledge ostensible allegiance to our values, and more importantly—allow the West access to their territory for strategic purposes and to their markets for economic and commercial ones.

This paper reflects the views of the author and not the views of the U.S. government, the Department of State, or the Special Operations Command.

In striking these Mephistophelian bargains with an assortment of thugs and dictators in the developing world with whom the democracies should ordinarily have been embarrassed to be seen associating, the United States and its allies incurred powerful costs by being seen as hypocritical neoimperialists by many peoples struggling to achieve for their own countries the sort of democracy the West professed to offer.

With the fall of the Wall and the death of the Bear, the Western democracies (and especially the United States) now have an opportunity to advance the core political, social, economic, and humanitarian values they say they hold and replace the criterion of "anticommunism" with a loftier test of how governments should comport themselves vis-à-vis their own people and their internal development processes.

This article does *not* join the current U.S. internal political debate over foreign aid or the reorganization/reinvention of the U.S. government and its foreign affairs agencies. It is, rather, an argument for shucking the simplistic "are you for us or against us" test of the past four decades (a test which some in today's U.S. internal political arena would actually have us *strengthen!*) that led us into partnerships with a variety of Latin American dictators, African thugs, and others—and seek, instead, "legitimate partners" in the new international environment.

The Cold War: Security Through Alliances

To preserve the freedom and independence of the Western democracies against an expansionist and imperially-minded USSR, the United States took the lead in crafting a series of formal mutual security agreements with countries closest to or most threatened by the Soviet Union and enlisted the cooperation of other states around the periphery of the USSR and PRC in looser arrangements whose ultimate purpose was the same as the more structured agreements—the "containment" of our strategic global adversary.

NATO, CENTO, SEATO, ANZUS . . .

Foremost among the formal security agreements was the North Atlantic Treaty—still the cornerstone of U.S. national security policy. Its language articulates the most precise and specific commitments of any of the multilateral agreements, declaring "an attack upon one [to be] an attack upon all"—binding *all* signatories to come to the aid of any North Atlantic Treaty Organization (NATO) member attacked by a nonmember state.

The Baghdad Pact included Turkey, initially Iraq, Iran, Pakistan, the United Kingdom, and the United States, and was created to protect the "southern tier" countries from Soviet encroachment across the Caucasus, Elburz, and Karakoram mountains. It was renamed the "Central Treaty

Organization" or CENTO, after a bloody revolution in 1958 murdered King Faisal II of Iraq (cousin of Jordan's King Hussein) and Prime Minister Nuri as-Said took Iraq out of the "Western" camp and into a growing radical Islamic one.

The Southeast Asia Treaty Organization (SEATO) overlapped CENTO by including both eastern and western wings of Pakistan and extended across the southern periphery of Asia to protect Thailand and the Philippines, incorporating a protocol covering the former French Indochina. It was the corresponding mutual security alliance hemming in the south and southeast Asian flanks of the USSR and China.

ANZUS, a trilateral alliance among the United States, Australia, and New Zealand, was established basically for the same purposes as NATO, CENTO, and SEATO—protection of the English-speaking countries of the South Pacific against a Soviet (or Chinese) attack.

Finally, in the northwest Pacific, the United States reached individual (and separate) mutual security agreements with Taiwan, South Korea, and Japan.

... and the Rio Treaty

In Latin America, the 1947 Treaty of Rio de Janeiro bound the nations of the Western Hemisphere to "consult" in the event of a security threat— which the United States intended to be understood as one coming from *outside* the hemisphere (i.e., Soviet-inspired). In fact, a year after the Rio Treaty was signed, a significant, albeit short-lived, uprising in Bogota, Colombia, during an Organization of American States conference attended by Secretary of State George Marshall, gave the United States a fright and served as a pretext for amplifying the alarm against Communist penetration in the Western Hemisphere.

Six years later (during which the United States and allied United Nations' forces had fought Communist aggression to a bloody draw on the Korean peninsula), similar concerns led the United States to offer clandestine assistance in 1953–54 to opponents of the Guatemalan government headed by Jacobo Arbenz, believed by some within the U.S. government to be a Communist. By then (1954), renewed forces of Asian communism were taking aim at the remaining outposts of French colonialism in Southeast Asia, John Foster Dulles was in full form, and the specter of a USSR-on-the-march led to widespread civil defense drills in U.S. schools and cities and round-the-clock alerts by U.S. Strategic Air Command B-36, B-47, and B-52 bombers.

By the time Cuba's Fulgencio Batista was overthrown by Fidel Castro at the end of 1959, however, the United States was beginning to experiment delicately with "peaceful coexistence" with a USSR led by Nikita Khrushchev (Josef Stalin mercifully having passed from the scene without starting a

nuclear-tipped World War III). Although it was clear soon after Castro came
to power that he would act against U.S. economic and commercial interests
in Cuba and probably harbored significant political and ideological differences with the United States, President Dwight (Ike) Eisenhower postponed
direct U.S. action against him until Ike's successor, John F. Kennedy, could
take office. The Cuban die had been cast, however, and Kennedy's first
major foreign policy engagement was a disaster whose effect was to shield
Castro—if not precisely immunize him—from more forceful U.S.
intervention for the next 30 years.

They Worked

Given the nature of the threat the alliance structures were devised to cope
with, any fair analysis of the cold war period would have to conclude that
the strategy of "containment" through alliances by and large served reasonably effectively to protect the Western democracies and their principal
partners from a rampant USSR. Despite occasionally expressed misgivings
about the merits of such arrangements in the U.S. Congress and among
some Americans and foreigners active in the discussion of international
relations, each of the formal agreements was ultimately ratified by the U.S.
Senate, each enjoyed substantial popular support in the United States and
other member states, and each worked: notwithstanding the nuclear
Damoclean sword under which the world lived during those times, no
member state of any of these formal security arrangements ever endured an
armed frontal attack from the USSR or PRC (Korea was not, in 1950, a
member of any of the regional security alliances and had, unfortunately,
earlier been declared by Secretary of State Dean Acheson a country to whose
independence the United States did not attach very much importance).
Every member survives today as a participant in the world community of
democratic nations (excepting, if one wants, Iraq and Iran, whose internal—
but non-Communist—nationalist revolutions currently place them in opposition to the United States).

Although the "domino theory" has taken some hard knocks, a considered review of the evidence from those 40 years suggests that communism
as an ideology and the Soviet Union as an "empire" were indeed on a roll
during the 1950s and 1960s—and that both the ideology and the empire
were intent on expanding their grasp by preying on neighbors and by
targeting the institutionally weakest of the countries associated with the
West or at large in the world. The system of regional alliances fathered
by a succession of United States secretaries of state from George
Marshall through John Foster Dulles was the means chosen to "contain"
communism—and it served its purpose remarkably well.

Friends ("Either You're with Us . . .")

Dulles elevated the concept of "friends-as-allies" to the level of theology by his declaration (apropos India's refusal to join SEATO) that "neutrality is immoral"—thereby not just writing off, but actively ostracizing the newly emerging nations of the Third World who gathered at Bandung, Indonesia, in 1954 to proclaim their intention to remain apart from the two superpowers' formal alliance structures. Thus continued the time-honored U.S. tradition of insisting that countries declare themselves as our *friends* or be proclaimed our *foes*. Sure enough, the United States wrote off, for the better part of the next two decades, half a dozen or more important and respected Third World leaders and their countries—men like India's Jawaharlal Nehru, Egypt's Gamal Abdel Nasser, Ghana's Kwame Nkrumah, Tanzania's Julius Nyerere, Indonesia's Sukarno, and others—even while continuing to try to curry favor with as many as possible of the remaining nonaligned nations through U.S. economic and security assistance programs, Peace Corps Volunteers, and other such stratagems.

In seeking to enlist as many countries as possible in what was portrayed as the "global confrontation" between democracy and communism, however, the United States let its standards for partnership drop to something less than the criteria that our erstwhile partners should be democracies and that their governments should be, for want of a better phrase, "of the people, by the people, and (*especially*) *for* the people." Although much lip service was paid to the principle of representative government (and, in later years, fealty to acceptable human rights norms), foreign policy and national security expediency drove us in the direction of simply accepting "anticommunism" as the major criterion for our friendship and its putative rewards. And—not to put too fine a point on the matter—many of these governments were hardly the sorts of partners a democracy should be proud of having.

The Western Hemisphere

In the Western Hemisphere, U.S. fear of "international communism" led the United States to turn a blind eye to the otherwise plainly obvious lack of support from their own people (and enormous brutalities visited against their own peoples) of many of the regimes the United States favored and rewarded. Our association with many of these fetid and squalid dictatorships increasingly complicated our relations with those in Latin America who sought to wrench that tortured region out of its sixteenth-century Iberian feudalism and haunted our search for legitimate partners in this hemisphere. One need only recall Gen. Gustavo Rojas Pinilla's brutal dictatorship in Colombia, Gen. Marcos Perez Jimenez's in Venezuela, Gen. Trujillo's in the Dominican Republic, Gen. Alfredo Stroessner's in Paraguay, Mrs. Somoza's little boys in Nicaragua, a succession of tin-pot dictators in Guatemala, and numerous other thugs whose primary claim to fame (apart from the resplendent military uniforms which clothed them all) was the proficiency with which they brutalized their own people and the thoroughness with which they looted their countries' treasuries.

Of course, their other claim to fame was the frequency with which they proclaimed that they stood shoulder-to-shoulder with the United States in the global war against godless atheistic communism. So deep-seated has been American paranoia about communism that even today, detractors of Haiti's Jean-Bertrand Aristide almost reflexively persist in describing him as "a left-wing anti-American priest"—despite the paucity of evidence of anti-Americanism on his part since he returned to his thoroughly ravaged (a condition thanks in no small part to the utterly misbegotten regime of U.S. economic sanctions which sought, in vain, to force Lt. Gen. Raoul Cedras to yield power) country.

For the better part of the four decades following the end of World War II, the United States watched silently and remained largely immobile (save for occasional spurts of altruism such as the Alliance for Progress and the work of thousands of Peace Corps Volunteers) as the elites clung (sometimes ferociously, as in El Salvador and Guatemala) to power in this hemisphere. Resentment against the "haves" grew among the "have nots"—resentment frequently coupled to anti-Americanism because of the perceived association of the United States with oppressive, usually military, dictatorships. U.S. economic assistance was mostly directed toward regimes which proclaimed their anticommunism the loudest. U.S. security assistance programs enabled those regimes to keep their own populations under control by strengthening Latin American military forces' abilities to maintain order in their own societies, the United States apparently not noting the irony, or seemingly not caring very much, that it doesn't allow its own military to enforce domestic tranquillity in the United States.

As a token of acknowledgment that Latin American military forces spent considerable energy and resources in wars against their next-door neighbors, the United States made an effort, with only limited success, to prevent the introduction of high-tech weaponry such as advanced military fighter aircraft into the hemisphere—an effort undermined by our West European allies who sold supersonic jets to half a dozen Latin American countries during the seventies and eighties. The Soviets capitalized on growing resentment against the United States by selling great quantities of military equipment to Peru (in addition to Cuba and, after the Sandinista revolution, to Nicaragua).

By the mid-1980s, most Latin American countries had experienced at least a whiff of anti-American (and anticapitalist) armed revolution or insurgency. By means ranging from traditional economic and military assistance to various forms of covert action and other clandestine programs, the United States helped the Latin American governments with whom we were aligned counter most of the threats to their continued control. Serious armed insurgent movements persisted in Colombia, Peru, and notably El Salvador, where the United States more directly sought to help a regime which professed to be anti-Communist fight guerrillas attempting to establish a government of social and political equality similar to the one which had taken power in neighboring Nicaragua. In the end, the U.S. effort in El Salvador was successful—in that the guerrillas did not achieve power and an at least minimally "democratic" government in San Salvador survived.

In terms of the potential for direct impact on the United States of Latin American social, economic, and political ferment, Mexico was—and remains—the greatest concern. With 1,500-plus miles of largely undefended southern border, the consequences for the United States of upheaval in Mexico are unpleasant to contemplate (although they could be dealt with if the United States had to and was willing and able domestically and politically to do so, by a considerable expenditure of resources and by reshuffling and relocating military personnel and equipment). The major problem would be (as it already is) the large-scale flight to the north by both poorer campesinos and better-off middle- and upper-class Mexicans that would inexorably attend any serious degree of instability, not to mention violent revolution, in the hopelessly overcrowded and underemployed valleys of central Mexico.

The number of Mexicans illegally crossing the border into the United States which has occasioned such a ruckus in California and the U.S. Congress would almost certainly become a flood tide. People flee insecurity. If there has been a single simple consequence of *every* social/political/ economic upheaval in the world during the past 50 years, it has been massive migrations of people trying to get themselves and their families out of the way of the physical violence and fighting which result from social and political instability. In this hemisphere, that has meant illegal migration (call it "economic" or whatever) toward the United States (Mexicans don't flee to *Guatemala* as a result of internal Mexican problems!).

The Middle East

The same sorts of effects also hold in other parts of the world. Let's look at the results of similar "illegitimacy" of governments in the Middle East.

We won't dwell for long here; the United States doesn't have a very good track record of objectivity when it comes to trying to reconcile (a) our national emotional attachment to the State of Israel, (b) recognition that Western economic interests lie overwhelmingly with good relations with the Arab world, (c) an incapacity to integrate justice for the Palestinian people into our emotional feelings about the Balfour Declaration (a "national homeland" for the Jewish people), and (d) a suspicion that the Arab governments which have been our traditional allies in that embattled region of the world may not be the ones which will prevail in the longer run of history.

The encumbrance of the Arab-Israel dispute is sufficiently well known not to require elaboration here. Let's just say that the West's association with and support for Israel have, whatever their other merits, led to a significant degree of alienation of Arabs (broadly identified) from the United States and its principal allies and trading partners—although the latter have, to a considerable degree, found ways to reingratiate themselves with much of the Arab world.

The simple fact is that the United States has ended up on the losing side of *every* revolutionary change of government in the Arab world since the end of World War II. *Every* revolutionary change has been explicitly proclaimed as anti-Western and anti-imperialist; in *every* case, the United States actively supported the losing side. From the military overthrow of Libya's King Idriss (who had allowed the United States to construct a major Strategic Air Command facility at Wheelus Field, outside Tripoli) in 1954 to General Naguib's overthrow of the corpulent and diseased Egyptian monarchy (followed by Colonel Nasser's overthrow of him), the Baathist revolts in Iraq and Syria and the upheavals in Yemen and Aden and Sudan and Algeria all were manifestations—at least in part—of popular discontent against pro-Western Arab governments which could be easily denigrated by radical revolutionary elements as "puppets" of Western imperialism.

Nor need we dwell on more recent events such as the overthrow of the shah of Iran, let alone dare think about the possibility of radicalism threatening the remaining royal houses of the Arabian peninsula/Gulf area—such an occurrence being almost too ghastly to contemplate. The longevity of each of these royal houses is, mercifully, a function of different internal political equations in each of their countries, and it would be wrong to say—and I am not saying—that each is equally in jeopardy. I would simply note that a cardinal characteristic of *each* of the governments which has been overthrown, and *each* of the royal houses which may be in jeopardy in the future, is its perceived *illegitimacy* in the eyes of a substantial number of its own people.

And Africa?

And Africa! Senator Jesse Helms (former ranking minority member and now chairman of the Senate Foreign Relations Committee) has frequently described foreign aid as "money poured down a rat-hole." Senator Mitch McConnell has called for tying U.S. aid to recipients' willingness to align themselves with U.S. national interests and purposes. Let's look at this in an African context.

In the 25 years from the close of the colonial epoch (the early 60s) to the end of Communist competition with the West on that continent (the late 80s), nearly 85 percent of all U.S. economic and security assistance in Africa went to just seven countries: Liberia, Chad, Sudan (before Bashir overthrew al-Mahdi), Ethiopia (before Mengistu overthrew Haile Selassie), Somalia (after Siad Barre flip-flopped to the West when the USSR switched its support to Mengistu's Ethiopia), Kenya, and Zaire. With the exception of Kenya (with whose government we are, however, barely on speaking terms because of human rights abuses), this dreary lineup includes a certain number of rat-holes by virtually *any* reasonable standard!

Two characteristics are common to all of those governments: first, questionable "legitimacy" in the eyes of their own people; and second, the willingness—nay eagerness—on the part of those regimes to allow themselves and their national territories to be used by the United States for U.S. national purposes.

It is not at all evident that the United States gained from this association and certainly the African peoples involved did not (even though their rulers *certainly* did). In Liberia, Sudan, Ethiopia, Somalia, and Zaire, the United States has nothing—*nothing*—to show for the several billion dollars it provided in economic aid and military assistance over nearly a three-decade period (although Ethiopia, with Mengistu gone, is now staging something of a comeback). Liberia and Somalia don't even exist as countries any more; their military forces, trained and largely equipped by the United States, have disappeared. Virtually nothing the United States helped create or build in Sudan and little that it provided to pre-Mengistu Ethiopia are still around. Zaire stands as an archetype of sorts (on a continent with a surfeit of such archetypes) of a "collapsed" state, and the United States is diligently seeking the removal of the potentate it literally wined and dined and otherwise supported for so many years and whose military the United States helped school and equip.

To be sure, we were afforded access to Liberia's international airport for many years before highway roadblocks and robberies by Liberia's armed forces of U.S. passengers and crews traveling from Robertsfield to downtown Monrovia finally led even the U.S. Air Force to fall back on Dakar's and Abidjan's safer environments; Chad allowed the United States to kick sand in Mu'ammar Qadhafi's eyes from its soil; the United States supported a faction in Angola's civil conflict from a Zairian airfield; and Kenya has been willing to allow the United States the use of its two major international airfields and the port of Mombasa to stage a variety of military, humanitarian, and international peace operations in East Africa and the Horn, diminishing any U.S. temptation to be more sharply critical of Kenya's authoritarian domestic policies. Other than these nominal tips-of-the-hat to U.S. interests, however, the United States doesn't have much to show for rather extensive and (relative to the intrinsic worth of the place) rather expensive involvement with Africa over the 30-plus years of the latter's postcolonial history.

South/Southeast/East Asia

Here the record is better, but it isn't at all clear how much is due to U.S. influence and how much to differences between Asian societies (political, economic, and social) and those in other parts of the world. We won't spend much time on them other than to note that where strong national societies existed, they have largely capitalized *by themselves* on their *own* strengths to build flourishing economies—but where the "legitimacy" of their regimes was in question, they have had greater trouble.

The ne plus ultras of U.S.-supported "illegitimate" governments obviously not having the loyalty of their own people were the Kuo Min-tang regime of Chiang Kai-shek on the mainland of China (from which it was driven into exile on Taiwan in 1949) and the South Vietnamese government, which folded under nationalistic revolutionary pressure in 1975. The latter marks one of the sadder U.S. failures to understand the concept of "legitimacy": despite all the retrospective agonizing over whether the United States should have acted more forcefully militarily in the early stages of the conflict (rather than taking a gradual step-by-step escalation of pressure against the North), whether we used the right "tactics" to counter a guerrilla insurgency, whether we tied one hand (or more) of the U.S. military behind its back as it sought to shore up the beleaguered Army of the Republic of Viet Nam and other Government of Viet Nam military forces, and whether we should have utilized village development schemes or refined the French "strategic hamlet" concept, the fact is that right up to the end of the conflict the United States was trying to support a government and a military that self-evidently did not have the support of their own people. That the people did not support the Viet Cong is obvious from their efforts to flee the latter. Nevertheless, fear of or dislike or distaste for the approaching Vietnamese Communist "liberators" did not overcome the unwillingness of the South Vietnamese people to support a regime which had done little or nothing to win over their allegiance.

That is the bottom line in any counterguerrilla effort: any government which cannot enlist the *active* support of its own people—not passive, but *active*—starts with a powerful handicap, because the guerrillas get to choose the times and places of their attacks, whereas the government has to defend all the places all the time.

Two other countries in Southeast Asia, Laos and Cambodia, also succumbed to Communist insurgencies, but it is easier to ascribe their insurgencies' successes to outside assistance (from China and, latterly, North Vietnam) than to failure of their own peoples to support their traditional monarchies. Various South Korean regimes likewise have faced problems stemming from lack of popular "legitimacy."

Enlarging Democracy

So, having described the problems of "illegitimate" governments with no standing in the eyes of their own people, and the complications for the United States (and our principal allies and trading partners) of our associations with them, where do we go from here?

If the United States proactively stands—or *should* stand—for anything, it ought to be for encouraging the growth of democracy, respect for human rights, and an enlargement of free markets and market-driven economic development.

A major problem for the United States is that it remains mired in its conviction that "political" democracy must take precedence over "economic" democracy. Furthermore, in much the same way that we demonized those during the cold war who did not subscribe to our insistence on the preeminent importance of opposing communism (and, conversely, rewarded those, no matter how unworthy, who simply proclaimed themselves our friends and anti-Communist), we now have a clear propensity to penalize those who don't practice *our* form of democracy (c.f., Fujimori's Peru), implement *our* ideas about human rights in their societies (c.f., Singapore and China), or follow the U.S. lead in fighting our new demons such as narco-trafficking (c.f., various Andean Ridge countries), international terrorism, and the proliferation of weapons of mass destruction.

Using Sanctions to Bring About Change

The United States, in fact, seems to have an almost mystical faith in the ability of sanctions to compel recalcitrant governments to do our bidding. The United States probably has more experience in the application of sanctions of various sorts—economic, political, financial, denial of foreign aid, denial of military equipment—than all other countries combined. Yet, there is scant evidence that the use of such pressures to persuade other governments to conform to our notions of how they should behave has ever had the desired effect.

The United States tried to isolate the People's Republic of China for nearly 25 years while the rest of the world increasingly switched from doing business with Taiwan to Beijing. We have applied sanctions against Cuba for nearly 35 years in an effort to bring down Fidel Castro (let's not dissemble: we weren't trying to achieve "behavior modification"; we were trying to bring about his ouster). We imposed sanctions against Gen.

Wojciech Jaruzelski's Poland after he beat up on Solidarity's Lech Walesa; and while Solidarity and Walesa ultimately triumphed, there is little reason to believe it was because of Western Pressure rather than internal Polish developments which made Jaruzelski's position untenable. We tried sanctions against the USSR after its invasion of Afghanistan; the Soviets finally threw in the towel on Afghanistan, but not because of U.S. sanctions: rather, Moscow finally concluded, as the United States had earlier in Vietnam, that it was increasingly bogged down in a quagmire. We applied sanctions against the Communist North Vietnamese regime in Hanoi which we are only now, 20 years after the fall of Saigon to Vo Nguyen Giap's Peoples' Army, beginning to ameliorate. We tried them against Nicaragua's Sandinistas; the Sandinistas were ultimately thrown out by Nicaraguans, but there is little evidence that U.S. sanctions added much to that battle. We used them against Argentina's generals because of their gross human rights violations (the Madres de la Plaza de Mayo ultimately triumphed, but not because of U.S. sanctions); and against Chile's Augusto Pinochet (the Chilean people ultimately forced him out, as the *Chilean* people overthrew Salvador Allende); and, of course, against Libya's Qadhafi, Iraq's Saddam Hussein, and the radicalized and hoary mullahs of Tehran.

If generalized conclusions can be drawn from the U.S. experience in the use of sanctions in an effort to persuade other governments to do things they've said they're not prepared to do, one could say (a) governments which have adopted strong, determined, and antagonistic positions are unlikely to change those positions simply because of *outside* pressures; (b) sanctions are generally effective *only* against governments that *care* what their impact is on their own people (Saddam and Qadhafi obviously don't); and (c) working with and helping *internal* forces press for change is more likely to be effective than trying to compel behavior modification from without.

This is not to say that the United States (or other nations, for that matter) shouldn't refuse to do business with regimes they consider to be politically reprehensible, morally repugnant, or otherwise "illegitimate," but simply to say that one should not have very high expectations of bringing about change as a result of outside pressure.

Otto von Bismarck was unlikely to give up his goal of unifying Germany simply because the outside world thought Bavaria and Westphalia and Schleswig-Holstein and other among the Teutonic princely states were entitled to national self-determination—nor Charlemagne just because Normandy, Brittany, and Picardy wanted to retain their independence; nor Garibaldi on account of the Tuscans and Umbrians; nor Ferdinand and Isabella toward anyone not from Castile, Leon, and Navarre.

So too, it is *irrational* to expect Slobodan Milosevic to be moved by foreign public or official opinion—or by bombs falling from NATO aircraft—to let significant portions of what used to be Yugoslavia revert to independent ethnic or religious ministates just because Western countries have recognized these ethnic homelands and brought them into the United Nations.

The Development of Democracy

The United States may, in fact, have a mistaken impression about the way democracy develops. It should by now be fairly clear from more than 50 years' worth of experience with economic development schemes that democracy does not create a middle class; *economic development* creates a middle class. The growth of that middle class leads, in pretty nearly a point-to-point relationship, to pressure for political and economic and social freedoms and for the right to participate in the governmental policy-making process.

Democracy is a middle class phenomenon. Democracy is not for the rich: the rich are simply asked to pay, through a transfer of resources from themselves to those at the other end of the socioeconomic spectrum, for programs to help raise the living standards and potential for economic advancement of the poor.

Nor is democracy for the poor: "democracy"—participation in the political, social, and economic policy-making *process*—is a distraction to the poor from their primary goals and objectives, which are food and housing, medical care and education for their families, and jobs. They want hard, cold, tangible, practical rewards—not the ephemera of "participation" in a political process in the hope of a long-term improvement in their conditions of life.

This has, in fact, been the entire pattern of political, social, and economic development in Western Europe and the United States, and now in the emerging Asian democracies, and it will soon be apparent in several Latin American countries.

The Concept of "Legitimacy"

I have used the concept of "legitimacy" (or lack thereof) in discussing the characteristics of governments with which the United States does its daily business—including governments whose *lack of* legitimacy has caused U.S. administrations problems ranging from an inability to win support from the American people or Congress or media, to loss of existing support, to the more serious problem of losing support from our principal allies and trading partners for U.S. strategic (not to mention commercial, political, or social) goals and objectives.

In Latin America, the "legitimacy" of regimes we have been closely associated with has been the most serious issue and has caused the most difficult complications for our overall policy objectives, partly because the social, political, and economic cleavages between the "haves" and the "have nots"—between the oligarchs (with whom the United States has traditionally been associated) and the masses (the *campesino* and urban laborer class)—have been so pronounced. The rising tide of disaffection in Latin America during the past half-century has led to bloody uprisings not infrequently aimed at least indirectly against the United States or U.S. citizens and businesses; it has resulted in the violent overthrow of several governments—in some cases, of regimes with long-standing ties to the U.S. government. And although insurgent threats to governments like those of Peru, Colombia, El Salvador, Guatemala, and others have (at least at present writing) been brought reasonably well under control and do not, at least for now, pose a serious threat to the stability of the Mexican government, no one should take satisfaction from the state of "democratic" government in the Western Hemisphere.

To say that "all Latin American governments," at least for the moment, are "elected democracies"—as the U.S. government has been stating since the 1994 ouster of Haiti's Cedras, is simply to pervert both words. Most Latin American governments remain, by and large, governments *of* the oligarchies, *by* the oligarchies, and *for* the oligarchies. Even in the case of a reasonable approximation of a "populist" democratic government such as that of Ecuador's President Sixto Duran Ballen, Peru's Alberto Fujimori, and Argentina's Carlos Saul Menem, *power*—economic, political, and social—remains in the hands of a few. The masses know it, and they're not happy about it. And they don't think of their basic human needs ("BHN," in the arcane language of the bureaucrats concerned with economic assistance and development programs) are being met, or even that very much effort is being made to meet them.

As long as this remains the case, U.S. interests ultimately will be in jeopardy in this hemisphere, not from international communism—now pretty well dead—but from movements and activists who hold the United States largely responsible for helping the oligarchs continue to hold onto power. The Oligarchs' trump card, in the end, is their willingness (and their ability, having prudently taken the precaution of stashing in U.S. or European financial institutions the loot they stole from their own citizens) to toss in their hands and flee to safety in the U.S. (and our unwillingness, not to say inability, to keep them from coming here). (Clapping a handful of Cuban and Haitian boat people in camps at Guantanamo hardly qualifies, in the face of some 7 to 14 million illegal immigrants already living and working in the U.S. as much of a deterrent.)

In Africa, the regret is that the United States has squandered significant (and now uncoverable and irreplaceable) resources on regimes (and, in some cases, on whole countries) which either no longer exist or have little or no popular support, for U.S. purposes once described as "strategic" but which are now pretty much irrelevant. At the same time, largely to punish (or at least penalize) countries whose governments chose not to associate themselves with the United States and our strategic purposes, we have withheld resources which might have been sensibly used by governments which enjoyed considerable popular support. A notable example is Ghana under Flt. Lt. Jerry Rawlings—whose popularity among Ghanaians, when he chased the moneylenders from the temples of government, was obvious and encouraging—but who didn't conform to U.S. notions of what the U.S. administration of the day said it wanted from a government of Ghana.

Africa suffers from too many crippling problems to try to comprehensively catalogue here, but—in addition to being victimized by 30-plus years of superpower rivalry—it has crippled itself by its fealty to the sanctity of its colonial borders. Largely on the grounds that "national borders" was a Pandora's box not to be tampered with, African governments have sought (and fought) to keep opposing (sometimes violently so) tribes together within national borders that could only charitably be described as whimsical, arbitrary, and capricious. It is hard to see peace returning to Sudan so long as Khartoum is determined to keep together a country—itself the creation of Whitehall's nineteenth-century fertile imagination—consisting of white Moslem Arabs and black Christian/animist Africans. Is it worth continuing the calamitous killing of innocent civilians in Angola, both Ovimbundu and Kimbundu, just to try to hold another whimsical, arbitrary, and capricious nineteenth-century European geographic confection together? It may, in the end, not be altogether fair to blame the strife between UNITA and the FMLA on Jonas Savimbi's bloody-mindedness—or that in KwaZulu on Mangosuthu Buthelezi's seeming megalomania—but how far would national disintegration go in Africa if the lid were removed from this incendiary continental tinderbox? Does that matter? The economic and political viability of African states is something for *Africans* to determine—not outsiders—and if the alternative is continued or even increased bloodletting occasioned by trying to persuade obviously and sometimes viciously nonconsenting adults to commit unnatural acts (i.e., living together peacefully "like good Christians"), then the fragmenting of existing national structures may be preferable. If Africans conclude that their ministates are not viable, then Africans can put together new national agglomerations on the basis of their own perceptions of their own tribal or ethnic or national self-interest.

I'll not touch the Middle East: it speaks for itself. The United States and its friends and trading partners need good, friendly, close working relationships based on mutual respect and mutual interest with the Arab/Islamic world. It's hard to say with a straight face that we now have them (except in the formal sense of our existing relationships with a bunch of increasingly anachronistic monarchies and the plutocracies with vested interests in supporting them). Of the sociopolitical split in the Arab/Islamic world, we're on the wrong side of history. It isn't clear how long the royal houses—our friends—will survive, but the long run of history (not to mention our own professions of preference for democracies) is not in their favor.

For better or worse, Iran is probably going to be the future power in that part of the world. There's a reason why the Persian Gulf is called the "Persian" gulf; for the past 2,500 years, the center of intellectual and technological creativity in that enormous part of what we call the "middle east" was located on the Aryan Plateau. Iran has the resources, the people, and the talent to emerge as an economic and political "tiger" in its area, in much the same way Korea and Taiwan and Thailand and Malaysia and Singapore have done in their part of the world. No other country in that region is likely to develop such a potential in the proximate future.

According to recent travelers to Iran, it may be safer to be an American walking the streets of Tehran today than to be a mullah. Iranian youth—not unlike young people in other parts of the world at similar times and in similar circumstances—avidly lap up whatever news and information they can get about the outside world, especially about technical, social, and cultural developments in the West and in the United States. Thirties-something Iranians—both men and, apparently, increasing numbers of women—are already on-line and wired in, faxing and networking and planning their future while the moss-encrusted mullahs squat cloistered in their seminaries, picking moodily at the scab of the Great Satan's relationship with the late House of Pahlavi.

The United States lost decades in developing a relationship with China because of our inability to accept a government which didn't conform to our notion of what it ought to be. The world, meantime, beat a path to Beijing's door. The United States has spent 35 years trying to isolate Castro's Cuba in an effort to bring Castro down. Castro will, in due course, pass from the scene, but the United States will have lost decades in trying to refashion a relationship with Cuba—each year of which will jack up even further the price that will have to be paid to rebuild that tormented island. Arguably it would have been politically impossible for the United States to have moved faster to reconstruct a relationship with Vietnam—but must the sulking *always* come from the U.S. side? If the United States is prepared to try to reach an agreement with a country like North Korea—unquestionably the world's most xenophobic, brutal, reactionary, and relentlessly and remorselessly hostile regime—why do we seem incapable of working to restore a relationship with a country like Iran? (It may not *only* be the mullahs who sit cloistered in their sanctuaries, picking moodily at the scab of a relationship filled with bitterness and hostility . . .) Is there some hidden logic that makes it possible for the U.S. to whip itself into a fervor about the righteousness of a minor tribe in Bosnia defending itself to the death? If the Bosnian Muslims, then why not the Chechens? Why not the Basques? Why not Tibet? Why Somalia but not southern Sudan, or Liberia, or the Tamil portion of Sri Lanka? (Indeed, why not Ulster! Or Quebec?)

Finding Legitimate Partners

So where does this lead us?

With the dissolution of the architecture that provided the basis for the conduct of international relations for the 45 to 50 years after the end of World War II, the United States now has an opportunity to take a new look at the way it structures its relationships with the rest of the world. It may help to set forth some simple and straightforward precepts:

1. The existing Western mutual security alliances and other arrangements have served all parties well and continue to be needed.
2. The USSR and Warsaw Pact are no more, but no one can predict with very much confidence how events in Eastern Europe or Russia will evolve over the next decade and beyond.
3. One thing *not* in U.S. or European interests is simply to move the border to NATO 500 miles eastward—hence 500 miles closer to an already paranoid-enough country, government, and people.
4. Nor can one derive much confidence from the way the United States is conducting its relations with one very clearly unstable part of the world—northeast Asia/the northwest Pacific. To pretend that the United States can contribute to long-term growth in interlocking relationships and economic and social policies in that unsettled region of the world by standing on our shore of the Pacific shaking our fists at China (over human rights), Korea (over South Korean human rights abuses and North Korean nuclear objectives) and Japan (over the imbalance in bilateral trade) appalls the imagination.
5. Relations among *states* aside, we will also see growth in other sources of instability, such as international terrorism, religious fundamentalism, the proliferation of weapons of mass destruction (chemical, biological, and nuclear), and international criminal networks. The United States has squandered far too many resources and far too much goodwill on a self-evidently futile effort to curb the flow of drugs from the producer-countries. Now one is left to hope that, in reaching the conclusion that this has been a waste of time, money, and lives, we don't also decide to forgo seeking "legitimate partners" with whom to cooperate in the struggle to prevent these new sources of instability from consuming our society.

To achieve these purposes, we need to take a harder and more selective look at what our objectives are, and which countries' support we should seek to enlist in working toward their achievement. Now that the cold war is over, we can begin to shift our efforts from countries and governments that simply allowed us to do as we wished from their soil toward supporting those countries and governments whose actions are consistent with our values and beliefs.

PART THREE

The Third Pillar: An Appropriate Management Structure for the Conduct of Contemporary Conflict

9

Organizing for Operations Other Than War (OOTW) in the Post–Cold War Era

Ambassador Edwin G. Corr and Ambassador David C. Miller, Jr.

This chapter addresses the third pillar of success for U.S. foreign policy in the post–Cold War era—the government's management, agency coordination, and policy implementation structure. The authors sketch the current international setting and challenges along with a brief description of the U.S. experience with low-intensity conflict (LIC), special operations, and operations other than war (OOTW). They examine the influence of attitudinal, legislative, and executive policy restraints, and the impact of recent conflicts on the U.S. capability to cope with low-intensity conflict and operations other than war. Finally, they assess the Clinton administration's policies and management of LIC and OOTW and make recommendations to improve management and performance in this area.

New elements in national security arise from a changing global situation. During the past decade communism collapsed in Eastern Europe, independent states emerged there, the Soviet Union disintegrated, Western Europe moved further toward economic and political integration, Japan and East Asia's growing economic and political might thrust the region increasingly into the international arena, and there was a remarkable movement in Latin America, Eastern Europe, and Africa toward the development of accountable governments—typically multiparty democracies. It is also clear that the world, at least for foreseeable future, is moving toward market economies, although many Third World thinkers remain skeptical of capitalism's ability to resolve the tremendous economic and social inequities of the developing world.

Reflection on the very large disparity in global allocation of income, the rapid growth of population in most developing countries with attendant degradation of the environment, the intensified religious and ethnic hostilities, the frustrations of minority groups in many countries, and the general inability of Third World governments to govern and to grapple successfully with challenges to their legitimacy suggest continued and heightened instability in many regions of the world. This instability poses and will continue to present serious security challenges to the United States.[1] The United States must be concerned about governmental organization and capabilities to deal with security threats, including the challenge of low-intensity conflict (LIC) and operations other than war (OOTW).

While U.S. public attention focused on the threat of nuclear war with the Soviets over the last half-century, there was great turmoil and hostility in the Third World. The 1988 Long-Term Integrated Strategy Report of the Defense Department pointed out that more than 30 wars and about twice as many guerrilla conflicts had killed more than 16 million people in developing countries during the previous four decades. Except for Greece, all the wars the United States has been directly or indirectly involved in since World War II occurred in what has been called the Third World.[2] For years there have been numerous internal and external wars throughout the world, most of them ignored by the American public. By 1991, after the events in Panama and Iraq and conflicts in other areas, the number of dead from such wars was estimated to be between 20 and 40 million.[3]

In the environment of the formerly Communist world and in the developing world, the resource base, both human and natural, is frequently limited. The political systems, even if formally democratic, are fragile; and in many cases the politicoeconomic structure is regressive. Armed hostilities are only the most immediately threatening of the many crises facing these societies. The challenge is, and has been, how to create justice and peace through restructuring societies to promote economic growth with equity and responsible legitimate governments.[4] As President José Napoleón Duarte of El Salvador used to say, prolonged conflicts must be met with prolonged strategies for peace, constitutional government, and democracy.[5] This idea is consistent with U.S. values, tradition, and history, and with the theme of this book.

The question is whether the U.S. government is organized in a way that allows it to make wise decisions and effectively implement a legitimacy theory of engagement in support of U.S. values and security interests, especially when lengthy, limited, and indirect involvement may be required. Will the existing bureaucratic and military structure enable and prepare the United States to respond to the range of actual threats to its national security? Are we preparing to fight the right wars? Are we organized to engage in prolonged operations other than war to defend our national interests and to support constitutional government, democracy, and economic growth? The cumulative effect of a series of losses by governments favorably disposed to justice, democracy, and the market economy could create disorder and violence that eventually could alter significantly the U.S. security situation and leadership position in international affairs.

The international environment and Americans' way of life will be greatly affected by global economic growth or deterioration of the developing nations as well as by developments in Western Europe and East Asia. The fastest growing markets lie in the emerging countries of the Third World. The dispersion of weapons of mass destruction and the acquisition of long-range delivery systems by irresponsible regional powers or even terrorists present clear threats to U.S. interests. Refugees seeking freedom from repression and improvement in economic conditions cause problems not only for the United States but also for countries with whom we trade, cooperate, and share values. The cancer of narcotics trafficking is aided and abetted by hostile governments and unstable societies. Even the containment of contagious disease is related to the maintenance and expansion of economically vibrant democracies. Low-intensity conflict (LIC) is a menace to national stability, democratic government, and expanding economies and therefore is in some cases a threat to our national interests.

U.S. Government Experience with Low-Intensity Conflict

U.S. involvement in special operations, LIC, and OOTW is marked by successes and controversy. The most glorious historical success was when American insurgents combined unconventional and conventional military action in the War for Independence, 1776–1781. Shortly thereafter, the United States Marine Corps' raid on Tripoli in 1804, immortalized in the Corps' hymn, was an early victory through special operations or limited war. The political-military struggle against Mexico to incorporate Texas, California, and other Western states that culminated in war with Mexico in 1845 had earlier contained elements of LIC. The Spanish-American War of 1898 set the stage for numerous U.S. interventions in internal wars and conflicts of Central America, the Caribbean, and the Philippines during the initial third of the twentieth century.

Support for partisan and guerrilla operations in Europe and Asia during World War II established a precedent for U.S. support to insurgents. The United States extended counterinsurgency support worldwide during the cold war and deployed large numbers of troops directly into combat during the Vietnam War. Although involvement in Third World conflicts was greatly discredited by defeat in Vietnam, indirect involvement in low-intensity conflicts continued integral to U.S. national security policy and actions, as witnessed in the cases of Angola, Afghanistan, and Central America, to name only a few.[6]

Notwithstanding a long and largely successful experience with special operations and LIC, the American people generally do not like limited wars that involve U.S. soldiers in land warfare, nor do they sympathize with prolonged security support for Third World countries in conflict. Americans prefer short wars supposedly fought on the basis of idealism and principles (as opposed to realpolitik, balance of power, and spheres of influence), in which victory is achieved rapidly with minimum losses through the use of massive firepower and high technology. The U.S. government's indirect support for insurgencies and counterinsurgencies, even when successful as in Afghanistan and Central America, was inevitably overshadowed in the media and public consciousness by short, successful, direct military actions in Libya, Grenada, Panama, and Iraq. Moreover, involvement in Somalia and, initially, Haiti further diminished public support for involvement in LIC and operations other than war.

Creating the Bureaucratic Structure: Earlier Presidential Efforts to Coordinate U.S. Agencies in Low-Intensity Conflict Efforts

Administrations since World War II have addressed low-intensity conflict situations with varying degrees of interest and success. President Harry Truman gained congressional approval for the 1947 National Security Act, which created the bureaucratic framework through which the national security strategy of containment would be implemented. Within this larger framework, Secretary James Forrestal created in the Defense Department the Office of Special Programs and gave it responsibility for unconventional warfare planning and psychological operations. The Office coordinated with the National Security Council (NSC), the Central Intelligence Agency (CIA), and the State-Army-Navy-Air Force Coordinating Committee. In 1949 the Office of Special Programs became the Office of Foreign Military Affairs. The same year, the Department of State established the interdepartmental foreign information coordinating Office for Political-Military Affairs. In 1952 a deputy assistant to the secretary of defense for international security affairs was created.

President Dwight Eisenhower established the Operations Coordinating Board to integrate implementation of national security policies, including covert operations and LIC. The Office of Special Operations of the Defense Department had responsibility for psychological warfare, unconventional warfare, and intelligence.[7]

The Kennedy administration merits special attention when examining previous government efforts to organize itself to cope with LIC. President John Kennedy came into office acknowledging the importance of unconventional forms of conflict and committed to reorienting the strategic focus. He was responding in large part to a statement issued by world Communist leaders in a meeting of November 1960 and to Premier Nikita Khrushchev's address of January 6, 1961, which clearly expressed Communist and Soviet support for "wars of national liberation."[8] President Kennedy involved himself personally in outlining a strategy for dealing with insurgency and subversion. His policies and the bureaucratic machinery established then were the United States' most comprehensive organizational effort to deal with LIC.

Kennedy began by stipulating in National Security Action Memorandum No. 2 (NSAM 2) that the armed forces place more emphasis on counterguerrilla units. He prodded the Departments of State and Defense to build up their LIC capabilities. Secretary of State Dean Rusk appointed a director for internal defense. Secretary of Defense Robert S. McNamara elevated and strengthened the Office of the Assistant to the Secretary for Special Operations and Deputy Secretary of Defense.

Kennedy was reportedly frustrated by the Department of State's reluctance to assert leadership in LIC. Seymour Deitchman, a senior Defense Department official during the sixties, wrote that the Department of State:

> appeared to consider problems of internal conflict a diversion from their main interest of foreign policy and diplomacy, and something that would, if played down long enough, eventually be resolved in the normal course of international relations.[9]

Chester Cooper, a CIA official on the NSC and later a member of Ambassador Averell Harriman's negotiating staff, described the State Department as ". . . resigned to playing a reactive, even peripheral, role during the early 60s. The war in Vietnam, it was felt, was the Pentagon's business."[10] Perhaps if the State Department had played a more active and aggressive policy role in the management of the conflict, the U.S. effort could have been more balanced and the results more favorable.

President Kennedy asserted leadership from the White House. He promulgated NSAM 124 in January 1962 to ensure a government-wide counterinsurgency effort. NSAM 124 declared subversive insurgency to be "equal in importance to conventional warfare." The memorandum established the Special Group (Counter-Insurgency) to integrate counterinsurgency into national security strategy. The Special Group consisted of the military representative of the president (chair), the attorney general (the president's brother, Robert), the deputy under secretary of state for political affairs, the deputy secretary of defense, the chairman of the Joint Chiefs of Staff, the director of Central Intelligence, and the special assistant to the president for national security affairs. Other department and agency representatives were invited as the subject under discussion required.[11] It is of interest that the State Department, nominally the lead player in foreign affairs, chose to be represented at a bureaucratic level lower than all the other participants.

The functions of the Special Group (Counter-Insurgency) were:

a. To ensure proper recognition throughout the U.S. government that subversive insurgency ("wars of national liberation") is a major form of politico-military conflict equal in importance to conventional warfare.

b. To ensure that such recognition is reflected in the organization, training, equipment, and doctrine of the U.S. Armed Forces and other U.S. agencies abroad and in the political, economic, intelligence, military aid, and informational programs conducted abroad by State, Defense, AID, USIA and CIA. Particular attention will be paid to the special training of personnel prior to assignment to MAAGs [Military Assistance Advisory Groups] and to embassy staffs in countries where counterinsurgency problems exist or may exist.

c. To keep under review the adequacy of U.S. resources to deal with actual or potential situations of insurgency or indirect aggression, making timely recommendation of measures to apply, increase or adjust these resources to meet anticipated requirements.

d. To ensure the development of adequate interdepartmental programs aimed at preventing or defeating subversive insurgency and indirect aggression in countries and regions specifically assigned to the Special Group (C.I.) by the President, and to resolve any interdepartmental problems which might impede their implementation.[12]

President Kennedy's intent was to establish a bureaucratic mechanism that could establish "broad lines of counterinsurgency policy . . . ensuring a coordinated and unified approach to regional or country programs, and verifying progress in implementation thereof."[13] The Special Group was sufficiently senior to make decisions on policy, but not so senior that members' responsibilities and demands prevented them from meeting.[14]

In August 1962, Kennedy issued NSAM 182, the Overseas Internal Defense Policy (OIDP) Memorandum. It asserted that the government would support friendly Third World governments threatened by guerrilla movements. NSAM 182 covered threat, objectives, and strategy and addressed strategy implementation. Methods of support for Third World nations in low-intensity conflicts included intelligence, land reform, civic action, community development, education, leader groups, and police. It touched on the role of multilateral organizations and defined specific roles for the Special Group (C.I.), the State Department, the Department of Defense (DOD), the CIA, the U.S. Agency for International Development (USAID), and the United States Information Agency (USIA). A model country internal defense plan was included as an annex.[15]

The Johnson administration replaced the Special Group (CI) with the Senior Interdepartmental Group (SIG), composed of key departmental representatives at the deputy secretary level and other key agency heads and officials. Underneath the SIG were five Interdepartmental Regional Groups, chaired by assistant secretaries of state for those regions.[16]

Despite the efforts of Presidents Kennedy and Johnson to involve all relevant government entities and these presidents' repeated insistence on the importance of the "other war" to achieve political objectives of security for the people, good government, and the people's well-being, the government normally gave higher priority to immediate military and geopolitical objectives. The result was that, although articulated, the political, social, and economic goals were consistently overshadowed. The considerable progress made in Vietnam in certain developmental areas at the local level was undone by the absence of a functional and legitimate South Vietnamese government.[17] The 1969 Nixon Guam Doctrine, to be discussed below, recognized this fatal weakness, but by that juncture it was probably too late. Even if not, the U.S. people and Congress were not willing to meet the commitments made by the Nixon administration to the South Vietnamese government to ensure a successful Vietnamization program.

By the end of the Johnson administration the momentum for LIC had stopped. Military budgets for the activity were cut back; and economic and security assistance funds for Asia, Latin America, and Africa were reduced. Diplomatic missions and the numbers and kinds of U.S. personnel assigned to embassies in Third World countries were curtailed.

Under the Nixon, Ford, and Carter administrations LIC received scant attention. Their bureaucratic structures related to LIC are not here described because in general, LIC issues were addressed on an ad-hoc basis.

The Reagan administration again elevated the importance of LIC, particularly as it related to insurgencies in Angola, Afghanistan, Nicaragua, and El Salvador. The bureaucratic arrangements and machinery established by President Ronald Reagan and by the Congress during his term remained, with slight alteration, the bureaucratic structure through which the Bush presidency dealt with LIC. This structure and the current policies, organization, and management mechanisms of the Clinton administration will be described and analyzed later in the chapter.

Executive Studies Affecting Low-Intensity Conflict Capabilities

There have been a number of important efforts to understand and to better government capabilities to deal with LIC.[18] Some of the significant studies and commission reports are as follows:

* Rockefeller Report   1958
* Draper Commission   1959
* Special Operations Research Office   1962

* Howze Board	1962
* Defense Science Board Report	1964
* Restricted Engagement Options	1973
* Holloway Commission	1980
* Joint Low-Intensity Conflict Project	1986
* Packard Commission	1986
* Integrated Long-Term Strategy	1988
* The Bottom-Up Review	1993

The early Rockefeller Report identified "concealed wars" as one of the most serious challenges facing the nation:

> These conflicts raise issues with which in terms of our preconceptions and the structure of our forces we are least prepared to deal.... Our security ... will hinge importantly on our willingness to support friendly governments in situations which fit neither the soldier's classic concept of war nor the diplomat's traditional concept of aggression.[19]

The 1958 presidential commission under William H. Draper evaluated U.S. foreign policy and aid in 1958 and 1959. The report suggested more aid for the internal defense of Third World countries, including funding for military education, engineering, and community services, to help countries cope with LIC threats.[20] The Special Operations Research Office was established at American University in 1962 and along with the Department of Defense's Special Warfare Directorate was asked to "facilitate and coordinate" LIC programs. Within the military, counterinsurgency courses were institutionalized at the Special Warfare School at Fort Bragg, North Carolina. The Howze Board called for increased indoctrination of U.S. military in counterinsurgency and for doubling the number of special forces.[21]

The 1973 Department of Defense "Restricted Engagement Options" proposed the creation of "an integrated, multipurpose, low cost, low visibility agency" to deal with low-intensity conflicts. The agency would have been at the same level as the Departments of State and Defense and the CIA.[22]

President Reagan established the Packard Commission (the President's Blue Ribbon Commission on Defense Management) in 1985, and in June 1986 it suggested sweeping changes in defense policy and organization. President Reagan issued National Security Decision Directive No. 219 in April 1986 and subsequent executive orders to implement the commission's recommendations. Many of these affected LIC and OOTW capabilities. Especially important was broader authority for the unified commands and flexibility for them to deal with situations in their regions. This change meant a greater focus on LIC for those commands in the Third World.[23]

The U.S. Army's Low-Intensity Conflict Project's two-volume report of

August 1986 painted a bleak picture of U.S. LIC capabilities, stating that "As a nation we do not understand low-intensity conflict. We respond without unity of effort; we execute our activities poorly; and we lack the ability to sustain operations." The Joint Special Operations Agency (JSOA) was established to ensure the involvement of the Joint Chiefs of Staff in special operations, and a number of initiatives were taken by the Department of Defense to strengthen capabilities in this area.[24]

The Commission on Integrated Long-Term Strategy, established in 1988, had a working subgroup that submitted a report on supporting U.S. strategy for Third World conflict that urged greater consensus among the executive, Congress, and American people to achieve legislative reforms, organizational realignments, resource allocations, and diplomatic initiatives needed for a strategy to protect and advance U.S. interests in the vital developing world. These interests included protecting our nation and our allies from threats (LIC, drug trafficking, terrorism) arising there; responding to challenges to the global economy; defending and promoting democracy, freedom, and human rights; ensuring access to allies, strategic regions, and critical raw materials; and creating constructive relations and peaceful dispute settlement. The report emphasized the need for unprecedented governmental coordination and for drawing upon U.S. technology. The working group said the entire strategy could be underwritten for only $12 billion per year.[25]

The Bottom-Up Review conducted by Secretary of Defense Les Aspin in 1993 defined four major dangers for the post–Cold War world, none of which specifically included LIC and Third World conflict other than in the sense of conventional regional wars and the risk that democratic reforms might fail in the former Soviet Union.[26] Despite its name, the review appeared to be in large part a Department of Defense exercise to protect its budget and institutions rather than an effort to discard entrenched historical perspectives and take a broader view of international threats to U.S. security. The report added little to OOTW and LIC theory, organization, or doctrine. What has evolved in this area during the Clinton administration has, as described later, flowed from the administration's efforts to respond to multilateral peace operations, referred to as operations other than war.

Attitudinal Constraints on U.S. Government Capabilities to Deal with Low-Intensity Conflict

A certain amount of bureaucratic rivalry is part of the U.S. system and is constructive. Excessive competition by some agencies, combined with neglect and stonewalling to defend turf by others, has an adverse impact, however. Loyalties to office, bureau, service, agency, and department sometimes dominate over comprehensive government objectives. Differences in bureaucratic cultures and institutional orientation often lead people to avoid rather than seek coordination with other agencies. Such differences may result from clashes between those having technical or functional responsibilities and those charged with regional or country-specific responsibilities.

There is also the difference in approach between the soldier and the diplomat. By training and experience the soldier seeks certainty and emphasizes victory through force. The diplomat is accustomed to ambiguity and emphasizes solving conflicts through persuasion. The soldier's principal expertise is in operations, and the diplomat's is in persuasion.

The dynamics of government and bureaucratic behavior are deeply ingrained in our culture and political system. It seems highly unlikely and probably undesirable that competitive tensions should be eliminated from U.S. bureaucracy. Nonetheless, to the degree that agency rivalries and lack of coordination are dysfunctional, preventing the United States from coping effectively with LIC, corrective actions should be taken.[27]

Attention to organization for LIC, especially in the armed forces, heightened during the Reagan administration. Low priority and lack of conscious and explicit organization to cope with LIC were more evident among the civilian agencies. Three former ambassadors to El Salvador identified coordination of policy and operations as among the most challenging problems during their tenures in that country,[28] and the managerial and bureaucratic structure on the civilian side changed little under Reagan.

As in the Kennedy administration, the Reagan presidency tried to force the bureaucracy to cope effectively with LIC. The Congress joined the president and legislatively mandated the Pentagon—kicking, screaming, and with many of its generals and civilian executives leaving their fingernails in the door frame as they were dragged through it—to create a special operations command (one of only 11 commands headed by a four-star general) and an assistant secretary for special operations and LIC. Similar reorganization and priority for LIC were not imposed on civilian agencies. Unfortunately, with the end of the Cold War and apparent successes through direct military intervention in Grenada, Panama, and Iraq, the momentum to implement significant organizational changes to manage LIC situations more effectively appeared to decline until renewed attention related to peace operations in Somalia, Bosnia, and Haiti.

The bureaucratic machinery and capacity to deal with LIC, as opposed to special operations, are still deficient in the mid-1990s. This was clear from the much-criticized U.S. performance in Somalia, although the Haiti operation was much improved by the high priority given to it by the Clinton administration, by the predominant role of the United States in the operation, and by luck.

Why has the United States been so reluctant to deal with the challenge of

LIC? The principal U.S. defense priority during the Cold War was rightly the prevention of nuclear war, with a primary focus on Europe, while, ironically, nearly all armed conflicts occurred in the Third World. Although it need not have been so, our preoccupation with preventing low-probability, high-intensity nuclear conflict detracted from our giving sufficient attention to and learning to deal efficaciously with existing low-intensity conflicts. We have been slow to adapt our thinking, organization, and resource allocations to high-probability LIC where our military's role is often relatively small and indirect, and where extraordinary support is required for civilian authorities in their developmental efforts. Meeting this challenge becomes more important as we exist in a world environment of greater instability and low probability of massive nuclear exchange.

Part of the difficulty in dealing with LIC has been caused by the "World War II syndrome," not just the "Vietnam syndrome." It was World War II that created for Americans an almost total unity and commitment with regard to war, and this experience set thought patterns that still strongly affect the way we think wars should be waged. During the great conflict from 1941 to 1945, the United States felt itself to be righteously, unconditionally, and totally in a crusade to crush fascist states and liquidate evil enemy leaders, and thereby permit the world to continue a natural evolution and progress toward prosperity and democracy. The perceptions of the simple culpability of leaders such as Hitler, Mussolini, and Tojo and the justice of their defeat were not confused by the stark reality of the developing world, where most conflicts occur and where the roots of hostilities are deeply embedded in historical, social, political, and economic inequalities. In those circumstances, the military resolution of conflict does not and cannot bring lasting peace, progress, justice, and democracy. Our struggle and defeat in Vietnam, over which there were tremendous national division and ambiguity, strengthened the World War II mind-set.

This misperception of low-intensity conflicts was reflected by the organizational and policy confusion of the U.S. government in Somalia. It was earlier reflected by congressmen and groups of citizens visiting El Salvador during the conflict there who inevitably asked: "When will the war end?" The American public and its officials are still too inclined to envision the termination of the conflict along the lines of V-E Day in Europe or the signing of peace with the Japanese on the *USS Missouri*, whereupon hostilities came clearly and finally to a halt. In the prevailing form of armed conflict and operations today, LIC and OOTW, nothing is so neat and definitive. Sometimes there are peace agreements and clear-cut victories for the governments or insurgents, but more often conflicts smolder for decades. Armed conflict may be halted temporarily, but as long as gray areas exist and the underlying social, economic, and political causes of discontent do not seem to be improving, the resumption of terrorism and insurgency is always a threat. With good fortune and solid programs, insurgencies dissipate and end as the guerrilla cause and guerrillas themselves seemingly tire and finally die of old age. More realistically, however, insurgencies are reduced over time to a tolerable, manageable level as a result of government legitimization and responsible and effective government counterinsurgency measures.[29]

In 1988 Secretary of State George Shultz spoke of new political complexities in "the ecology of international change" and noted that "In this decade, I believe Americans have come to recognize that we are not likely to face either an era of total war or of total peace."[30] Professor Stephen Sloan, however, argued that U.S. governments have failed to convey sufficiently to the public that coping with LIC in the Third World is generally long term. The British, for example, with a world-class armed force after World War II, and in a period when human rights were not the political concern they are today, required 15 years to defeat Malaysian insurgents. Sloan suggested that quick strike and withdrawal operations, such as the Libyan raid, Grenada, Panama, and the militarily successful Iraq war, have acted as a barrier to popular and governmental understanding that most low-intensity conflicts are not quickly resolvable.[31] The U.S. experiences with Somalia, Bosnia, and Haiti have added to public understanding that coping with LIC is difficult; but, even with increased understanding, and perhaps because of it, the Congress and U.S. people are even less inclined to make long-term commitments to engage in Third World protracted conflicts. Increased understanding will have little consequence unless it is accompanied by changes in our priorities, the will to persist, a modified legal framework, and an organizational structure to implement national policy.

The evolution of international law on wars, the development of our national defense and foreign policy organizations, our laws, and our national psyche are built largely on a clear distinction between "war and peace."[32] Traditionally, just as we have defined war and peace as mutually exclusive states, civil and military roles and organizations within the government have been clearly separated. Our laws and budgeting process prohibit mixing of civil and military functions and thereby impede cooperation, coordination, and integration of U.S. military and civilian programs. Such has been the case particularly in the implementation of foreign economic and development assistance in combination with security and military assistance. The contemplated changes in foreign economic assistance by both the Clinton administration and the Republican Congress will probably make matters worse.

Another problem with protracted conflict is that without appropriate organization, Washington (as well as the U.S. public) soon tires, and the priority of a specific LIC situation drops. It degenerates to "in-box" issues dealt with in a routine, inflexible manner on personnel assignments, resource allocations, and response time to changing events and crises.[33]

Legislative Constraints on Coping with Low-Intensity Conflict

Congress decided that national defense and especially Third World contingencies were too important to leave in the hands of the president and the generals. In addition to oversight and the annual requirements included in funding legislation, the Congress adopted the War Powers Resolution in 1973. It reflected a struggle between the executive and legislative branches over the control of foreign policy and war-making and was seen by Congress as a safeguard against the executive's engaging the country in other Vietnam-like quagmires. The resolution requires the president to:

1. "In every possible instance" consult with Congress before committing U.S. troops in "hostilities or into situations where imminent involvement in hostilities" is likely;
2. Inform Congress within 48 hours after the introduction of troops if there has been no declaration of war;
3. Remove U.S. troops within 60 days (or 90 days in special circumstances) if Congress does not either declare war or adopt a joint resolution approving the action.[34]

The Congress also claimed power to end U.S. military involvement before 60 days by passing a concurrent resolution, which does not require the president's signature and therefore cannot be vetoed. This claim was found unconstitutional by the Supreme Court in *U.S. vs Chadha* in 1983, but the court has not ruled on the rest of the War Powers Resolution.

Every president since the resolution was adopted has questioned the resolution's constitutionality. Presidents have acknowledged the need to consult with congressional leaders before committing U.S. military forces. They also have submitted reports to the Congress but have fulfilled War Powers Resolution requirements only in part, and they always made clear implicitly or explicitly the view that the executive was not bound to render such reports.[35]

The Goldwater-Nichols Department of Defense Reorganization Act of 1986, drawing on the Packard Commission Report, endeavored to make the Defense Department more effective, including in the area of LIC. The act mandated additional guidelines aimed at enhancing LIC capabilities; in this regard, the creation of the United States Special Operations Command (USSOC) was particularly significant.[36] As a follow-on to the Goldwater-Nichols Act, the Defense Authorization Act of 1987 created an assistant secretary of defense for special operations and low-intensity conflict.[37] The act also directed the president to establish a Low-Intensity Conflict Board within the National Security Council and recommended that a deputy assistant to the president for low-intensity conflict be designated.[38]

Many of the executive branch and congressional initiatives met resistance within the armed forces, the Defense Department, and the national security establishment as a whole. The warnings and advice of presidential commissions and important strategic thinkers over the last 40 years have not been sufficiently heeded.

Executive Policy Restraints on Coping with Low-Intensity Conflict

Two national defense policies or doctrines have had and continue to have an important influence on the U.S. approach and capabilities to cope with LIC: the Nixon Doctrine and the Weinberger Doctrine. Yet to be evaluated is the Clinton Doctrine that is discussed later.

The Nixon (or Guam) Doctrine was enunciated in 1969 by President Richard Nixon as an outgrowth of events in Vietnam. Public and congressional opinion was moving strongly against the country's involvement in Vietnam and against U.S. intervention in other countries generally. The Nixon Doctrine emphasized that henceforth the United States would assist friendly nations but would require threatened nations to provide the manpower and be ultimately responsible for their own defense. The United States, when its national interests were at stake, would play a supporting role by providing political, economic, and military support.

The Nixon Doctrine was implemented in the "Vietnamization Program." Lack of pledged support with U.S. resources, combined with lack of legitimacy and will on the part of the South Vietnamese government, permitted the North Vietnamese to triumph, however. The Nixon Doctrine nevertheless has become a cornerstone of U.S. policy on LIC and OOTW.

The Nixon Doctrine implies that the United States will avoid direct combat involvement of its own troops in an insurgency, that there must exist indigenous civilian and military elements with real or potential strength that the U.S. government can support, that there must be enough time to train and equip indigenous forces for their self-defense, and that there must be sustained U.S. political and economic support to allow political, economic, social, and justice reforms to occur.[39] This doctrine was put to the test in Central America, Afghanistan, and Mozambique.

The range of action was broadened by the Reagan Doctrine, which stated that the U.S. government would assist "freedom fighters" (insurgents) fighting to overthrow Marxist regimes.[40] It was, in a sense, a return to a policy similar to that of World War II when the United States supported partisan and guerrilla groups in France, Italy, and Yugoslavia. (It also could be related to President Eisenhower's and Secretary of State John Foster Dulles's earlier concept of "rollback" of Communist governments.)

Despite this broadening of the use of LIC by President Reagan, a policy pronouncement by Reagan's secretary of defense greatly inhibited U.S. actions in Third World conflicts. The Weinberger Doctrine was enunciated by Secretary Caspar Weinberger in a 1984 speech to the National Press Club. He outlined six major criteria to be met before the United States would commit military forces abroad:

* Vital interests of the United States or its allies must be at stake
* We must be willing to commit enough forces to achieve our objectives
* We must have clearly defined political and military objectives
* We must subject our involvement to continuous reassessment
* Prior to deployment of troops, there must be reasonable assurances of public support
* The use of combat power should be a last resort[41]

The main purpose of these criteria, Weinberger said, was to keep the United States from being gradually pulled into a combat role.

Whereas the Nixon Doctrine serves to prevent overinvolvement of U.S. military forces and to place the major responsibility for countering insurgency on the supported government, the Weinberger Doctrine has been regarded by many as inhibiting nearly all involvement in low-intensity conflicts. This impediment resides chiefly in interpretation of the requirement for prior U.S. public support, which many see as prohibiting involvement in Third World conflicts.

Executive Branch Organizational Deficiencies for Coping with LIC and OOTW on the Eve of the Clinton Administration

David Miller, one of the authors of this chapter, while serving under President George Bush as the special assistant to the president for national security affairs, and senior director for Africa and international programs, led an NSC review of government procedures and structure to meet the threats of LIC, both prevention and resolution. The purpose was to examine how the government formulates, coordinates, provides resources for, and implements national strategy and policy toward countries threatened by or engaged in LIC. In addition to extensive reviews with Washington agencies and meetings with outside experts, an interagency team visited key embassies involved in implementing U.S. policies in LIC situations.

A major issue of the review was interagency unity of effort. The review team concluded that the existing array of actors and of interagency coordinating arrangements was inadequate to respond to unusual and urgent requirements for economic, developmental, informational, and military assistance, either in anticipation of a growing conflict or over a sustained period. The need for coordination from the NSC level down through country teams was stressed.

The underlying problem was twofold. First, there existed no effective interagency forum to address generic issues irrespective of geographic location (e.g., training of U.S. personnel to work together in a low-intensity conflict situation and on nation-building procedures). Second, there existed no effective interagency forum below the level of the Deputies Committee of the National Security Council that could identify and ensure provision of functional expertise and a coordinated flow of resources to country teams for country or region-specific programs, especially in times of crisis. Given the workload of the Deputies Committee, it is unrealistic to expect it to provide the needed support on a sustained basis.

Unity of effort among departments and agencies is also a function of intradepartmental structure. As long as geographic boundaries and functional responsibilities among departments and agencies are roughly equal, coordination is facilitated. When responsibilities are unequal, as is frequently the case, coordination is impeded. Unfortunately, agency structures often have been and continue to be incompatible for optimum coordination.

The Impact of Recent Conflicts on LIC and OOTW

On top of these congressional actions and executive policies or doctrines must be put the effect of U.S. combat experiences in Libya, Grenada, Panama, and Iraq, and subsequently with Somalia, Bosnia, and Haiti. The euphoria that much of the U.S. government, military, and public felt over the apparent successes of military actions on the first group of countries had an impact on thinking, or lack of thinking, about LIC (as opposed to special operations, for which there has been increased emphasis). Americans elatedly projected fighting the kinds of wars and engagements that the armed forces and the public prefer—a superiority of U.S. firepower and technology, short duration, and few casualties. Satisfaction with these victories and realization that the proxy wars of the cold war were over temporarily caused attention to LIC to fade.

Presentations to the Congress by Department of Defense representatives during 1991 acknowledged impending cuts in the armed forces but stressed military might as the principal solution to future contingencies, with little comment on LIC by military leaders, although there was rhetorical recognition of it as a threat by President Bush and Secretary of Defense Richard Cheney. General Colin L. Powell, chairman of the Joint Chiefs of Staff, was quoted as saying, "We have overwhelming power, and we have demonstrated a willingness to use it."[42] Army Chief of Staff General Carl E. Vuono, describing restructuring plans for the 1990s, wrote "the preponderance of the Army will be based within the continental United States and will be focused on the projection of land combat power quickly and massively anywhere in the world."[43] An Air Force presentation stated that in "this new world we are rapidly moving into plays to Air Force strengths—rapid, deployable, long-range, flexible, and lethal capabilities, which can deter, provide a tailored response or punch hard when required."[44] Representative Les Aspin, while still chairman of the House Armed Services Committee, said, " . . . whenever you use military force it has to be quick and low in casualties."[45]

Nonetheless, President Bush in his August 2, 1990, speech at Aspen, Colorado, using another of the many terms for LIC, "peacetime engagement," said that the United States would remain "every bit as constant and committed to the defense of our interests and ideals in today's world as in the time of conflict and Cold War."[46] Department of Defense official documents, in contrast to some of the selected citations above that suggest less attention to LIC, interpreted "peacetime engagement" to include "strategy missions and activities in all environments short of large-scale conventional and nuclear war; that is, ranging from peacetime up through major contingency operations but not including general war."[47] The March 1991 Joint Chiefs' "Military Net Assessment," while stating that military planning had moved to major regional contingencies, such as renewal of Iraqi hostilities or a North Korean attack on South Korea, also indicated more attention to lesser regional contingencies and to counterinsurgency as well as to terrorism and counternarcotics operations.[48]

Secretary of Defense Cheney, in testimony to the Senate on February 21, 1991, noted that the " . . . cooling of superpower rivalry decreases the chances that a regional conflict will escalate into global war . . . " but that there also " . . . is a risk that the end of the bipolar world could unleash local, destructive forces that were previously kept in check." He said that " . . . we face the sobering truth that local sources of instability and oppression will continue to foster conflicts small and large virtually across the globe," and that "Separate and apart from the broad regional conflicts . . . there is another set of demanding threats. They are low-intensity conflicts, including insurgencies, terrorism, and drug trafficking."[49]

Speaking before the House two weeks earlier, Secretary Cheney assured Congress that the Department of Defense officially is aware of and officially gives priority to LIC:

> To help deter low-intensity conflicts and promote stability in the Third World, we must have innovative strategies that support representative government, integrate security assistance, and promote economic development. Our approach for doing this is "peacetime engagement"—a coordinated combination of political, economic, and military actions, aimed primarily at counteracting local violence and promoting nation-building.[50]

Clinton Administration Policies and Organization of the U.S. Government for Low-Intensity Conflict Engagements

With the emergence in the Bush administration of Somalia, Bosnia, and Haiti, not to speak of several upheavals in the former Soviet Union, concern about LIC had again increased. Discussion focused on resolution of such problems through UN peace operations. The Clinton administration reinforced this tendency, while rebaptizing LIC and "peacetime engagement" as OOTW. The frustrations of coping with these later intractable or difficult LIC problems served to make the American public, their elected legislative representatives, and military commanders even more reluctant for the United States to be involved in LIC. How have the Clinton administration's policy and management performance for LIC and OOTW evolved?

Policy Evolution of the Clinton Administration

Caught up in the euphoria of President Bush's proclaimed "new world order" that was to result from an end to the cold war and the end of deadlock in the UN Security Council, and influenced by victory in the Gulf War with Iraq under the auspices of the United Nations, the Clinton administration has built upon, extended, and modified the Bush administration's policy. William Clinton's campaign oratory and early statements were that U.S. security interests could best be protected and advanced in most cases in the Third World with minimum political and resource costs through UN peacekeeping, peace enforcement, and peace-building. This attitude framed policy and doctrine. The Clinton administration's policies, doctrine, and organization for dealing with LIC are based on what it inherited from previous administrations and have taken form in the uncertainty of the post-cold war international environment. Especially important were initial efforts to respond to conflicts and problems in the Third World through multilateral institutions.

The negative experiences of Somalia and Bosnia, and the frustrations of Rwanda and Haiti, have provoked criticism about Clinton policies, actions, and nonactions. Concerns about the United Nations' competence and usurpation struck a responsive chord among Americans with a historical preference for unilateralism in foreign policy. Complaints about placing U.S. military units under foreign commanders were even stronger. By September 1993, President Clinton shifted U.S. policy by laying down specific criteria for determining whether the United States would involve itself in specific multilateral operations. These were put forth by National Security Adviser Tony Lake and Ambassador to the United Nations Madeline Albright, and, finally, by President Clinton himself in a speech to the UN General Assembly. The criteria were further refined and articulated in Secretary of Defense Les Aspin's *Annual Report to the President and Congress,*

January 1994, and the president's report, *A National Security Strategy of Engagement and Enlargement, July 1994*. Department of Defense and other U.S. government agencies have incorporated the guidelines into their documents and manuals.

The Clinton administration posed specific questions for determining whether to support a particular U.N. peace operation:

> These include an assessment of the threat to international peace and security; a determination that the peace operation serves U.S. interests as well as assurance of an international community of interests for dealing with the threat on a multi-lateral basis; identification of clear objectives; availability of the necessary resources; and identification of an operation's endpoint or criteria for completion.[51]

The administration identified four basic principles upon which the use of force might be used "to respond to key dangers—those posed by weapons of mass destruction, regional aggression, and threats to the stability of states":

> First, and foremost, our national interests will dictate the pace and extent of our engagement. . . . Risks of U.S. military involvement must be judged to be commensurate with the stakes involved. . . . Our use of force will be decisive and, if necessary, unilateral. . . .
>
> Second, as much as possible, we will seek the help of our allies or of relevant multi-lateral institutions . . . [and] on those matters touching directly the interests of our allies, there should be a proportional commitment from them. . . .
>
> Third, in every case we will consider several critical questions. . . . Have we considered non-military means . . . ? What kinds of U.S. military capabilities should be brought to bear, and is the use of military force carefully matched to our political objectives? Do we have reasonable assurance of support from the American people. . . . Do we have timelines and milestones that will reveal the extent of success or failure. . . . Do we have an exit strategy?
>
> Fourth, our engagement must meet reasonable cost and feasibility thresholds. . . . The United States will be actively engaged at the diplomatic level.[52]

The Clinton Administration's Management of LIC and OOTW

The principal government actors today in LIC situations in which the United States is involved are the NSC, the Department of State, DOD and the armed forces, the CIA, AID, USIA, the Department of Justice (DOJ), the Department of the Treasury (DOT), the Department of Commerce (DOC), the Office of Management and Budget (OMB), and embassy country teams. Upon assumption of their duties, key national security Cabinet members of the Clinton administration announced plans for reorganization of their departments and agencies to better deal with the changed international environment. These were only partially implemented because of congressional and bureaucratic resistance and political controversy over appointments.

The problem remains that overall responsibility for LIC and OOTW does not belong to any one agency; there is no continuous center of authority; and it is very difficult to sustain an integrated effort. Washington's lack of responsiveness to some urgent requests from author Ed Corr while he served as ambassador to El Salvador is testimony to Washington's organizational and operational difficulties.[53] Officials who have been involved in managing LIC situations have long felt that interagency coordination is inadequate. We will briefly survey some managerial problems of the Departments of State and Defense.

The Department of State. If LIC is that ambiguous area between conventional war and peaceful relationships among nations, in one sense the Department of State has been managing LIC fairly successfully in the normal conduct of diplomacy since World War II. Nonetheless, with respect to specific countries where high levels of violence and insurgency prevail, the Department of State, where for many the lead for managing LIC properly belongs, is poorly organized, understaffed, and lacking in resources.

Regional assistant secretaries maintain their status as *primus inter pares*, and the assumption remains that the ambassador should turn to the regional assistant secretary for coordination of support from Washington. The assistant secretary theoretically accomplishes this coordination through a Regional Policy Coordinating Committee (PCC) constituted by his regional bureau and other pertinent departments and agencies. For a multiplicity of reasons, the PCCs, although effective bodies to develop policies, are not effective bodies for the management of resources to support the policy. In addition, the regional PCC typically will be managing policy toward many countries and be supporting country teams in a number of crises simultaneously.

Competent and experienced ambassadors seldom have problems in achieving good country team coordination and effort "in-country" toward commonly agreed U.S. objectives. The ambassador's authority is fairly well established and recognized by his staff regardless of their parent agency, and the close proximity and sometimes dangerous circumstances within which U.S. officials work in low-intensity conflicts help to mold them into a single team. The ambassador's challenge is to obtain promptly and consistently from Washington via the Department of State the kinds of staffing and correct mix of resources needed to do the job.

Both authors feel strongly that the mechanism for development of LIC policy under the NSC and with the principal foreign affairs departments is good but is only the preplanning stage of a 60-minute game, the success of which depends on teamwork and execution. This teamwork means effective management and coordination of personnel and resources from an array of often competing agencies that frequently have predetermined agendas. In effect, between the NSC Deputies Committee and the country team—a bureaucratically long distance—the United States government has no effective mechanism to manage and support LIC efforts.

Up to and until the Haiti operation, Department of State lines of authority and organization for LIC have been lacking. There was no consistent overall direction, coordination, or coherence. Thus, for example, on a complicated LIC engagement such as counternarcotics, which has components of regional policy, military assistance, and counterterrorism, the Department of State rarely presents a unified position unless matters for decision reach the deputy secretary level.

The Department of State is chronically short of personnel for the responsibilities assigned, is slow to make personnel assignments, does not order people to post without great difficulty, and is frequently limited in the awards that can be offered to personnel assigned to high-threat countries. The contrast between State and Defense Department abilities to assign people rapidly was stunningly illustrated in the Andean region counternarcotics effort, where the uniformed services produced on a moment's notice a wide range of personnel who were apparently enthusiastic about their assignments. Although this contrast is inherent in the difference between military and civilian organizations, the civilian agencies must find the personnel resources and procedures to become more responsive. Moreover, depending on the U.S. armed forces for the bulk of the advisory manpower and expertise to help local democratic leaders move toward a civilian-dominated government ironically undermines the very concept of military submission to civilian authority.

The Department of Defense. The Defense Department and armed forces reluctantly have accepted important organizational changes, such as Congress's creation of the United States Special Operations Command and the Office of the Assistant Secretary of Defense for Special Operations and Low-Intensity Conflict. The strength of the Department of Defense and the armed forces in the management, coordination, and execution of U.S. resources in a LIC situation resides in the regional command structures and their greater amount of personnel and resources. The regional commanders, in some ways analogous to the assistant secretaries of state, do in fact have command and control over all military resources dedicated to the effort. The assistant secretaries of state do not have adequate control over all civilian resources. If the regional commander gives LIC a high priority, he is far better equipped with the needed resources and personnel than any other U.S. government official.

The Defense Department and the armed forces as a whole, nevertheless, appear less than enthusiastic about a type of warfare that requires relatively limited resources and manpower (compared with mid- and high-intensity conflict), that seldom permits U.S. military forces a direct combat role, and in which the lead department is normally State rather than Defense. The enthusiasm for LIC is further tempered by the ambiguous environment of such hostilities and the lack of clearly achievable objectives and neatly won victories.

Discussions with armed forces personnel and the emphasis of some of their public comments cast doubts on their seriousness and commitment to LIC and whether the Defense Department and armed forces have escaped from their half-century of almost exclusive focus on nuclear deterrence and high-intensity conventional warfare. One is reminded of the Kennedy-Johnson years when there was much talk about the preeminence of political, economic, and social goals over military and geostrategic ones, but in the end the latter goals appropriate for U.S.-Soviet confrontation monopolized attention and resources.

Recommendations

The authors note that of five recommendations for improved management of LIC and OOTW made in a previous book, *Low-Intensity Conflict: Old Threats in a New World*, three have been partially implemented by the Clinton administration. While claiming no cause and effect, we are pleased to note this progress in areas that were of great concern to us.

The Progress

First, the Department of State did move under the Clinton administration to strengthen its ability to manage low-intensity conflict challenges. State created an assistant secretary of state for the Bureau of International Narcotics and Law Enforcement Affairs, with broad responsibilities for international narcotics and criminal matters. As predicted, it proved impossible to gain congressional support for including counterterrorism in this office. Just as important as creating the post, the State Department named an experienced and energetic officer, Ambassador Bob Gelbard, to the position.

In addition, after the failure of Somalia, the State Department recognized the need to appoint a senior officer to work exclusively on the effort in Haiti. By all accounts, Ambassador Jim Dobbins, special Haitian coordinator, did a superior job of managing the Haitian program. By the appointment of Dobbins, the State Department "bureaucratically recognized" that regional assistant secretaries simply do not have the time to manage a major crisis in their region and take care of all the other day-to-day responsibilities. As we write, the State Department is wrestling with the issue of developing a permanent office to deal with crises such as Haiti, but no definitive structure or staffing has been reached.

Second, while no formal changes in DOD organization were made, the emergence of the assistant secretary of defense for special operations low intensity conflict as a more active player in the policy dialogue is important. The assistant secretary has developed an effective working relationship both with the director of the Joint Staff and equally important with the J3 (Special Operations) component of the Joint Staff. This has been a major step toward implementing in reality a strong Defense Department office to manage low-intensity conflicts.

Third, the Office of Global Issues and Multilateral Affairs of the National Security Council (NSC), the successor to the NSC's International Programs Office under President Bush, has continued to assume greater responsibility for the oversight and management of low-intensity conflicts. This office, led by former Assistant Secretary of State for Politico-Military Affairs Dick Clarke, supported by Randy Beers, has again demonstrated that in crises authority and responsibility will naturally flow to those who can effectively manage low-intensity engagements.

Although the authors are pleased to see these developments, it is important that the administration continue this progress and, insofar as possible, institutionalize these changes.

The Failures

In our previous writing, the authors pointed out the absolutely critical need to rethink USAID and other economic assistance programs when they are to be deployed in low-intensity conflict engagements. There has been no progress made on this recommendation whatsoever. The dramatic political/military failure of the Somalia intervention precluded the requirement for an effective economic assistance program there. In Haiti, the Clinton administration, through effective coordination, the expenditure of a great deal of money to support U.S. armed forces, and a certain amount of luck, intervened militarily to restore to power democratically elected President Jean-Bertrand Aristide. Now that the bulk of U.S. forces have withdrawn and the operation has been turned over to the United Nations, however, it is questionable if the U.S. public—in a time of budget cutting and public revulsion to foreign economic assistance—will allow the U.S. government to provide sufficient development assistance over an extended period of time to allow the Haitians truly to consolidate democracy. This will be even more the case for crisis areas further from U.S. shores.

We say again that as part of the rethinking of USAID and U.S. economic assistance in general, specific focus must be given to the mechanisms of providing economic assistance in areas of crisis where we have made a national judgment to intervene.

The second recommendation upon which no action has been taken is the creation of courses or training facilities designed to include all personnel, uniformed and nonuniformed, from all United States government (USG) agencies that we expect to be involved in low-intensity engagements. Whether these courses are developed at the Foreign Service Institute or at one of the educational facilities of the uniformed services, over the long run it is most important that all USG agencies and their personnel who will engage in operations other than war have an opportunity to train and think together before being sent to the field.

New Recommendations

During the time that has elapsed since our last publication on this subject, roughly three years, operations in Somalia, Rwanda, Haiti, and in the ongoing areas of counternarcotics and counterterrorism have led the authors to make two new recommendations.

First, as in all conflicts, intelligence is critical. Intelligence is a service industry, a support function. It exists to provide information to its ultimate client, the National Command Authority, on current and future threats. As the threats change so must collection and analytic capability. Although it is hard to gather intelligence in Somalia or Rwanda or Haiti or against international terrorist organizations or narcotics traffickers, as the threat and our country's desire to project force shift from the old Soviet Union to these new challenges, it is imperative for the director of Central Intelligence to lead the effort to develop intelligence assets targeted at these new challenges.

These are dark days indeed for the Central Intelligence Agency, but dark days frequently present an opportunity. It is time to rethink, to restructure, and to reallocate intelligence assets. It seems dark humor indeed to argue that the current situation may offer the ideal opportunity to do exactly that.

Second, the authors would recommend that the National Security Council lead an effort to determine how operations other than war could be conducted at substantially lower costs to the taxpayer. The interventions in Somalia, Rwanda, and Haiti, if government estimates are accepted, cost the taxpayers something in the range of $4 to $5 billion. It is instructive to contrast this to the entire African USAID budget, which in recent years has been approximately $800 million per annum with promise of substantial cuts in fiscal year 1996. If we are to continue to pursue operations other than war, there *must* be an effort to do so at a more reasonable cost.

In addition, the cost of the "postmilitary intervention" must be determined and committed *before* the intervention. Haiti, the authors predict sadly, will illustrate this point graphically over the coming years. It is illogical to commit so many military assets and lives, at great cost, simply to restore Aristide to power. If the justification is to produce a new Haiti (that will not generate a continuous stream of refugees), then a large economic assistance package should have been a necessary component of planning and commitment for the operation.

To conclude, the United States has a long history of coping with low-intensity conflict and operations other than war and has been fairly successful in this area of national security. Official commissions have repeatedly pointed out the need to organize and prepare better for low-intensity conflict situations that threaten U.S. interests. Substantial progress organizationally (but less attitudinally) has been achieved within the Department of Defense and the armed forces. There remains a need for greater priority and attention to organizational matters within civilian departments and agencies, and to the president's overall coordination and implementation of LIC and OOTW through the National Security Council. Advances have been made by recent presidential administrations through the pragmatic management of specific LIC challenges and these are applauded. Given the nature of the post-cold war era and the increasing likelihood of LIC situations, there is a need to ensure that the management and implementation pillar that is key to national security and successful foreign policy is well constructed and strong for LIC and OOTW as well as for conventional warfare.

Notes

1. Ambassador David C. Miller, Jr., "New Elements of National Security," (speech to the Seventeenth Annual Wirth Washington Seminar, Washington, D.C., April 26, 1991), pp. 1–2.

2. Commission on Integrated Long-Term Strategy, Report by the Regional Conflict Working Group, *Supporting U.S. Strategy for Third World Conflict* (Department of Defense, June 1988), pp. 1–6; and Commission on Integrated Long-Term Strategy, *Discriminate Deterrence* (Washington, D.C.: GPO, January 1988), p. 13. General Paul Gorman, former commander in chief, Southern Command, was the leader and principal author in the Regional Conflict Working Group.

3. "After the Thaw: 'The Residual Role for the Military,'" Interview with Robert S. McNamara, former secretary of defense and former president of the World Bank, *New York Times International*, February 3, 1992, p. A6.

4. Ambassador Edwin G. Corr, "Preface," in *El Salvador at War: An Oral History*, ed. Max G. Manwaring and Court Prisk (Washington, D.C.: National Defense University Press, 1988), p. xxxiv.

5. Ambassador Edwin G. Corr, "The Salvadoran Report Card" in *El Salvador at War*, p. 452.

6. Todd R. Greentree, "The United States and the Politics of Conflict in the Developing World," Center Paper no. 4, Center for the Study of Foreign Affairs, Foreign Service Institute, U.S. Department of State, October 1990, p. 24.

7. *Strategy and Policy Background: Umbrella Concept for Low-Intensity Conflict*, vol. 1 (prepared by Booz-Allen & Hamilton, Inc. for Headquarters, U.S. Special

Operations Command, May 1989; finalized by Headquarters, U.S. Special Operations Command, August 1989), p. A–1.

8. Ibid., pp. 2–19.

9. Seymour J. Deitchman, *The Best Laid Schemes: A Tale of Social Research and Bureaucracy*, 1976, pp. 86–87 as cited in *Umbrella Concept for Low-Intensity Conflict*, p. 2–3.

10. Chester L. Cooper, *The Lost Crusade: America in Vietnam*, 1970, p. 255, as cited in *Umbrella Concept for Low-Intensity Conflict*, p. 2–4.

11. *National Security Action Memorandum No. 124 (NSAM 124)*, the White House, January 18, 1962, declassified on August 11, 1978, p. 1.

12. Ibid., p. 2.

13. Ibid.

14. Ibid., Annex.

15. *National Security Action Memorandum No. 182 (NSAM 182)*, the White House, August 24, 1962, declassified on January 5, 1980, pp. 1–31.

16. *Umbrella Concept for Low-Intensity Conflict*, p. A–3.

17. Greentree, "United States and the Politics of Conflict," p. 18.

18. This list is adapted from *Umbrella Concept for Low-Intensity Conflict*, p. 3–1. The "Rockefeller Report" and the "Restricted Engagement Options" were added; the former taken from *Supporting U.S. Strategy for Third World Conflict*, p. 6, and the latter from Greentree, "United States and the Politics of Conflict," pp. 39–40. Also added were the "Integrated Long-Term Strategy" and the "Bottom-Up Review."

19. *Supporting U.S. Strategy for Third World Conflict*, p. 6.

20. Ibid.

21. *Umbrella Concept for Low-Intensity Conflict*, pp. 3–4, 5.

22. Greentree, "United States and the Politics of Conflict," pp. 39–40.

23. *Umbrella Concept for Low-Intensity Conflict*, pp. 3–8.

24. U.S. Army Joint Low-Intensity Project: Final Report, vol. 1, *Analytical Review of Low-Intensity Conflict*, U.S. Army Training and Doctrine Command, August 1, 1986, as cited in *Umbrella Concept for Low-Intensity Conflict*, p. 3–11.

25. *Supporting U.S. Strategy for Third World Conflict: Report by the Regional Conflict Working Group submitted to the Commission on Integrated Long–Term Strategy* (chaired by General Paul P. Gorman), Washington, D.C.: Department of Defense, June 1988, pp. 1–3.

26. Les Aspin, Secretary of Defense, *Annual Report to the President and the Congress, January 1994*, Washington, D.C.: U.S. Government Printing Office, 1994, pp. 11–27.

27. Greentree, "United States and the Politics of Conflict," pp. 36–37.

28. Manwaring and Prisk, ed., *El Salvador at War*, pp. 111, 244, 245, 399, 400, 485, 486, 489.

29. Corr, "Conclusion," in *Uncomfortable Wars: Toward a New Paradigm of Low-Intensity Conflict*, ed. Max G. Manwaring (Boulder: Westview Press, 1991), pp. 127–129.

30. Secretary of State George Shultz, "The Ecology of International Change" (speech before the Commonwealth Club of California, San Francisco, October 28, 1988).

31. Stephen Sloan, "The Reagan Administration and Low-Intensity Conflict: An Enduring Legacy or a Passing Fad?" *Military Review* (January 1990): 42–29.

32. J. Bacevich, James D. Hallums, Richard H. White, and Thomas F. Young,

American Military Policy in Small Wars: The Case of El Salvador (Washington: Pergamon-Brassey's, 1988).

33. Corr, "Conclusion," in *Uncomfortable Wars*, pp. 129–130.

34. Glen P. Hastedt, *American Foreign Policy: Past, Present and Future*, 2d ed. (Englewood Cliffs, N.J.: Prentice Hall, 1991), p. 102.

35. Ibid., pp. 102–105.

36. Chapter author Ed Corr served as a member of one of the advisory Red Teams created to help the USSOC commander organize his command.

37. *Umbrella Concept for Low-Intensity Conflict*, pp. 3–8, 9.

38. Ibid., p. 1–2.

39. Barbro Owens, "Military Power and Low-Intensity Conflict—Can LIC's Be Licked Without the Use of Threat or Force" (Individual study project for the U.S. Army War College, Carlisle Barracks, Pennsylvania, March 18, 1989), pp. 4–6.

40. Henry A. Kissinger, *Diplomacy* (New York: Simon and Schuster, 1994), pp. 773–774.

41. Owens, "Military Power," p. 9.

42. Don Oberdorfer, "Strategy for a Solo Superpower: The U.S. Plans to Keep Its Powder Dry," *Washington Post National Weekly Edition*, May 27 – June 2, 1991, pp. 8–9.

43. Ibid.

44. Ibid.

45. Ibid.

46. President George Bush, "United States Defenses: Reshaping Our Forces" (speech at the Aspen Institute, Aspen, Colorado, August 2, 1990).

47. Office of the Assistant Secretary of Defense for Special Operations and Low-Intensity Conflict, "Peacetime Engagement" (Working paper from the Peacetime Engagement Conference sponsored by the assistant secretary of defense and hosted by the Army-Air Force Center for Low-Intensity Conflict, July 10–12, 1991), p. 1.

48. Oberdorfer, "Strategy for a Solo Superpower," p. 9.

49. Secretary of Defense Richard Cheney, "Conflicting Trends and Long Term Defense Needs," prepared statement to the Senate Armed Services Committee, February 17, 1991, in Department of Defense, *Defense Issues* 6, no. 6: 4,5.

50. Secretary of Defense Richard Cheney, "U.S. Defense Strategy and the DOD Budget Request," prepared statement to the House Armed Services Committee, February 7, 1991, in Department of Defense, *Defense Issues* 6, no. 4: 3.

51. President William J. Clinton, *A National Security Strategy of Engagement and Enlargement, July, 1994*, Washington, D.C.: The White House, 1994, p. 22. See also speeches by President William J. Clinton, "Confronting the Challenges of a Broader World" at the UN General Assembly, September 27, 1993; National Security Adviser Anthony Lake, "From Containment to Enlargement" at Johns Hopkins University, September 21, 1993; Ambassador Madeline K. Albright, "Use of Force in a Post–Cold War World" at National Defense University, September 23, 1993.

52. Ibid., pp. 15, 16.

53. It took two years to fill a vacant legal officer position vital to country team efforts in the area of human rights. The U.S. armed forces required almost 18 months to send an urgently requested mobile training team for counterintelligence and two years to provide a Spanish-speaking army adviser to help the Salvadoran armed forces restructure their irrational recruiting, pay, and reenlistment systems.

10

The Principle of Unity of Effort:
A Strategy for Conflict Management

John T. Fishel

Among the Anglo-American principles of war, unity of command is nearly paramount. Yet, in interagency operations and coalition warfare, unity of command often is impossible to achieve. As a result, unity of effort may well be the only realistic goal. This chapter examines the challenge of achieving unity of effort as a part of political-military theory that is at once empirical and normative. Based on classical writing and observed recent events (the latter serving the same purpose they did for the classical theorists), the chapter focuses on three specific problems. First, it addresses multiservice, or joint, issues; second, it considers those of the civil-military arena; lastly, it looks at multinational challenges in settings of mature alliances and ad hoc coalitions.

The Classical Theorists

Over two thousand years ago, in China, the warrior sage, Sun Tzu, wrote of the importance of unity, the price of its lack, and the ways to achieve it . Similarly, to achieve victory, he argued the need to attack the enemy's unity. "When he is united, divide him."[1]

> *Chang Yu*: Sometimes drive a wedge between a sovereign and his ministers; on other occasions separate his allies from him. Make them mutually suspicious so that they drift apart. Then you can plot against them.[2]

The views expressed in this chapter are those of the author and do not necessarily reflect the official policy or position of the Department of the Army, Department of Defense, or the U.S. government.

Sun Tzu, however, was not finished. He addressed various aspects of unity, the first being the enemy's strategy, "Thus, what is of supreme importance in war is to attack the enemy's strategy;[3]

> *Tu Mu*: . . . The Grand Duke said: 'He who excels at resolving difficulties does so before they arise. He who excels in conquering his enemies triumphs before threats materialize.'
>
> Li Ch'uan: Attack plans at their inception. In the later Han, K'ou Hsun surrounded Kao Chun. Chun sent his planning officer, Huang-fu Wen, to parley. Huang-fu Wen was stubborn and rude and K'ou Hsun beheaded him and informed Kao Chun: 'Your staff officer was without propriety. I have beheaded him. If you wish to submit, do so immediately. Otherwise, defend yourself.' On the same day Chun threw open his fortifications and surrendered.
>
> All K'ou Hsun's generals said: 'May we ask, you killed his envoy, but yet forced him to surrender his city. How is this?'
>
> K'ou Hsun said: 'Huang-fu Wen was Kao Chun's heart and guts, his intimate counsellor. If I had spared Huang-fu Wen's life, he would have accomplished his schemes, but when I killed him, Kao Chun lost his guts. It is said: "The supreme excellence in war is to attack the enemy's plans." '[4]
>
> Next best is to disrupt his alliances.
>
> *Tu Yu*: Do not allow your enemies to get together.
>
> *Wang Hsi*: . . . . Look into the matter of his alliances and cause them to be severed and dissolved. If an enemy has alliances, the problem is grave and the enemy's position is strong; if he has no alliances the problem is minor and the enemy's position is weak.[5]

Finally, Sun Tzu asserts the "almost obvious" positive argument, "He whose ranks are united in purpose will be victorious."

> *Tu Yu*: Therefore Mencius said: "The appropriate season is not as important as the advantages of the ground; these are not as important as harmonious human relations."[6]

Thus, Sun Tzu staked out the position that in war, unity of effort is what Carl von Clausewitz would call "a center of gravity."

Count Carl von Clausewitz, in his treatise, *On War*, articulated the principle of unity of command for the modern student. Nevertheless, he states that, "Friction is the only concept that more or less corresponds to the factors that distinguish real war from war on paper."[7] In that friction lies the challenge not only to unity of command but also to the broader notion of unity of effort. Clausewitz notes

> The military machine . . . is basically very simple and therefore seems easy to manage. But we should bear in mind that none of its components is of one piece: each part is composed of individuals, every one of whom retains his

potential for friction. In theory it sounds reasonable enough: a battalion commander's duty is to carry out his orders; discipline welds the battalion together.... A battalion is made up of individuals, the least important of whom may chance to delay things or somehow make them go wrong.[8]

In essence, Clausewitz is saying that in the friction of war unity of command is not enough to guarantee unity of effort. Rather, the military leader must, through the training of his men, make certain that unity is achieved in the effort that is the engagement or campaign. Consider, then, how much more difficult it is likely to be to attain effective unity in a campaign conducted by multinational forces in coalition. Clausewitz comments on this point when he says:

If two or more states combine against another, the result is still politically speaking a single war. But this political unity is a matter of degree.[9]

As a matter of degree it will vary with the circumstances. When, as in the Second World War, the very survival of all of the allies was at stake, the supreme allied commander could enforce both unity of command and unity of effort. When, however, the survival of no member of the coalition is at stake, as is perceived to be the case in the "drug war" in South America today, unity around the strategic and operational goals will be loose, at best.

It is, then, here that Clausewitz gives us a major assist in understanding the nature of unity of effort when he posits that, "This unity lies *in the concept that war is only a branch of political activity; that it is no sense autonomous.*"[10] In other words, for Clausewitz, unity of effort rests on the proposition that there is agreement among the coalition partners on the nature of the political objective. Clausewitz merely hinted, however, at two aspects of modern war that have come to the forefront since his day. The first of these is its multiservice or joint nature, while the second is its interagency civil-military complexity. Before addressing these two issues, however, it is necessary to focus on another and equally preeminent principle—the *objective* or *end state*.

The End State

The concept of the end state is fairly simple. It is what we wish the battlefield to look like after the fighting is done. If, however, there is no battle, then "battlefield" becomes a figurative term but one that in no way vitiates the concept of end state. In other words, the end state refers to the descriptive outcome of the operation, but one that may also be prescriptive in the sense that it is what our plans call for. The end state is also more than the objective. Rather, it is a painting of the landscape on which the objective is located. In a commonplace combat example, the objective may well be a particular hill on which is located an enemy observation post in a farm-house. The objective will be given as the hill. The end state might be described as the occupation of the hill and the farmhouse with our troops and the removal of the enemy troops. It might be further described as the farmhouse intact, the enemy troops prisoner or dead, but unable to consti-tute a counterattack. This brings us to one other aspect of the end state; it is not simply a single outcome but rather a range of acceptable outcomes. In our simplistic example, the outcome described is near the maximum end of the acceptable. Toward the minimum end would be the following: the hill occupied, the farmhouse destroyed, the enemy driven off with sufficient losses that he is unable to regain the hill with a determined counterattack. Clearly, this end state is not as desirable as the first, but it does fall within the acceptable range.

Another important aspect of the end state is that it needs to be the subject of agreement among the decision makers engaged in the operation. It does little good for the commander to envision an end state while his subordinate air and naval commanders envision different end states. If the political leaders have still another vision, then the force commander may well find himself in some other job much sooner than he expected. Furthermore, if other, nonmilitary government agencies are involved and their view of the end state is different, then a successful outcome is problematic, at best. Finally, if other nations, intergovernmental organizations (IGOs), and/or nongovernmental organizations (NGOs) are involved, then their desired end states must be accounted for as well.

In another context I have written that:

> We have shown that achieving unity of effort is often elusive and that the premier pitfall is in the failure to reach agreement on the desired end state or strategic objective. If there is no agreement on the range of outcomes that can be defined as acceptable end states, then there will be no effective unity of effort. Lack of an agreed upon end state clearly dooms any effort to failure.[11]

This principle has been operative in conflicts throughout the Cold War and the post–Cold War period, to varying degrees. Even cases of apparent success have been marred by the lack of a coherent political-military end state. At best, those cases leave the United States with an interminable military commitment as in Korea or northern Iraq; at worst, the United States is forced to withdraw its forces ignominiously as in Lebanon (1983) or Somalia. In between are ambiguous cases like Panama and Desert Storm, where the immediate military objective was achieved but the strategic political end states of democracy (in the former) and regional stability (in the latter) continue to be beyond our collective reach. This ambiguity, then, leaves the nagging question of whether the entire effort will have to be undertaken again at some future date to finally resolve the unresolved issues.

While the end state is critical to strategic success, that is not to say that it is unessential at the operational level. Rather, this essay strongly argues that operational, as well as strategic, success depends on an agreed-upon end state. At the operational level, however, the end state is more military than political; but it is not exclusively military. An example of an appropriate operational end state from Operation Desert Storm was the occupation of Kuwait City by Arab coalition forces including the Kuwaitis, aided by U.S. forces (especially Special Operations Forces and including Civil Affairs) in a way that ousted the Iraqis, restored the Kuwaiti ruling family, and precluded extrajudicial reprisals.[12]

Despite the demonstrated criticality of the end state, it is an insufficient condition for unity of effort. Without an agreed-upon objective defined as an end state, there will be no unity. Nevertheless, the mere existence of such an end state in no way guarantees unity of effort. Rather, there are many shoals on which a ship may founder.

The Shoals of Jointness

The new "American way of war" is joint warfare—that is, it encompasses the forces of several services. Although Americans have fought jointly since their Revolution, jointness in the modern sense dates only from the 1986 Department of Defense Reorganization Act, known for its sponsors as Goldwater-Nichols. Prior to 1986 all "joint" U.S. military operations were conducted by the individual services pulled, kicking and screaming, into harness. Goldwater-Nichols shifted the focus of operations away from the services to the unified commander and gave him the new authority required to effectively practice real joint operations.[13] That authority is summarized by the command relationship called combatant command. Under this authority the commander in chief of a unified command has combatant command of any assigned or attached forces in his operational area. Combatant command, essentially consists of operational control and directive authority for logistics. Operational control gives the commander in chief the authority to direct his forces *and* task organize them, while "directive authority for logistics" allows him to task one service component to provide logistical support for another. Combatant command, thus, gives the commander in chief the authority to mold the joint team in ways that were impossible prior to 1986.

One example of what I am talking about is drawn from the planning for what became Operation Just Cause in Panama in 1989. In this case, the commander in chief, General Fred F. Woerner, determined that he needed operational control of naval forces supporting his operation. The navy argued that its normal procedure was to operate "in support of" a commander in chief, not under his operational control. What General Woerner objected to in such an arrangement was the idea that the naval commander "in support" could undertake some other mission, thus depriving the commander in chief of forces he was counting on. With the battle lines thus drawn on the bureaucratic map, the issue was referred to the chairman of the Joint Chiefs of Staff, Adm. William Crowe, for resolution. Admiral Crowe surprised his fellow admirals when he ruled in favor of General Woerner. Nevertheless, the issue was not completely dead. It raised its head again during Operation Desert Shield in the Persian Gulf; this time the commander in chief, Pacific, or Adm. Arthur Larson, sided with his fellow commander in chief, Gen. H. Norman Schwarzkopf and "chopped" the naval component to U.S. Central Command in operational control status, relieving the commanding admiral for his continued objections in the process.

Jointness does not mean that forces are wholly interchangeable or that the United States is engaged in a Canada-like experiment of merging all services into one. Rather, jointness means that each service brings its unique capabilities to the operation to be used in the most effective way possible with the capabilities of the other services. The U.S. military is getting pretty good at this most of the time, as we have seen in Operations Just Cause, Promote Liberty, Desert Shield/Storm, Provide Hope, and the ongoing mission in Haiti. In spite of our general success in attaining effective unity of effort in joint operations since 1986, we still face significant challenges.

The principal vehicle for conducting a joint operation is what is known as a joint task force (JTF). By doctrine, the joint task force is an organization made up of two or more services for an operation of limited duration.[14] In spite of this definition, at least one joint task force has achieved an endurance record of eleven years.[15] When creating a joint task force, a commander in chief is faced with two basic choices: he can create it from the base of an existing organization or build it, ad hoc, from scratch. In the first case, the joint task force will have the advantage of a staff that has worked together but it will also have the flavor of its parent service (with all the associated parochialism). In the second case, the joint task force will likely be specifically tailored to the mission with (one hopes) the precisely proper mix of forces, but its staff will almost certainly be a bunch of strangers who will have to learn to work together while at the same time learning each other's service language (as well as the joint language).[16]

As examples of what we are discussing let us consider Joint Task Force South, which carried out Operation Just Cause, Joint Task Force Restore Hope (also known as UNITAF) in Somalia, and Joint Task Force Provide Comfort in Turkey and Northern Iraq. Joint Task Force South was the XVIII Airborne Corps plus augmentation from the air force, marines, navy, and army forces assigned to Panama. In essence it was an army organization and did business the army way. Even the fact that its staff had to be significantly augmented did not change this fact very much because most of the augmentation came from the staff of the army component permanently assigned to Panama. Joint Task Force South clearly demonstrates both the advantages and disadvantages of achieving unity of effort in this way. The Airborne Corps staff had worked together as well as having worked with the army component staff in Panama; they knew each other and shared a common worldview. Nevertheless, Joint Task Force South was a very parochial organization that clearly did not understand the nature of the threat posed by the Panama Defense Forces, its enemy.[17] Similarly, Joint Task Force Restore Hope, built around the First Marine Expeditionary Force, was an augmented Marine Corps staff. Essentially, it did business in the Marine Corps way and, although successful in accomplishing its stated mission, was subject to criticism for its methodical approach.[18]

By contrast, Joint Task Force Provide Comfort was an ad hoc organization built around the doctrinal concept of a foreign internal defense augmentation force (FIDAF).[19] As such, its organization was specifically tailored to the mission. Its staff was more clearly joint, but it had the definite disadvantage of having to learn to work together from scratch. This problem was mitigated by the use of a number of staff elements that had worked together in both the two subordinate task forces and the joint task force itself.[20]

As we have shown, the U.S. armed forces are becoming more and more used to playing the joint game. Moreover, it is being taught to field grade officers (majors and lieutenant commanders) at the several staff colleges with a selected group intended to be joint staff officers attending a 12-week second phase at the Armed Forces Staff College. Thus, the future commanders in chief, their staffs, and the service chiefs and their staffs are being nurtured in soil well fertilized with "jointness." This is not to say that parochialism has gone away. Rather, it continues to appear in battles over budget and doctrine, as well as in conflict over roles and functions. "However, because the joint game is far more institutionalized than any of the other games, it is far more subtle. The joint game has been played in the U.S. military for years and even such major rule changes as the Goldwater-Nichols legislation have only changed the game at the margin, although in some very profound ways."[21]

The Interagency Problem

In modern conflict, the joint game will hardly be the only one in town. Rather, for U.S. forces involved in the conflicts of the post–Cold War age there has been and will continue to be a bewildering array of governmental and nongovernmental players. In the first phase of this discussion, we will limit ourselves to the problems of unity of effort among the agencies of the U.S. government and the nongovernmental organizations (NGOs) that are U.S. based, leaving to the next section intergovernmental organizations (IGOs) and non U.S. NGOs. The principal question to be considered in this environment is, "Who is in charge?"

The environment of modern conflict tends to put U.S. military forces into situations where the U.S. command structure is less than totally clear. In most of the instances cited above, U.S. civilian governmental agencies and structures were in place where the operations were taking place. The single exception is Operation Provide Comfort in Northern Iraq—an important difference. In all the others, an American ambassador was on the ground, which sets some particular ground rules for how business is done. The only problem with the rules is that their interpretation can, sometimes, lead to conflict. Every American ambassador appointed to post since the presidency of John F. Kennedy has received the same letter of instruction. In essence, this letter states that the ambassador is the personal representative of the president and is responsible for every action undertaken by the U.S. government or its representatives in that country.[22] The exceptions to this are personnel assigned to international agencies and "major military commands."[23]

What constitutes a major military command to create the exception is somewhat undefined. It is, for example, quite clear that the U.S. ambassador to Panama does not have jurisdiction over Headquarters, U.S. Southern Command located in that country nor over the service components of the command that are also based there. On the other hand, it is equally clear that Joint Task Force Panama (consisting of the army component and much of the air force, navy, and marine components) is in support of the ambassador and must respond to his guidance. In the more normal environment, where the military is represented by a Defense Attache Office and a Security Assistance Office, officials from both are members of the ambassador's country team. Both are subject to his policy guidance, and can be ordered out of country by him, and their senior members receive "letter input" to their formal ratings from him.

What this means during a significant military operation where war has not been declared and the president has not specifically stated that the ambassador is to support the military forces, is that the letter of instruction still sets the ground rules. In other words, the ambassador is, formally, "in charge." The real relationship, however, is one of negotiating with the ambassador and the other agencies on the country team (or represented in country) to try to achieve common objectives and mutually supporting actions. Interagency coordination can founder on the shoals of turf battles, personality conflicts, and petty disputes, as well as on real policy disagreements.

The kinds of turf battles, personality conflicts, and petty disputes contemplated tend to be aggravated by the porous boundary between the strategic and operational levels of operation. As suggested above, the strategic end state tends to be more political than military, while the operational tends toward the reverse. If the boundary between the two is unclear, then the probability of conflict between the wielders of the military and political instruments of power increases with the increasing lack of boundary definition. A good example of sharp boundary definition was that of the Gulf War, where the political leadership of the coalition determined that the only way to achieve the desired political end state was through the exercise of the military instrument. The plan of the campaign was then worked out by General Schwarzkopf and agreed to by General Khalid and supported by the diplomatic representatives of the coalition and their civilian governments. By contrast, the decision to use the military instrument of U.S. power to defend Saudi Arabia was led by the political instrument in diplomatic guise and supported with military assets, most notably Schwarzkopf himself.

The second part of the interagency problem has to do with U.S. NGOs. As the term suggests, these are private agencies not under the control of the U.S. government. They are in country, usually, by agreement with the host government (or with an international agency), but they still expect to be supported by the U.S. government organizations in place, much as any citizen would. Moreover, the U.S. government often finds them to be of use in carrying out its policy, which it may do by funneling resources through these NGOs. This funneling is commonly done by the U.S. Agency for International Development (USAID) Office of Foreign Disaster Assistance, thus creating a symbiotic relationship with the NGOs. All of this is supposed to be coordinated by the senior U.S. governmental officer present, typically the ambassador, but this situation, too, is complicated by personality and organizational culture. What happens when the "take charge" organizational culture of the military meets the "studied ambiguity" of the State Department, the "street cop" smarts of the Drug Enforcement Agency, (DEA), the "developmentalism" of USAID, and the "single minded goal orientation" of an NGO? Confusion is likely to reign unless the several organizational leaders can develop the empathy necessary to achieve unity of effort.

Multinational and IGO Games

The last problem area brings us back again to the classical theorists that we considered at the beginning of this essay. Both Sun Tzu and Clausewitz remarked on the problems of alliances. Nevertheless, in the last two decades of the twentieth century we have rediscovered the difficulties of multinational operations but have also added some new angles to the classical problem. In the process, we appear to have resolved some old issues only to have raised new ones.

In the classical multinational game, we have two basic kinds of relationships: alliances and coalitions. Although alliances are usually thought of as being longer term, more institutionalized, and more stable and coalitions are perceived as more ad hoc, such is not always the case. At the beginning of the First World War, Europe was divided by a system of alliances and coalitions. On one side was the Triple Alliance of Germany, Austria-Hungary, and Italy; on the other was the entente built around a formal alliance between Russia and France and informal understandings and combined military maneuvers between France and England. In that event the coalition arrangement proved stronger than the formal alliance.[24]

In spite of such cautionary facts, formal alliances may well be the key to achieving unity of effort among both military forces and their governments. The American experience in Operation Provide Comfort is a case in point. As will be recalled, this operation was an intrusive humanitarian assistance mission into Northern Iraq to protect the Kurds who had fled their homes in the wake of their failed revolt against Saddam Hussein following the Gulf War in 1991.[25] In this operation, under the command of American Lt. Gen. John Shalikashvili, with a mainly U.S. force but one with significant augmentation from a large number of countries, it was most important and helpful that most of the participants were members of the North Atlantic Treaty Organization (NATO). While Provide Comfort definitely was not a NATO operation, General Shalikashvili conducted it using NATO procedures, which gave all the critical participants a common way of doing business and a common language. In such a case, it is difficult to discount the impact of such a long-term organization, even when it was not acting as such.

Although the lack of such common ground does not preclude success, it does make it more difficult to achieve. During the several operations in Somalia from 1990 to 1994 (to be addressed in detail in the next chapter), some of the difficulties faced by the coalition forces were the result of a number of nations that had rarely worked together. We may conclude this portion of the discussion by noting that recent experience indicates that a coalition is more likely to achieve effective unity of effort if its members are familiar with each other's way of doing business by virtue of being members of an alliance of long standing with an integrated command and control system. Nevertheless, that familiarity will not overcome the divisiveness of conflicting political objectives and differing end states, as we have seen in the recent difficulties suffered by peacekeeping operations in Rwanda and Bosnia.

As is true in the single nation interagency environment, the multinational one is also complicated by nonmilitary and nongovernmental players. Among the more important nonmilitary players are the IGOs, especially the United Nations (UN) family of IGOs. Many erroneous expectations about the UN abound—the central one being that it is a single organization that acts in the same way a government does. The UN is not a single entity; it is, instead, a family of IGOs, each of which can act in its own sphere only to the extent that its members allow it to do so. Thus, a UN Security Council resolution is binding on all UN members (if the Great Powers that are the five permanent members are willing to enforce it). A resolution of the General Assembly is merely a recommendation. Loan conditions imposed on a member by the International Monetary Fund (IMF) can be very powerful and compelling while, at the same time, in complete conflict with the policy positions of the secretary general. In short, it is not unlikely to find, in a UN-mandated operation, UN IGOs working at cross purposes with each other.

Again, as all this is taking place we have the nonmilitary agencies of several national governments (not all of which are members of the coalition) working in the area of the operation along with a host of international NGOs. Although we are not faced with a wholly anarchic international system, we do have one that, without concerted effort, verges on the chaotic. Achieving unity of effort in this environment requires both diplomatic and political skills on the part of all key players. It also requires a strategy.

Achieving Unity of Effort

Through the development of a strategy one can, perhaps, come to closure with the problem of unity of effort. A strategy consists of three parts: ends, ways, and means. The ends can be stated in general terms as goals or aims, or in more specific terms as objectives. An effective strategy will do both and carry the process a step further by describing one or more acceptable end states. Ways answer the question of "how." They are best laid out as courses of action and may be usefully detailed in a campaign plan. Among the key parts of the courses of action should be a description of the nature of the controlling relationships for the operation or activity. Finally, means refer to resources, financial, material, and personnel. This strategy, then, should be tested against the three critical questions of strategic development. First, will the courses of action proposed accomplish the goal? Second, can they be executed with the resources that are available or can be made available? Third, is the cost—human, social, political, material, and financial—acceptable? If not, then, unity of effort is unlikely to be achieved and the strategy is likely to fall short.

A successful strategy to achieve unity of effort requires the knowledge to determine which of the several possible games are being played. In the post–Cold War world it is almost certain that all three games will be taking place simultaneously. This simple fact requires that each key player's real objectives be understood. Merely agreeing to vote for a resolution in the UN Security Council, or offering to contribute troops to a peace operation authorized by that resolution, does not mean that a government has the same objectives as does your government. Moreover, no government wholly gives up its freedom of action in any kind of operation. The first prerequisite of successful unity of effort is for the leaders to know the goals, objectives, and aims of their partners. This is equally true of the military services, government agencies, IGOs, and NGOs.

Once the leadership has identified the objectives of the players, it must determine where the common ground with respect to the objective and its attendant end state lies. That common ground provides the necessary but insufficient condition for unity of effort. Mutually compatible goals and objectives will provide the leadership a clue as to how best to organize the effort without asking any player to do something that is not in keeping with its objectives.

The next step in the development of a strategy is to determine the ways to achieve the common objectives as well as how to best prevent the attainment of those that are clearly not compatible with one's own. Objectives that are "value neutral" can be left to those who desire them—they need neither to be helped nor hindered. In approaching the decision as to ways, one needs to consider the procedures available because they offer the operational and tactical common ground that makes it easier to achieve unity of effort, if they exist, or more difficult, if they do not. It is here that long-standing alliance relationships can come into play.

The final step in developing a strategy is to assign resources against objectives. The general principle to be followed here is that assets should be assigned against objectives that a coalition partner or cooperating organization has identified as its own. At the same time, care must be taken to avoid giving an asset the opportunity to undertake an objective that is contrary to the common goals of the mission.

This, in turn, brings us to the question of basic command and control procedures for any particular mission. For the United States, it is especially useful if the president will make a decision as to whether the ambassador or the military commander is in charge of the mission. Experience shows that American political authorities are reluctant to do this. It, therefore, is incumbent on the operational planner to make every attempt to force a decision. This is best done by stating the force commander's intent to "take charge" in the formal planning process that is referred to the president and secretary of defense for approval. In this way, a decision on civilian or military authority may be forced.

Unfortunately, this approach will not solve the basic problem in the multinational setting. Still, one can reduce the problem to the extent that the participating nations understand and follow common procedures. The evidence suggests strongly that the most effective unity of effort has been achieved when the coalition is dominated by nations who have long worked together in a standing alliance with an integrated military command and well-established political institutions.

Finally, the process of achieving unity of effort with IGOs and NGOs is mainly accomplished in two ways. First, the operational leader can be of use to the individual IGO and/or NGO. By creating some dependency, he can to some extent control their behavior. He should also be aware that there is a great likelihood that a mutual dependency will be created and that to the extent it is, he will be influenced by the IGO or NGO he wishes to influence. Second, the operational leader can cut off support for the IGO/NGO he wishes to influence. The danger in this approach, however, is the access that organization has to the operational leader's political authority.

Achieving unity of effort in modern conflict is a complex process. At its base it entails effective politics and skillful diplomacy. Neither of these qualities is thought to be the common currency of military leaders. Throughout history, the successful military leader has possessed them both in abundance as demonstrated by such as Alexander, Napoleon, Eisenhower, and Schwarzkopf.[26] Less successful military leaders may well have been deficient in these skills.

Concluding Thoughts

This chapter has explored the concept of unity of effort in some detail. It first looked at what the classical military theorists, Sun Tzu and Clausewitz, had to say with respect to the subject. In many respects, theory suggests that the concept represents a center of gravity (or a potential one) at all three levels of operation, strategic, operational, and tactical. Although the classical theorists had considered some significant "modern" problems involving unity of effort, they had not wrestled with the complexities of joint and interagency operations. Neither had they considered the subtlety of the nuances of multinational operations that have developed over this century.

Our exploration led us into the notion that a necessary but insufficient condition for achieving unity of effort was a common objective defined as an end state among the key decision makers. Even the existence of such an agreed-upon end state does not guarantee that unity will be achieved at any level of operation. Rather, the way in which the operation is organized will play a significant role in determining the degree of unity to be achieved. We noted that the United States has developed some effective procedures for joint operations over time, but especially during the past decade. Some of this success has carried over into the combined or multinational arena with the effective use of NATO procedures in several non-NATO operations. The common procedural ground among the members of the alliance provided a solid foundation on which coalition operations could be conducted.

Far less successful were operations conducted in the interagency arena, whether they were unilateral U.S. or multinational. Part of the problem lies in the different organizational cultures represented, while another part lies in the lack of political direction as to who is in charge in any particular case.

These issues will be discussed again in the next chapter, which will focus on how they played out in three relatively recent cases. The case studies will allow us to examine the theory and the observations here in significantly greater detail. The result will be an informal test of the hypotheses implicit within this discussion. We may anticipate that some of our observations will be supported while others will be modified and some others may even have to be discarded. The following chapter will develop these themes in the "real world."

Notes

1. Sun Tzu, *The Art of War*, trans. and introduced by Samuel B. Griffith (New York: Oxford University Press, 1963), p. 69.

2. Ibid., p. 69.

3. Ibid., p. 77.

4. Ibid., pp. 77-78.

5. Ibid., p. 78.

6. Ibid., p. 83.

7. Carl von Clausewitz, *On War*, ed. and trans. Michael Howard and Peter Paret (New York: Alfred A. Knopf, 1993), p. 138.

8. Ibid., pp. 138-139.

9. Ibid., p. 721.

10. Ibid., p. 731.

11. John T. Fishel, "Achieving the Elusive Unity of Effort," in Max G. Manwaring, ed., *Gray Area Phenomena: Confronting the New World Disorder* (Boulder, Colo.: Westview, 1993), p. 124.

12. See John T. Fishel, *Liberation, Occupation, and Rescue: War Termination and DESERT STORM* (Carlisle, Penn.: Strategic Studies Institute, 1992).

13. See Gary Bryant, *What is COCOM?*, MMAS Thesis, U.S. Army Command and General Staff College, 1993.

14. See U.S. Army, FM 100-5, *Operations*, 1993 and Joint Pub 3-0, 1993.

15. This is the case of Joint Task Force B, at Soto Cano Air Force Base, Honduras, established in 1983 and scheduled, finally, to be stood down in 1994.

16. These considerations are not well addressed in doctrine.

17. See John T. Fishel, *The Fog of Peace: Planning and Executing the Restoration of Panama* (Carlisle, Penn.: Strategic Studies Institute, 1992), especially ch. 4.

18. Press, various.

19. U.S. Army, FM 100-20, *Military Operations in Low Intensity Conflict*, 1990, Appendix A.

20. Fishel, *Liberation*, ch. 6.

21. Ibid., p. 6.

22. Robert Hopkins Miller, *Inside an Embassy* (Washington, D.C.: Institute for the Study of Diplomacy, 1992), p. 3.

23. Ibid.

24. See Barbara Tuchman, *The Guns of August* (New York: Dell, 1962).

25. Fishel, *Liberation*, ch. 6.

26. Rick Atkinson, *Crusade: The Untold Story of the Persian Gulf War* (Boston: Houghton Mifflin Company, 1993).

11

The Management Structures for Just Cause, Desert Storm, and UNOSOM II

John T. Fishel

The terms leadership and management—concepts respectively dear to the military and civilian communities—both attempt to deal with the question, "Who is in charge?" The military notion of "command *and* control," perhaps, best summarizes the complexity of the issue. We are not dealing here merely with the issue of authority but also of how that authority is used, not used, or misused. In turn, we must also address who can influence the situation and how that influence is exercised. In short, we are looking at one of the major issues of political science, the exercise of power. Here we are considering it within the context of three post–Cold War military operations and, therefore, are approaching it from a public administration—specifically a bureaucratic politics—perspective.

In each case, we will consider the relationship between civil and military authority. In Just Cause we will observe that it is essentially a simple case involving only the U.S. government (and the host country). Desert Storm was a more complicated picture because of the involvement of other nations but within the context of a United Nations (UN)- authorized coalition. Finally, UNOSOM II picks up from a similar coalition and attempts to operate a truly multinational United Nations coalition with a fully multinational management system.

This chapter, drawing on the last, will suggest that there are common links in both the successes and failures of all three operations. It will show that while we learned a significant amount from Operation Just Cause and

The views expressed in this chapter are those of the author and do not necessarily reflect the official policy or position of the Department of the Army, Department of Defense, or the U.S. government.

applied it to Desert Storm, we appear to have forgotten some of the important lessons of both (and/or misapplied) them when it came time to plan and execute a mission in Somalia.

Operation Just Cause (and Promote Liberty)

Operation Just Cause, the December 1989 invasion of Panama, and its attendant, postconflict operation, Promote Liberty, were the result of a command and control structure significantly modified by the 1986 Goldwater-Nichols Department of Defense Reorganization Act.[1] This act had given the commanders in chief of the unified commands, including United States Southern Command, significantly greater authority than they had in the past. It had also strengthened the role and power of the chairman of the Joint Chiefs of Staff at the expense of the service chiefs.[2] The full impact of the new law, however, had yet to be felt. Rather, it was a process of bureaucratic revolution by evolution taking place in some of the minor skirmishes over command relationships, among other engagements, discussed in the last chapter. Thus, in 1989, while the extent of combatant command still was not exactly clear, it was significantly greater than the command relationship that had existed a mere six years before during the U.S. led invasion of Grenada.[3]

From February 1988, when planning for what became Just Cause began, until September 30, 1989, the commander in chief of U.S. Southern Command was Gen. Fred F. Woerner. A scholarly Latin Americanist who was a superior troop leader, General Woerner had attempted to stay ahead of the military implications of the constantly shifting sands of U.S. policy toward Panama since the beginning of the "crisis" the day after he took command in June 1987. Although he disagreed with many aspects of that policy, he loyally implemented it and took the lead in attempting to achieve realistic civil-military positions that stood a chance of success in attaining the objectives of the U.S. policymakers, which included the departure from power and Panama of the de facto dictator, Gen. Manuel Antonio Noriega, peacefully and without any obvious U.S. intervention.[4]

Woerner's efforts resulted in a plan that he called Fissures. Fully coordinated with the State Department, it attempted to divide the Panama Defense Forces (PDF) from the civilian supporters of the regime and drive a wedge between the PDF and Noriega. Woerner sent the plan through his channels to the Joint Chiefs of Staff and when he heard nothing developed a revised version called Fissures II. This he sent forth with his recommendation that it be adopted as a complete package. He specifically requested that he not be ordered to execute individual paragraphs of the plan because it had been developed as a unified concept with each part dependent on every other part in concert with the other agencies of the U.S.

government. All he ever was directed to execute were individual, unrelated paragraphs.[5]

This abortive effort at interagency planning marked the boundaries of the interagency process through the execution of Operation Just Cause and well into Operation Promote Liberty. An activity that had been developed in coordination among several agencies clearly belonged to no agency and, therefore, was hardly worthy of serious consideration. The joint military planning process that produced Operations Orders Blue Spoon and Blind Logic, by contrast, were well established as part of the Joint Operations Planning System Crisis Action Planning. As such, conflicts, which indeed existed among the several planning commands, were played out according to fairly well-established rules.[6]

The most significant military planning conflicts occurred during the period from May 18, 1989, through October 1989. During this period, General Woerner, on the advice of his director of operations, Brig. Gen. Marc A. Cisneros, had activated the XVIII Airborne Corps as Joint Task Force (JTF) C to take over the execution planning for Blue Spoon (the combat operation), thereby relieving JTF Panama (U.S. Army South plus augmentation) of this planning responsibility. The reason for this was that the army component was being stressed so hard that its theater responsibilities were suffering.[7] This entailed, in addition, the coordination between the Airborne Corps planners and the Southern Command staff who were responsible for the commander in chief-level orders. Moreover, it required coordination with the Civil-Military Operations planning cell who were developing the commander in chief's Civil-Military Operations Order as well as the Operations Order for the Civil-Military Operations Task Force. In the event, action officer-level agreements that had been incorporated into the Civil-Military Operations Order (Blind Logic) were not included in the Corps' plan.[8]

Part of this had to do with the fact that General Woerner's retirement was announced on July 20 and scheduled for September 30 while his successor, Gen. Max Thurman, was announced at the same time. The Corps was not particularly happy with Woerner's Blue Spoon and felt that the Southern Command staff was dictating how they should conduct their mission rather than what that mission should be. For its part, Southern Command was concerned that the Corps planners showed not the slightest amount of understanding of the political-military nuances that characterized the Panama situation.[9]

When General Thurman assumed command on September 30, he formally activated the Corps as JTF South for planning purposes. Between July and September, however, he had been working with the Corps to completely restructure General Woerner's concept of the operation. Interestingly, this restructuring was in the direction of some rethinking that the new director of operations at Southern Command, Brig. Gen. William Hartzog, initiated.[10] Hartzog's predecessor, General Cisneros, had taken command of U.S. Army South in late June and, in an ironic twist, in his new capacity as Joint Task Force Panama commander, had become somewhat resistant to the idea that the Corps was needed.

Nevertheless, Thurman was very explicit about one thing. He wanted unity of command and designated the Corps commander, Lt. Gen. Carl Stiner, as his "warfighter" and sole subordinate commander for the operation. As a result, the Corps staff took charge of the planning. Some of the friction of this time is reflected in an article by "Tacitus" (a pseudonym for one or more staff officers from the 193d Brigade and/or U.S. Army South or USARSO):

> U.S. Army South (USARSO), in its role as Joint Task Force-Panama (JTF-PM), was thought to lack the organization and experience to execute the original plan, so the XVIII Airborne Corps was designated the war-fighting headquarters. But the Corps wasn't deployed to the theater; instead, XVIII Corps, like JTF-South (JTF-SO), stayed in CONUS until just before the attack. It then tried simultaneously to deploy, absorb the JTF-PM staff, assume command of in-place forces, and control the flow of H-hour and follow-on forces. This was a prescription for failure.[11]

When Operations Orders Blue Spoon and Blind Logic were executed respectively on December 19 and 20, 1989, as Operations Just Cause and Promote Liberty, there was no question as to who the commander of all combat operations was—Stiner was the "warfighter." When General Thurman activated his director of strategy, plans, and policy, Brig. Gen. Benard Gann as commander, Civil-Military Operations Task Force, however, there was some question as to whom Gann worked for. He was directed to execute a separate commander in chief plan in addition to his duties as a director of the Southern Command staff. Moreover, General Stiner later declared that he had no responsibilities for restoration operations. Yet, for several days, commander, Civil-Military Operations Task Force formally was located under Joint Task Force South, after which it was returned to the commander in chief's control. At no time did Stiner take effective control over it.[12]

The issue of command and control of commander, Civil-Military Operations Task Force vindicated General Woerner's concept that the civil-military operation to restore government services to Panama was both the key to political-military success and that it was much too sensitive to leave in the hands of the joint task force commander. Thus, a separate headquarters, reporting to the commander in chief, was appropriate, especially so that the commander in chief himself would determine the priorities between the requirements of the joint task force and those of commander, Civil-Military Operations Task Force.

Nevertheless, General Thurman's effort to centralize all of the operations directed by Operations Order Blue Spoon was also appropriate. Where Woerner had three separate headquarters reporting to him and carrying out a combination of combat and civil-military operations, Thurman only had two headquarters, one that dealt with combat operations while the other addressed civil-military issues. The key was that the Joint Special Operations Task Force (JSOTF) now was subordinate to the joint task force. This decision, indeed, resolved a point of conflict that had been very much in evidence prior to Thurman's assumption of command.[13]

One additional unity of effort issue that needs to be addressed in this case is that of civil-miliary cooperation and coordination with respect to the operations orders. In the planning phase of the operation, the U.S. embassy only was aware of Operations Order Klondike Key (the noncombatant evacuation) in any detail and only loosely aware of the existence of Blue Spoon.[14] With respect to Blind Logic, the order with the greatest policy implications, the chief planner was refused permission to coordinate with the embassy and allowed to discuss the U.S. government's goals for a post-Noriega Panama in only the most general way.[15]

Once Promote Liberty was being executed, significantly more civil-military coordination took place. When Deane Hinton arrived as U.S. ambassador, he clearly was in charge of all activities by elements of the U.S. government, including the military, but only to the extent that he actively took action. In a number of areas he allowed separate agencies, nominally under his control, to continue bureaucratic infighting long after any such conflict might have been productive. This was particularly true of the relationship between the U.S. Military Support Group (successor to commander, Civil-Military Operations Task Force) and the International Criminal Investigative Training Assistance Program. Also a player in this conflict was the Administration of Justice Program of the U.S. Agency for International Development or USAID.[16] Nevertheless, all three organizations were either officially or de facto members of the ambassador's country team, so there was a specific forum available for the resolution of conflict. The existence of such a forum hardly suggests that it will be successful—success is driven by personality, institutional position, and power in-country and in Washington. Suffice it to say that the civil-military arena was somewhat more chaotic than the joint military one.

We may summarize unity of effort in Just Cause and Promote Liberty as being a significant improvement over what had gone before in the joint arena. Under both Woerner's and Thurman's concepts, span of control was limited. Where Woerner had, perhaps, retained too many decisions in his own hands, Thurman, possibly, had not intended to retain enough. The civil-military environment, on the other hand, was hardly unified at all. Initially, that is, in the planning stage, this lack of unity was due to two factors. First, for much of the critical period no ambassador was in country. Second, when dealing with operations orders under the Joint Operations Planning System, the planners were specifically prohibited from coordinating outside of military channels. Finally, after the operations were under way, civil-military coordination was hampered by a somewhat laissez faire approach to control on the part of the ambassador and the parochial interests of the several agencies on the ground. The country team mechanism, although it provided a forum for conflict resolution, was not sufficient to achieve a real unity of effort in the absence of leadership willing to force the contending parties to resolve their differences. A final manifestation of interagency conflict was the perception in the Joint Staff that the Department of Defense had been left holding the financial bag for other agencies in Panama despite commitments made at the time.[17]

One other conclusion can be drawn from Just Cause and Promote Liberty. Where the military objective of destroying the PDF as a fighting force was clear, there was unity of effort. Similarly, where the political-military objective of restoring government services was clear, there was also unity of effort. Where the political objectives were not clear and different nuances were understood by different players, however, then there was no unity of effort.

Operations Desert Shield/Storm

Unity of effort in and during the Gulf War had a significant advantage over Panama in that the principal strategic objectives were relatively clear and the end state reasonably well defined. This was done in a series of policy pronouncements, United Nations Security Council resolutions (SCRs), and the campaign plan and operations plans of U.S. Central Command and the coalition.[18] The immediate strategic/operational objective was the deterrence of Iraq from any further aggression into Saudi Arabia and its withdrawal from Kuwait. The end state was defined as the restoration of the legitimate government of Kuwait, the elimination of Iraq's ability to make aggressive war (including the elimination of its weapons of mass destruction), and stability in the region. The latter was further defined as leaving Iraq intact as a state and preventing its dismemberment into its three ethno-religious components—the Shia of the south, the Sunni of the Mesopotamian heartland, and the Kurds of the north.[19] A complicating factor lay in the escalation of President George Bush's rhetoric, which, at times, suggested that the United States would not be averse to an Iraq divided, "like all of Gaul," into three parts.[20] This factor, however, would hardly come into play until the end of the campaign. We will return to this discussion of objectives and end states as we delve into the command relationships of Desert Shield/Storm.

U.S. command in Desert Shield/Storm was fairly uncomplicated and informed by the Goldwater-Nichols Act of 1986. Because these were military operations taking place on the sovereign territory of a number of countries in the Middle East, it was clear that the military commander was the dominant U.S. player. U.S. ambassadors generally were "in support of" the military effort.

Military command was the combatant command of U.S. Central Command and its commander in chief, Gen. H. Norman Schwarzkopf. Thus, all U.S. forces operating in the commander in chief's area of responsibility were under Schwarzkopf's direct control. Combatant command, importantly, includes "directive authority for logistics," which means that the commander in chief can task his service components to provide logistical support to other elements of his force. In turn, the parent services provided the required support. In addition, inherent to combatant command is operational control, the authority not only to order forces to do something but also to organize and reorganize them.[21]

In practice, this authority meant that Schwarzkopf could—and did—attach U.S. Army forces to U.S. Marines and cross attach forces between units. It also meant that Army Lt. Gen. Gus Pagonis's 22d Support Command provided logistical support to all U.S. Central Command forces. It further meant that all air assets (at least on Day 1 of the air campaign) were tasked by a single air tasking order developed by the staff of the Joint Forces Air Component commander, Lt. Gen. Chuck Horner, USAF.[22] These included not only U.S. Air Force and Navy planes but Marine Corps aircraft and Army helicopters. (Later army aviation was not included and marine aviation was granted authority to give highest priority to sorties to close air support in accordance with Marine Corps doctrine.)

Like the air, maritime operations came under the operational control of the commander in chief. This was only the second time that U.S. Navy forces had ever been under operational control to a commander in chief from another service—the first time had been in the Panama planning. The U.S. Navy, historically, preferred to operate "in support of" a ground-based commander, and operational control was not accomplished without some conflict. When it was finally sorted out, the U.S. Central Command naval component, under the commander in chief, had operational control of all U.S. naval forces in the Gulf area.[23] This discussion leads to one last command relationship, tactical control. In this relationship a force may be given a mission by a commander who does not acquire the authority to task organize that force. Thus, when naval air was given a mission by the Joint

Forces Air Component commander under the air tasking order, the Joint Forces Air Component commander was exercising tactical control.

Although these relationships describe the command and control situation within U.S. Central Command, they do little justice to the arrangements among the U.S. unified commands or with coalition forces. The U.S. command and control system begins with the president of the United States as the constitutional commander in chief of all the armed forces and runs through the secretary of defense to the commanders in chief of the unified commands. Under the law, the chairman of the Joint Chiefs of Staff is not in the chain of command but is in the chain of communication. The chairman is the conduit through which all orders are relayed, in addition to being the principal military advisor to the president. Thus, it would be a rather foolhardy commander in chief who would choose to challenge the chairman directly.

When a conflict is taking place within a commander in chief's area of responsibility, all other commanders in chief and service chiefs operate "in support of" the primary commander in chief to the degree directed by the president. In Desert Shield/Storm that degree was nearly absolute. The general rule is that the "supported" commander in chief tells the "supporting" commander in chief what he needs and the supporter provides it. Again, the system worked as the textbook said (with the usual minor glitches, mostly unintentional) during the Gulf War. Thus, commander in chief, Pacific and commander in chief, Atlantic provided ships to commander in chief, Central Command's naval armada. Meanwhile, commander in chief, Europe provided a joint task force (JTF Proven Force), under tactical control to commander in chief, Central Command, to conduct the second front of the air campaign out of Turkey.[24]

Command and control of coalition forces was quite a bit more complicated. During the Gulf War there was no formal alliance among the coalition partners. Nevertheless, the North Atlantic Treaty Organization (NATO) relationships were important to the overall success of the coalition. Forty years of maneuvers and the development of common procedures and vocabulary stood the members of the coalition who were also NATO members in good stead. This was especially true of the coalition's air forces and naval forces. For the ground forces, it applied to the U.S., French, and British. Even where there was no alliance relationship, however, procedural unity had developed through many years of security assistance and combined exercises, which served the same end. Egyptians, Saudis, and members of the Gulf Cooperation Council had been recipients of U.S. equipment and training over the years and had conducted a number of combined exercises. Together, these factors went a long way toward putting disparate forces on the same procedural footing.[25]

Formal command and control was parallel, which is to say that the

United States and Saudi Arabia were, officially, equal partners. Saudi Joint Forces Commander Lieutenant General Khalid was General Schwarzkopf's formal equal. It was important that their headquarters were in the same building, making direct coordination between the two commanders physically easy. What, in fact, made this arrangement workable was the Coalition, Coordination, Communication and Integration Center (C³IC), which was formed under the lead of the U.S. Army component (ARCENT).

> The C³IC became a clearinghouse for coordination of training areas, firing ranges, logistics, frequency management, and intelligence sharing. Manned by officers from all Coalition forces, the C³IC served as the primary tool for the coordination of the myriad details inherent in combined military operations. It soon expanded and was divided into ground, air, naval, logistics, special operations, and intelligence sections. The C³IC became a vital tool in ensuring unity of effort among Coalition forces, remaining in operation throughout Operations Desert Shield and Desert Storm.[26]

This set of arrangements allowed the forces of the coalition to pursue effectively their common goals. When Desert Storm began, some coalition forces were rearranged so that British and French forces operated under tactical control to U.S. forces.[27] Arab coalition forces operated under the control of Khalid's two commands, Joint Forces Command North and Joint Forces Command East. Although not under Schwarzkopf's command, these forces acted in full coordination with the U.S. developed plans. The preservation of formal independence of operation permitted the practical integration of Khalid's forces with Schwarzkopf's, given that the coalition was fully united on its operational objectives.

One other tool for achieving unity of effort was the use of, primarily, U.S. Special Forces as liaison with the Arab coalition partners. These liaison elements provided an effective communication link among elements whose technical communications were not compatible, and who did not fully share doctrine or experience. The Special Forces liaison teams often were the glue which made the coalition effective at the tactical level.[28]

A final area for the discussion of unity of effort in Desert Shield/Storm is found in the management structure for planning postconflict operations in Kuwait and the command and control system for their execution.[29] As with Generals Thurman and Stiner in Panama, postconflict operations in Kuwait were the least of the worries facing Schwarzkopf and his subordinates when planning for the war. In Washington, however, the assistant secretary of defense for special operations and Low Intensity Conflict (ASD-SO/LIC) recognized that this would become a necessary mission. At the same time, the G5 of the 352d Civil Affairs Command, a Reserve unit, Col. Randall Elliott, who in civilian life was the Middle East desk officer in State Department's Bureau of Intelligence and Research and a close friend of the ambassador designate to Kuwait, Edward "Skip" Gnehm, saw a similar need, Together, Elliott and the SO/LIC staff, with Gnehm's support, energized the bureaucracy to begin postconflict planning. It finally got under way with the activation of the Kuwait Task Force under Elliott's direction with the call-up of a number of Reserve Civil Affairs officers.

The Kuwait Task Force was controlled by an interagency steering committee group from the Departments of Defense and State. Although it was supposed to be in coordination with U.S. Central Command, this never materialized to anyone's satisfaction. Thus, when the Kuwait Task Force arrived in Saudi Arabia in late January its plans were not synchronized with those of U.S. Central Command or the U.S. Army component. They did, nevertheless, provide a basis for the long-term reconstruction of Kuwait. Moreover, once the Kuwait Task Force arrived, it became under combatant command to the commander in chief, thereby alleviating much of the confusion as to the role of the Kuwait Task Force.

The Kuwait Task Force soon was incorporated into the Combined Civil Affairs Task Force built around its parent unit, the 352d Civil Affairs Command. During Desert Shield, U.S. Central Command had given "executive agency" for civil affairs to Army Central Command. Executive agency, an anachronism from pre-Goldwater-Nichols days, was hardly the appropriate vehicle to plan and/or execute postconflict operations. This was especially true because the commander in chief had retained command of the land component himself, thus precluding the Army Central commander from effectively planning and controlling all civil military operations.

When the time finally came to execute plans for the restoration and reconstruction of Kuwait, the Army Central commander established a combined task force, Task Force Freedom, under his deputy. It included not only the Combined Civil Affairs Task Force but also combat, combat support, and combat service support elements, as well as coalition units from the British, Saudis, and Kuwaitis. Of special import was that Task Force Freedom had inherited, with the Kuwait Task Force and Combined Civil Affairs Task Force, an interagency subordinate element, a Disaster Assistance Response Team from the USAID's Office of Foreign Disaster Assistance (OFDA). The Disaster Assistance Response Team came with its own civilian contractor support. Nothing like this interagency arrangement had been seen since the disappearance of the CORDS (Civil Operations and Revolutionary Development) organization of the Vietnam War. Finally, Task Force Freedom greatly resembled the U.S. Military Support Group-Panama, which had been developed from a doctrinal construct now called the Foreign Internal Defense Augmentation Force. In short, whether intentional or not, a large number of command and control lessons had been learned as a result of the Panama experience, coupled with trial and error.

Operations Restore Hope and Continue Hope

The two operations addressed here derive a significant amount from the two already discussed in this chapter. Restore Hope, in terms of its management structure, a joint task force, resembles Panama. It also resembles the Gulf Coalition in that it was a multinational operation undertaken with a UN mandate. Yet, it differs from both in a significant number of ways. Continue Hope, by contrast, was a different kind of operation altogether— a UN-mandated peace enforcement mission under Chapter VII of the United Nations Charter, executed by a UN "peacekeeping" force. Because the two operations are so closely related that they are, in fact, phases of the same mission, we will consider them here jointly.

> On 3 December 1992, the United Nations took an unprecedented step to resolve the problems of starvation, famine, and lawlessness in Somalia. It was significant in two regards. It was the first attempt by the international community to deal with a new post-Cold War phenomenon referred to as the "failed nation state." It has further significance in that the United Nations expanded its traditional role of Chapter VI peacekeeping operations to a more ambitious Chapter VII peace enforcement intervention authorizing participating states of the coalition to use "all necessary means" to execute the parameters of the Security Council mandates.[30]

This action was embodied in UN Security Council Resolution (SCR) 794, unanimously adopted, which endorsed "the offer *by a member state* to constitute and lead an international force for the purpose of protecting humanitarian relief operations in Somalia."[31] Although the resolution grants a similar type of authority to the United States as was given before Desert Storm, the purpose as stated in the wording is much more ambiguous. U.S. forces defined the end state of their mission as the creation of "an environment in which the UN and NGOs can assume full responsibility for the security and operations of the Somalia humanitarian relief efforts."[32] What was implied by these words, however, would haunt the missions of Operations Restore Hope/Continue Hope and the U.S., multinational, and UN task forces charged with their execution.

Any careful reading of the Security Council resolution and the end-state definition leads to the logical conclusion that the security mission required the effective reduction of the capabilities of the several Somali factions to make war and terrorize both the citizenry and the community of relief organizations. In turn, this reduction demanded a significant degree of disarmament of the factions. Although this "implied task" was, from time to time, recognized by U.S. military commanders in the early days of the operation, it was staunchly denied by President Bush and Secretary of Defense Richard Cheney, at the same time as it was just as staunchly affirmed by UN Secretary General Boutros Boutros-Ghali.[33] As a result, the ambiguous wording of the resolution was allowed to stand without clarification. Indeed, the disagreement over the objective of the operation between President Bush and Secretary General Boutros-Ghali was merely papered over while everybody waited for the incoming Clinton administration to resolve the issue.

One problem, however, was that the Clinton administration had not fully analyzed the implications of its predilection for multilateral action through the UN. Had it done so, it might not have been so ready to support Boutros-Ghali's interpretation in the succeeding resolution, 814, which established the UN peacekeeping mission. In the meantime, from January 20, 1993 until the passage of Security Council Resolution 814, ambiguity with respect to long-term objectives in Somalia reigned. Because of that ambiguity, unity of effort was very much at risk.

Operation Restore Hope initially was executed by a U.S. Joint Task Force, JTF Somalia, later renamed United Task Force (UNITAF) to accommodate the forces of other contributing nations. JTF Somalia was built around the First Marine Expeditionary Force augmented by army, navy, air force, and special operations forces. Given a U.S. joint task force that was larger than a division—this one had a marine and an army division plus assorted combat support and combat service support elements—the choice of joint task force base was severely constrained to one of the two military organizations with a staff sufficiently large enough to handle the command and control complexity presented by such a large operation. Thus, the choice was between an army corps and a marine expeditionary force.

That the choice came down to the First Marine Expeditionary Force may have had as much to do with personality as with anything else. General Joseph Hoar, USMC, was the commander in chief of U.S. Central Command in whose area of responsibility the mission was to take place. Hoar had been the chief of staff of Central Command just before Desert Shield and his replacement was Robert Johnston, now a lieutenant general and commander of the First Marine Expeditionary Force. Perhaps equally important was that Hoar perceived the mission as coming "from the sea." In any event, the First Marine Expeditionary Force, augmented by staff and forces from the other services, provided the base of the joint task force.

To accommodate the multinational forces, General Johnston chose to follow the example of Gen. John Shalikashvili in Operation Provide Comfort and exercise tactical control through liaison officers. In addition, Johnston gave the foreign contributors their own humanitarian relief sectors in which to operate. This decision clearly reduced the amount of supervision that the United Task Force staff would have to exercise.[34] The use of liaison officers and common procedures among the NATO countries participating in the operation created significant common procedural ground to pursue the common objective of establishing security for the delivery of relief supplies throughout the operational area.

Another factor affecting the unity of the U.S. operation was President Bush's naming of Ambassador Robert Oakley as special envoy to Somalia. Because there was no formal U.S. diplomatic representation to the Somali government—there was no such government—Oakley was not the accredited U.S. ambassador and, therefore, was not armed with the presidential letter of instruction making him responsible for everything the U.S. government does in that country. Yet, neither had President Bush directed General Hoar, as commander in chief, to assume that responsibility. Rather, Hoar was given a mission that he directed Johnston to execute, and Oakley was told to, figuratively, "go forth and do good." As Oakley put it, "The President was also urged to name a senior political representative who would complement the military commander."[35]

Generally, the ambiguity of the relationship between Oakley and Johnston caused no problems that were not resolved through direct and regular consultation. Indeed, Ambassador Oakley played the critical role in opening up the humanitarian relief sectors in the interior of the country, paving the way as "advance man" for the military forces.[36] On at least one occasion, however, conflict between Ambassador Oakley and General Johnston erupted when the latter took a significant military action that had major political consequences without previously consulting the ambassador. The ensuing discussion between the two reportedly was brief and pointed and without resolution of whether there was a requirement to consult, coordinate, or inform.[37] Such conflict, however, was rare.

Although the United Task Force mission was defined as "security," it had any number of important humanitarian and civic assistance aspects. Roads were built, supplies distributed, civic action conducted, rudimentary police forces and other local institutions established.[38] Most of the humanitarian relief, however, was being conducted by the same organizations that had done so before the operation began, the nongovernmental, private voluntary organization community (NGO/PVO). As had been done prior to the operation, the military sought to coordinate its relationship with the NGOs and PVOs through a civil-military operations center. During the airlift of supplies prior to December, the civil-military operations center had been established in Mombassa, Kenya, under a marine colonel from Central Command. When Restore Hope began, the civil-military operations center was relocated to Mogadishu under the command of the same marine colonel.

Into this situation one must now insert a unique organization of the U.S. government, the Office of Foreign Disaster Assistance (OFDA) of USAID. The Office of Foreign Disaster Assistance is a small office with about 50 staff members worldwide who are armed with legislative wording that allows them to use U.S. government resources from any agency "notwithstanding any other legislation" so long as the disaster is declared by the appropriate authority (and certain other minimal conditions are met).[39] The Office of Foreign Disaster Assistance first engaged in fully cooperative efforts with the military during Desert Storm in Kuwait City and again in northern Iraq during Provide Comfort.[40] From those efforts the organization had learned a great deal and felt fairly comfortable working with the military as well as with the NGOs. Indeed, it had been fully integrated into the civil-military operations center in Mombassa. When the civil-military operations center moved to Mogadishu, the Office of Foreign Disaster Assistance moved with it and that, in the words of the head of its team, was a mistake.[41]

What the Office of Foreign Disaster Assistance found was that as the operation unfolded, major decisions affecting humanitarian relief activities were not being made in the civil-military operations center. Rather, many were being made by the joint task force staff (particularly the J3, director of operations, Maj. Gen. Anthony Zinni). The Office of Foreign Disaster Assistance team chief, himself a general officer equivalent, discovered that General Zinni liked to sit by his tent in the evenings smoking a cigar and reflecting on the events of the day. A smoker himself, the team chief would often join Zinni and raise issues he deemed critical that had not reached the J3 through channels. Although this approach resolved many problems, some issues simply had to be addressed by the United Task Force commander and there was no guarantee that Zinni would prioritize them in the same way that the Office of Foreign Disaster Assistance did.

The Office of Foreign Disaster Assistance team chief determined that the way to solve his problem was through a similar informal coordination mechanism. Unfortunately for him, Johnston was not a smoker like Zinni, so that avenue of approach was not available. Johnston did, however, have an exploitable side; he was a runner. Although the team chief was not a runner, one of his senior staff members was, and it did not hurt that she was also attractive. As a result, she took to joining General Johnston on his daily runs, occasionally carrying messages for the Office of Foreign Disaster Assistance that the team chief felt were so important that the issues had to be raised directly with the joint task force commander. Despite the unorthodox nature of the approaches, these ad hoc coordination mechanisms were quite successful.[42]

This analysis suggests that the United Task Force was relatively successful in its execution of Operation Restore Hope for several reasons. First, the mission was fairly clear and the end state reasonably well demarcated, even if it was only an interim one. Thus, the mission was to provide security for the delivery of humanitarian relief and, in so doing, achieve as an end state an environment that was secure enough to turn the mission over to the United Nations. Second, the organization of the forces was a fairly "standard" U.S. joint task force building on the base of the relatively large staff of the First Marine Expeditionary Force, which had long established working procedures that could, and did, accommodate the required augmentations. Third, many of the multinational forces were NATO allies who were well accustomed to working together using common command and staff procedures. Finally, nations generally were given their own humanitarian relief sectors in which they could operate as they saw fit within the general limits of the mission.

Problems were inherent in the transition to the UN. What had been left unresolved by President Bush and Secretary General Boutros-Ghali would now be resolved by the stance of the new U.S. administration with respect to the UN and Security Council Resolution (SCR) 814, which was fully supported by the United States. Indeed, SCR 814 called on the UN to rebuild the failed Somali state, clearly resolving the issue in favor of Boutros-Ghali's interpretation. Thus, SCR 814 gave the UN a mission that was in many ways different from the one executed by the United Task Force under SCR 794. Although both resolutions authorized the use of force under Chapter VII of the Charter, SCR 814 gave the responsibility for enforcing peace *and* rebuilding the political infrastructure to the UN mission, UNOSOM (United Nations Operation in Somalia) II. Unlike UNITAF, UNOSOM II could not muster anything like the overwhelming combat power of its predecessor. At its peak UNITAF numbered some 37,000 troops, of which 28,000 were U.S., UNOSOM II was planned to have a total of 28,000 troops, of which only 1,200 were to be U.S. combat forces configured as a quick reaction force.[43] In fact, when UNOSOM II was activated on May 4, 1993, its strength was only 17,200.[44]

Given the specifically different mission and the significantly weaker force structure, it was clear that Somali forces who had not been thrilled with the idea of Operation Restore Hope would seek to modify its outcome. Chief among those forces was the Somali National Alliance, led by Gen. Mohammed Farrah Aidid. Aidid, who saw the only appropriate/legitimate outcome of the crisis as the confirmation of himself and his political faction as Somalia's national leader, was well prepared and positioned to take advantage of the transition to UNOSOM II.

What made UNOSOM II so much weaker than the United Task Force was not only its lack of combat power but also its formal structure and informal organization. In this it suffered both from U.S. planning and a lack of real commitment by the United States to its own plan.

In general terms the formal organization of UNOSOM II looked little different from that of countless other UN peacekeeping missions. Responsible to the Security Council through the secretary general was the special representative of the secretary general (SRSG). He, in turn, was responsible for the political, administration, and humanitarian relief divisions, the zone directors, and the UN force commander. In addition, the NGOs were linked in communication with the special representative of the secretary general.

The force commander and his deputy had operational control of national forces assigned to UNOSOM II.[45] Here, however, the traditional picture becomes more complicated.

At the insistence of the United States, the special representative of the secretary general was Adm. Jonathon Howe, U.S. Navy, retired, who had been deputy national security adviser to President Bush on the National Security Council. This appointment gave the appearance of continuity between the two U.S. administrations but one that was more apparent than real. Second, the deputy force commander was Maj. Gen. Thomas Montgomery, U.S. Army; and key members of the UN force staff, especially the operations officer, were also U.S. Montgomery, however, wore a second hat as commander of U.S. Forces, Somalia. These forces included the Quick Reaction Force from the Tenth Mountain Division, the Central Command Intelligence Support Element, Special Operations Forces, and the UN Logistics Support Command.[46]

The command relationships of the components of U.S. Forces, Somalia (USFORSOM), were somewhat convoluted. Most conventional was the UN Logistics Support Command, which was under the operational control of the UN force commander. The Central Command Intelligence Support Element provided direct support to General Montgomery. Both the Quick Reaction Force and the Special Operations Forces, however, remained under the operational control of commander in chief, Central Command. As Thomas Daze describes it:

> The command relationship between UNOSOM II and the U.S. Quick Reaction Force (QRF) was prescribed by the Commander, U.S. Central Command and outlined in the Terms of Reference for U. S. Forces in Somalia. The QRF, located in Somalia, was under the operational control (OPCON) of CINCCENT. Tactical Control (TACON) of the QRF was delegated to the Commander, USFORSOM (Deputy Force Commander) for "normal training exercises within Somalia," and "in situations within Somalia that exceed the capability of UNOSOM II forces and *required the employment of immediate combat power* for a limited period or show of force operations." Any tasking of the QRF outside of these guidelines required explicit USCINCCENT approval.[47]

This discussion of command relationships within the U.S. elements and between U.S. Forces, Somalia and UNOSOM II has left out a critical player, the force commander. The fact that the force commander was Turkish Lt. Gen. Cevik Bir, an officer from a NATO nation with extensive NATO experience, makes these command relationships particularly confusing.

UNOSOM II had placed political authority in the hands of a U.S. admiral as special representative of the secretary general. His subordinate force commander was a Turk, an officer from a NATO nation, completely familiar with NATO and U.S. procedures. His deputy commander was another American, as were his key staff officers (while others were largely from NATO nations). In other words, UNOSOM II was a U.S. and/or NATO organization in everything but name, such that operational control of most U.S. forces—especially the Quick Reaction Force—was the most appropriate and effective command relationship. Neither the Quick Reaction Force nor the Special Operations Forces were under the operational control of even the U.S. Forces, Somalia commander, however, let alone UNOSOM II. Rather, only tactical control was granted, and that in the most restrictive of circumstances.

> The terms of reference provided adequate flexibility for the UNOSOM II Deputy Force Commander to employ the QRF in emergency situations. However, to conduct of critical, yet non-emergency combat operations which exceeded the capability of UNOSOM II forces, the terms of reference proved to be quite inflexible.[48]

The truth of this assertion would be seen in the events of October 3 and 4, 1993.

The Rangers' battle with General Aidid's militia resulted from events that took place shortly after the UN replaced the U.S.-led coalition. On June 5, about a month after UNOSOM II had taken charge of operations in Somalia, Aidid's militia ambushed a force of Pakistani peacekeepers, killing 24. Admiral Howe recommended a strong UN response, and the Security Council passed a resolution calling for the "arrest and detention, prosecution, trial and punishment" of the responsible parties.[49] Then, after little success had been achieved in response to this resolution, a Pentagon spokesman announced on August 25 that, " A task force of Rangers and other elements of U.S. Special Operation Command had deployed to Mogadishu."[50] This task force, known doctrinally as a Joint Special Operations Task Force, was under the commander of the Joint Special Operations Command (JSOC), Maj. Gen. William Garrison, whose command relationship with UNOSOM II and U.S. Forces, Somalia was even more restrictive than that of the Quick Reaction Force. As a result, when the Rangers got in trouble during their October 3 mission, UNOSOM II, U.S. Forces, Somalia, and the Quick Reaction Force were ill equipped and oriented to come rapidly and effectively to their assistance. Although the force commander and his deputy had authority to veto such an operation, the allowance of only 30 minutes notification for security reasons did not allow the UNOSOM II leadership much time to react and hindered the effective use of the Quick Reaction Force and other UNOSOM II forces. In short, the U.S. failure to trust the management structure that its own diplomacy had created played a major role in UNOSOM II's inability to carry out its mandate effectively.

As a result of the October 3-4 events, the Clinton administration decided to withdraw U.S. forces from Somalia by March 31, 1994. To facilitate this effort and give the appearance of strength, the president directed that U.S. Forces, Somalia be augmented with a separate Joint Task Force built around the Tenth Mountain Division. Rather than giving command of joint task force Somalia to the division commander, however, Maj. Gen. Carl Ernst was named. Ernst, frocked as a major general,[51] was serving in the Army's Training and Doctrine Command at the time. Although the mission of Joint Task Force Somalia was to cover the U.S. withdrawal through a show of force, its relationship to U.S. Forces, Somalia, in practice, was never entirely clear. That lack of clarity produced sufficient bureaucratic conflict that when General Ernst returned to his previous duty after only a couple of months, Major General Montgomery resolved the issue by the simple expedient of putting on the additional hat of commander, Joint Task Force Somalia.[51]

The particular lessons of the United Task Force and UNOSOM II focus on the principle of the objective and its attendant end state, as well as on the appropriate organization to achieve that end state. The first problem encountered was that the strategic end state was not defined adequately to ensure the long-range success of the mission. The disagreement between Boutros-Ghali and Bush was papered over rather than resolved, leading to the passage of UN Security Council Resolution 814, which the new administration supported without realizing its full implications. Nevertheless, the operational success of the United Task Force caused the United States and the UN to believe that they were on their way to strategic success. Unfortunately, the United States, which had manipulated the organization of UNOSOM II so as to ensure unity of effort, failed to allow the systems it had created to work as intended. In turn, this failure made it impossible to accomplish the objective of the mission. Rather than fixing the structure in the face of adversity, the United States and the UN decided that the identified objective was not worth the effort. The result was a face-saving attempt to close down the operation. For the United States, this effort compounded failure, as neither the function nor the command relationships was particularly clear until General Montgomery added the joint task force command hat to the others he was wearing.

Conclusion: Lessons from the Cases

The three case studies discussed here support the arguments put forth in the previous chapter. First, and foremost, there can be no effective unity of effort, no matter what the management structure, organization, or command and control arrangements, if there is not agreement on the objective and its associated end state. Given this assertion, however, it is clear from the cases that agreement on the objective may take place at any or all of three levels. If it exists at any one level, then there is some ground to expect mission success at that level. In Panama and the Gulf, there was a high degree of agreement on the objectives and the end states at the tactical and operational levels and a reasonable amount of agreement at the strategic level as well. Thus, Just Cause and Desert Storm clearly were operational successes and arguably strategic successes, at least in the near term. By contrast, what characterized Restore Hope was a profound disagreement on the strategic objective and end state between key players. Papering over the differences allowed the agreement that existed on operational objectives to carry the mission forward. Nevertheless, it set the stage for strategic failure even with the formal agreement on strategic objectives set by UN Security Countil Resoluon 814 because the United States never did understand the implications of the end state envisioned by the resolution until it was too late. When it finally comprehended the cost, it withdrew its commitment to the objective, guaranteeing that the end state would not be attained.

Agreements on objectives and end states are necessary conditions for unity of effort. They are not, however, sufficient conditions. Sufficiency is achieved by adding an appropriate management structure or command and control system. The United States has developed over the last decade a fairly effective set of command and control systems for joint military operations that revolve around the unified commands, joint task forces, and organizational bases within the services, as well as doctrinal variants. These combinations give the United States an extremely flexible and effective system to conduct joint military operations. It is not a system without conflict and it still suffers growing pains, but it does seem to work rather well. Not the least contributory to its growing success is a rapidly developing common language supporting joint procedures.

Following closely on the success of joint organization is the rapidly increasing level of competence in the conduct of combined or multinational military operations. Desert Storm and Restore Hope showed just how effective the United States has become in leading coalitions in combat or near-combat situations. Part of the strength that has developed lies in the experience of 40 years of NATO planning and exercising. NATO developed common language and procedures over those 40 years such that it was relatively easy for its member nations to work together in the ad hoc coalitions symbolized by these operations.[53] With respect to the non-NATO coalition partners, common procedures, language, and equipment had been developed to varying degrees over the years through training exercises, international military education (mostly in U.S. branch and staff schools), and the purchase of some U.S. equipment. These factors were augmented by the imaginative use of (mostly) U.S. Special Forces soldiers as liaisons.

Desert Storm illustrates, however, both the importance of these factors and their proper place in the entire picture of unity of effort. Although they all facilitated success, the coalition would have operated in a relatively unified fashion even if several of them had not worked. That operational unity was, again, due to the very strong agreement among the coalition partners on the operational objectives focused on removing Iraq from Kuwait and depriving it of any fruits of that conquest. As a result, the coalition sought out mechanisms and procedures to make its working unity not only possible but a fact.

Although Restore Hope reinforces these conclusions, UNOSOM II clearly demonstrates that the most elaborately crafted management structure will fail to ensure unity of effort when the player who crafted it does not have confidence in its efficacy. The crafting of UNOSOM II took into account all the lessons the United States thought it had learned in the previous cases as well as several other operations. As discussed above, it was a U.S. command in all but name. Despite this, the U.S. Department of Defense rejected its implications and restricted the permissible command relationships to the point where the system almost inevitably would fail. The degree to which these restrictions reflected the previously identified discord over the end state implications of the mission is unclear, but it seems a reasonable hypothesis that the correlation is high.

If the United States and its partners have become fairly competent in the joint and combined military arenas, then the same cannot be said of the civil-military games. Rather, all three cases show a significant amount of discord among civil-military players, although Desert Storm handled that by generally ignoring the problem. Real discord in the civil-military arena did not appear until after the events addressed here, the latter stages of postconflict operation.[54] At the same time the cases demonstrate significant organizational learning taking place. The pivotal player in this learning has been the USAID Office of Foreign Disaster Assistance, which provides the critical interface among the humanitarian assistance community of national governmental organizations, IGOs, NGOs, and the military.

One result of these cases and others has been significant intellectual ferment seen in conferences involving academics, military, and civilian practitioners from all the communities represented. Books and articles like this have been appearing with increasing regularity, as have a number of joint and army manuals that address these subjects. Similarly, the Office of Foreign Disaster Assistance has produced a doctrinal field manual.[55] This ferment should produce the "doctrine, tactics, techniques, and procedures" to conduct more effective interagency operations in the future. A final note of caution is in order. Knowing how to do something right is no guarantee that it will be done right. In the civil-military arena, as much as in the other two—and perhaps more—the common objective and end state are essential for unity of effort. Only then can the mechanisms of management, leadership, and command and control work to create that unity required for mission success.

Notes

1. This discussion derives from multiple sources on Operations Just Cause and Promote Liberty, including the participant observation of the author (hereafter cited as Participant Observation) and interviews with participants. See also John T. Fishel, *The Fog of Peace: Planning and Executing the Restoration of Panama* (Carlisle, Penn.: Strategic Studies Institute, 1992).

2. See Department of Defense Reorganization Act, 1986 (Goldwater-Nichols), Title 10, USC.

3. Operational command (OPCOM) is the term that preceded COCOM. While it did include operational control (UPCON), it did not give directive authority for logistics. Although the term no longer exists in joint terminology, it is still a current NATO command relationship.

4. Interviews with General Fred F. Woerner, May 1991, Dr. Gabriel Marcella, 1991–1992, and Participant Observation.

5. Interview with General Woerner.

6. John T. Fishel, *Liberation, Occupation, and Rescue: War Termination and Desert Storm* (Carlisle, Penn.: Strategic Studies Institute, 1992), ch. 1.

7. Participant Observation.

8. Fishel, *Fog of Peace.*

9. Interviews, 1991 and Participant Observation.

10. Interview with Major General William Hartzog, April 1991.

11. Tacitus, "Few Lessons Were Learned in Panama Invasion," *Armed Forces Journal International*, June 1993, p. 54.

12. Fishel, *Fog of Peace*, p. 75.

13. Interview with Col. (Ret.) Chuck Fry, former commander SOCSOUTH, Oct 1994.

14. Interview with John Maisto, former deputy chief of mission, U.S. Embassy, Panama, October 1992.

15. See Fishel, *Fog of Peace*, Participant Observation.

16. Ibid.

17. Fishel, *Liberation, Occupation, and Rescue.*

18. Ibid., Department of Defense, *Final Report to Congress: Conduct of the Persian Gulf War*, Pursuant to Title V (Public Law 102–25), hereafter cited as Title V.

19. Ibid.

20. Fishel, *Liberation, Occupation, and Rescue.*

21. Gary Bryant, *What is COCOM?*, MMAS Thesis, Fort Leavenworth, Kansas, 1993, and AFSC Pub 1, *Joint Staff Officers' Guide*, Norfolk, Virginia, 1993.

22. Title V, p. 93

23. Interviews with Col. Douglas Craft, former chief, Policy and Strategy Division, J5 USCENTCOM, 1991–1992.

24. Title V.

25. Title V, p. 487, and Fishel, *Liberation, Occupation, and Rescue.*

26. Title V, p. 44, and Robert H. Scales, *Certain Victory: The U.S. Army in the Gulf War*, (Fort Leavenworth, Kansas: U.S. Army Command and General Staff College Press, 1994), p. 122.

27. Title V. See pp. 555–559 for discrepancies between command and control as depicted in the text and the graphics. I have followed the text, as it is more in accordance with both doctrine and common sense.

28. See Scales, *Certain Victory*, pp. 103–106.

29. This section is drawn from Fishel, *Liberation, Occupation, and Rescue*.

30. This quote is from the USFORSOM After Action Report, Strategic Studies Institute, Carlisle, Penn., 1994 as quoted by Thomas Daze in ch. 1 (Draft) of his MMAS Thesis. LTC Daze was one of the drafters of the report and executive officer to UN Force Commander LTG Cevik Bir.

31. Robert B. Oakley, "An Envoy's Perspective," *Joint Forces Quarterly*, Autumn 1993, pp. 44–55.

32. CALL, *Operation Restore Hope*, Revised Final Draft, August 16, 1993, p. I-14.

33. See *Los Angeles Times*, December 12, 1992, p. 87; December 13, 1992, p. A-14; *Wall Street Journal*, December 14, 1992, pp.B5A & A5E; *New York Times*, December 19, 1992, pp. 1 & 3; *Newsweek*, December 21, 1992, pp. 24–25; *Washington Post*, December 22, 1992, p. A18.

34. UNITAF Briefing Slides, nd.

35. Oakley, "Envoy's Perspective," p. 46, also interviews with former Restore Hope staff officer, 1993–1994.

36. Tenth Mountain Division, *U.S. Army Forces, Somalia*, After Action Report, June 1993, p. 22.

37. Interviews with Restore Hope staff officers, 1993-1994.

38. CALL and Tenth Mountain Division reports.

39. Interview with William Garvelink, deputy director, OFDA, December 1993.

40. See Fishel, *Liberation, Operation, and Rescue*.

41. Garvelink interview.

42. Ibid.

43. Daze, pp. 17–18.

44. Ibid., p. 21.

45. Ibid., p. 24.

46. Ibid., pp. 22–23.

47. Ibid., p. 23; internal quote taken from USFORSOM AAR.

48. Ibid.

49. *Army Times*, June 28, 1993, p. 13; and *Army Times*, September 6, 1993, p. 6.

50. *Time*, October 18, 1993, p. 46.

51. The term "frocked" is used for an army officer selected for promotion to the next higher grade who is allowed to serve in that grade without the increase in pay until the effective date of promotion for the convenience of the government.

52. JTF Somalia training Task Force papers and interviews with JTF Somalia staff officers and UNOSOM II staff officers, 1994.

53. It should be noted again that lack of agreement over objectives and end states can result in very serious problems of unity of effort even among NATO allies in this kind of operation. See Daze, ch. 2, forthcoming, for some elaboration.

54. See Fishel, *Liberation, Occupation, and Rescue*.

55. Among the conferences held were a working meeting in San Francisco in December 1993, sponsored by the 351st Civil Affairs Command, the Civil Affairs Association meeting in Portland, Oregon, June 1994, and a conference on Peace Operations at Fort Leavenworth in October 1994. For documents see my *Fog of Peace* and *Liberation, Occupation, and Rescue*, various SSI publications, MMAS Theses, SAMS Monographs, articles in military and military oriented professional journals, and doctrinal manuals such as FM 100-23, *Peace Operations*, the four service Humanitarian Assistance manuals, and OFDA's *Field Operations Guide*.

PART FOUR

Additional Challenges in Confronting the New World Disorder

12

The Implications of the Organized Crime Phenomenon for U.S. National Security

Graham H. Turbiville

At the mid-point of the 1990s, an explosion of the most virulent forms of organized criminal activity in many regions of the world has moved crime from an issue of "public safety" to one of "national security" in those areas most affected. These organized criminal activities—increasingly linked regionally and internationally—are challenging domestic and foreign policies of states around the world in multiple ways and are especially threatening to the cohesiveness and sovereignty of new and fragile democracies.[1]

While the impact of organized crime per se—to include drug and arms trafficking, sophisticated financial crimes, strategic material smuggling, extortion, and bribery among other forms—is a major concern in itself, *the increased association of organized crime with other security problems* promises to be a particularly difficult challenge for U.S. officials charged with developing and implementing effective security programs for the twenty-first century. It is instructive, therefore, to address some of the more important aspects of this association, and also to address ways in which more traditional or dormant forms of criminality have gained new vitality and changed in accord with new opportunities.

The merging of state and criminal agendas has been one prominent feature of the growth of international organized crime for a number of states in which existing institutions have been unable either to meet basic national needs, or to resist strong, aggressive criminal enterprise. In such instances, the question of what is criminal—and what is not—has become blurred or

---

The views expressed in this chapter are those of the author and do not necessarily reflect the official policy or position of the Department of the Army, Department of Defense, or the U.S. government.

distorted within these states, as have issues of sovereignty and legitimacy. Arguments by Latin American drug cartel representatives touting the national wealth they generate, for example, have in some ways echoed and perverted the observations of fifth century Christian theologian St. Augustine, who identified issues of sovereignty and legitimacy still fundamental 1,500 years later:

> what are bands of brigands but petty kingdoms? They also are groups of men, under the rule of a leader, bound together by a common agreement, dividing their booty according to a settled principle. If this band of criminals, by recruiting more criminals, acquires enough power to occupy regions, to capture cities, and to subdue whole populations, then it can with fuller right assume the title of kingdom, which in the public estimation is conferred upon it, not by the renunciation of greed, but by the increase of impunity.[2]

For some peoples and regions, criminal enterprise acting with impunity has become a better choice than an ineffective government with weak or flawed institutions, or an environment where economic opportunity, social justice, and basic order are absent.

Increased levels of crime have always been associated with conflict and political or social disarray. When the old order dies or weakens, and when ethnic antagonisms or national aspirations and tensions become acute, banditry and other forms of criminality appear, either as traditional types or altered to reflect new realities or technologies.[3] This association has extraordinarily increased, however, in the post–Cold War period, where the sudden appearance of many new states, the resurfacing of dormant antagonisms, unprecedented levels of individual global mobility, the nearly universal access to modern communications means, and the potential for enormous profits have provided ready opportunities and incentives for combatants and criminals to interact in pursuit of their own agendas. As a consequence, substantial criminal content has appeared in most dimensions of conflict in the 1990s.

It is clear also that the resolve of a number of government and law enforcement organizations to attack organized crime in many states abroad is minimal or nonexistent. In this regard, both U.S. and foreign government representatives concerned directly with such matters have judged recently that lack of government responses to increasing European organized crime have been much the same as lack of Western responses to the rise of fascism in the 1920s and 1930s—with the consequences of inaction being of parallel magnitude.[4] Similarly, the commitment of states to combating drug trafficking, money laundering, and other criminal activities has been questioned on every continent. In substantial measure, bribery and systemic institutional corruption have been identified as major contributors to inaction or ineffectiveness by states and institutions engaged in anticrime programs. Corruption, then, has become a familiar feature in reform pro-grams ranging from the creation or rebuilding of sound financial institu-tions to the restructuring of military and police forces. It is, of course, most debilitating for new states or states dealing with crises.

Overall, in terms of scope, diversity, and innovation, the development of organized crime is proceeding far faster than warnings about its impact and consequence are being addressed.[5] While this development has profound implications for U.S. domestic policies and programs, it is equally important in its foreign dimensions, where crime and other security issues have become more closely intertwined. This chapter addresses what may be some of the most challenging concerns for U.S. planners and policymakers concerned with foreign affairs: the threat of organized crime to the development or consolidation of democracy in new or fragile states generally; the increased association of crime with conflict; and the impact of crime on some of the most important of state institutions—the security and military forces that are expected to provide an environment suitable for promoting such basic U.S. foreign policy and security objectives as sustained democratic reform.

Organized Crime and States in Crisis

As suggested above, organized crime is a particularly acute problem for fragile democracies facing—or emerging from—periods of civil war or conflict, as well as for newly constituted democracies such as those estab-lished in Eastern Europe and the former Soviet Union (FSU). Institutions in these kinds of states especially are affected in numerous ways by criminal enterprise. Examples from around the world are numerous and diverse. They include among many others:

- the heightened level of organized and random crime in El Salvador following the 1992 Peace Accords that threatens continuing progress in establishing a stable society;[6]
- threats to institutional integrity in Guatemala, where efforts to end the weakened Guatemalan National Revolutionary Unity (URNG) insur-gency and begin a process of national reconciliation have been com-plicated by violent crime, drug trafficking, and corruption;
- continuing coca production and processing in Peru, joined by the cultivation of opium poppies and high levels of general crime despite the serious setbacks dealt to Sendero Luminoso (the Shining Path) and the virtual destruction of the Tupac Amaru Revolutionary Movement (MRTA);[7]
- widespread criminal problems of all types in South Africa following the end of apartheid, successful national elections, the establishment of a new government, and initially promising efforts to create new security institutions;[8]

- the intermixing of drug trafficking and other crime, political activity, insurgency, and the economy in Mexico, to the point of making criminal and other agendas indistinguishable;[9] and
- invigorated alliances of organized criminals and terrorists in many regions of India, which have been identified by the Indian Prime Minister Narasimha Rao recently as a growing threat to national stability.[10]

Affected states often characterize the most serious criminal problems in analogous, familiar ways. To focus briefly on one of these states, the government of Guatemala last year identified narcotics trafficking (among other forms of criminality) as a major threat to local and regional institutions and the "consolidation of the democratic system," setting out what it sees as some of the many difficulties faced, to include corruption and a weak military support infrastructure:

> Drug dealers pose the greatest threat to regional stability. These corrupt organizations not only undermine the government's authority but also weaken the social structure of the nation and endanger our national sovereignty. With their enormous economic resources they bribe political figures, buy votes, force [into office] their own political candidates, and have the flexibility to move their operations. . . .
>
> The guerrillas benefit from drug traffic, when their illicit operations are successful. Governmental control has been weakened by corruption, thus aiding drug trafficking. Some positions within the security forces have been appointed using narcotrafficking funds. As a result, governmental attempts to stop drug activities have been frustrated. Governmental officials and security forces rely on the local acceptance of their presence to supply their basic necessities which are, in many instances, completely controlled by the narcotraffickers. In consequence, some security forces are compelled to overlook obvious illicit activities. Those that don't, have found themselves immobilized and dependent on periodic governmental support.[11]

Certainly, the newly established democratic regimes in Eastern Europe and the FSU face analogous problems to those in Guatemala and elsewhere that seem to defy early solution. These problems may be generally characterized as daunting economic and resource constraints; complex political and social problems; enduring ethnic schisms and animosities, weakened national military and security establishments that are in the turmoil of reduction and restructuring programs characterized as "military reform"; the existence of military and security forces that are regarded with suspicion by the general population (and often the elected political leadership as well); and a host of serious transnational security problems—burgeoning international organized crime, narcotics trafficking, terrorism, and serious environmental problems.

In addition, the national and ethnic tensions that already have sparked active conflicts in a number of areas of the FSU and Eastern Europe promise to generate further armed clashes or local wars in the future. Even states in the region not directly involved face a real or potential flood of political and economic refugees. Legal and illegal immigration—in the view of many security officials in the regions affected—have facilitated the operation of organized criminal activities through establishing ethnic populations bases where criminal elements may hide and operate.

In short, many states around the world that are facing crises of one sort of another have become, in effect, laboratories for the development of the most pernicious forms of organized crime, where the interest of local, regional, and international criminal groups has coincided with the appearance of disrupted economies, requirements for hard currency, and reduced law enforcement effectiveness. In most of the states so affected, there has been no shortage of countermeasures discussed, legislation offered, and cooperation proposed. Nonetheless, most states are faced with a plethora of economic and political problems that they must address; severe resource constraints that limit the training and equipping of effective law enforcement organizations; and levels of institutional corruption that undermine those anti-crime measures actually put into effect. The presence or threat of armed conflict serves as a catalyst for the development of organized crime and fuels its growth.

Organized Crime and Its Association with Conflict

Criminal enterprise, to perhaps a greater extent than in the past, is often closely associated with insurgencies, terrorism, and ethnonational conflict. Indeed, new or reinvigorated centers of interethnic conflict, insurgency, and various forms of terrorism have acquired an organized crime content that in some cases blurs the distinction between political and criminal agendas. In addition, heightened levels of political, criminal, and random violence beyond the capabilities of conventional law enforcement to handle have made the crime problem a greater daily concern for citizens in a number of nations around the world.

In a number of areas of the world, organized criminal groups have acquired armed components that can hold areas, protect criminal enterprise, and resist government interference. This is the case, for example, in some regions of Mexico, where armed trafficking (or insurgent) groups in states like Guerrero have long been able to successfully challenge government control over drug and arms trafficking areas.[12] The Shan "Opium" Army of Khun Sa in the heart of Southeast Asia's Golden Triangle is an extreme case in point,[13] while the armed militias of drug traffickers and contrabanders like Tajikistan's regionally notorious Abdulamon

Lyombekov("Alyosha the Hunchback")—who controlled substantial opium trafficking routes leading from Afghanistan to Russia and the West—are now as common a feature in areas of the former Soviet Union as they are in other areas of the world.[14]

French unconventional warfare specialist Roger Trinquier, drawing on his experience in Algeria in the 1950s and applying it to future conflict, judged that "even a band of gangsters, lacking any political ideology at all, but without scruples and determined to employ the same methods (as terrorist groups using bombs, assassinations, and terror), could constitute a grave danger" to stability and government control. As has become so apparent five years into the post–Cold War period where such gangs and groupings are proliferating, the development of effective countermeasures is lagging well behind the growth of the problem. The consequence of inadequate response can be especially great. As Trinquier also assessed, timid, inadequate police operations would "fail pitifully" and only "encourage a goodly number of adventurers to team up with the original outlaws, who will rapidly develop into rebels."[15] As things have developed in a number of regions of the world, the opposite has turned out to be true as well—"rebels" have increasingly turned to crime after their defeat, negotiated termination of conflict, or the lure of criminal profits. Several dimensions of crime and conflict are worth examining briefly.

Crime, Insurgency, Civil War, and Ethnonational Conflict

Historically, crime has been a particularly close companion of unconventional warfare in its various forms, and there has often been difficulty in distinguishing among the various criminal and political agendas present. A number of diverse groups and regions—some well known and others less so—serve to illustrate the analogous ways organized crime has become a component of regional conflict.

In this regard, World War II India's "Quit India Movement" (of the Indian National Congress) presented the British with major law and order problems at a time when most forces were otherwise engaged. Following successful British efforts to repress the movement, however, dacoit (bandit) gangs formed from the remnants began to appear, which subsequently formed alliances with the socialist Azad Dastas organization. It soon became difficult to distinguish whether actions carried out by this alliance were criminally or politically motivated, a feature of much subsequent conflict in India.[16] Indeed, more than half a century later, the emergence of a "drug mafia" in the northeastern Indian state of Nagaland has become closely associated with the insurgency there and now combines criminal enterprise with a separatist goal.[17] Islamic insurgent groups in the state of Jammu and Kashmir are also heavily involved in drug trafficking to support their activities and for profit.[18]

In parts of Latin America, "the transition from politicized armed struggle to banditry" and the clear existence of "guerrilla-bandits" and "political bandits" in the more distant and recent past has been well documented.[19] Colombia is a particularly good case in point, where the distinction between guerrillas and bandits has often been an ambiguous one.[20]

In addition to its premier role as a center for narcotics trafficking by the cocaine and heroin cartels, Colombia also faces two major insurgencies, the National Liberation Army (*Ejercito de Liberacion Nacional*—ELN) and the Revolutionary Armed Forces of Colombia (*Fuerzas Armadas Revolucionarias de Colombia*—FARC). It is the Colombian government's view that the guerrillas have become increasingly involved in organized crime to include—but far from limited to—narcotics trafficking. As one Colombian government minister put it:

> We think the guerrillas have forsaken their self-attributed ideals of struggling for the redemption of the lower classes. We are in the presence of a large, profitable criminal organization that takes advantage of every mechanism of the capitalist economy and that has abandoned any revolutionary ideals its members might have had in the past.[21]

In other words, the insurgents have become largely criminal groupings rather than ideologically motivated revolutionaries. Although some analysts would judge this view to be overdrawn, considerable data have been mustered by government spokesmen to support their assertions.[22]

The most profitable insurgent criminal enterprise, according to the Colombian police, military, and government, is the per gram charges for coca leaf, paste, and processors.[23] Not much is known about the Colombian insurgents' relationship with poppies and heroin production, there are only some rough calculations that indicate this business is growing at an accelerated rate and, in terms of income, already may represent for the FARC one third of that illicit income received from coca.[24] The FARC is judged by some Colombians to garner close to 70 percent of its income between coca and poppies.

In Europe, the nine to ten fronts of Basque (ETA) separatists largely finance their terrorist activity and other support needs through "revolutionary taxes" obtained through extortion and ransoms.[25] The Irish Republican Army (IRA) makes heavy use of tax fraud and extortion activities (as well as more overt fundraising to include donations from sympathizers in North America).[26] The IRA's very substantial, institutionalized involvement in a variety of organized criminal activity has been detailed by law enforcement specialists, as has the extensive involvement in racketeering of Irish Loyalist (Protestant) paramilitary organizations. The bitter secular rivalries, however, have not prevented cooperation among rival Catholic and Protestant paramilitaries in the criminal sphere.[27]

The Kurdish Worker's Party (PKK), operating inside and outside of Turkey, has the aim of setting up an independent Kurdish state in the region.[28] Criminal and terrorist charges associated with the PKK over the last year include obtaining large sums of money from narcotics trafficking in Europe and the Middle East;[29] producing counterfeit Turkish banknotes in cooperation with the Italian Mafia, for distribution principally in the larger cities of western Turkey;[30] producing large revenues through the extortion of money from the 130,000 to 150,000 Turkish workers residing in that country;[31] cooperating with Armenian terrorist organizations like the Armenian Secret Army for the Liberation of Armenia (ASALA) and establishing bases in the former Soviet republic of Armenia;[32] and attacking Turkish targets in the German cities of Frankfurt, Karlsruhe, and Mainz and in Brussels, Belgium among other locations.[33]

In the former USSR, the growth of every dimension of organized crime is well enough known to negate the need for lengthy discussion here. Ethnic Russian (and Ukrainian and Belorussian) criminals clearly constitute the majority of the region's criminal population. It should be stressed, however, that a number of the 3,500–4,000 organized criminal groups that existed in the Soviet Union in its closing days,[34] and the 2,500 to 3,000 groups estimated to exist in Russia at the mid-point of the 1990s are "ethnic criminal groups formed on the basis of national communities. . . . "[35] Indeed, one of the criteria used to classify organized crime groups in much of the vast Central Eurasian region has been by ethnic affiliation.[36] Because of their ethnonational content, affiliations and location, these groups have become actors in the various centers of interethnic conflict. Security service representatives in the former Soviet Union judge that criminal groups variously provide material support to, encourage, or simply take advantage of the disruptions and opportunities presented by the various ethnic "hot spots" and tensions. Three examples illustrate this view.

In the Caucasus, an array of active Georgian, Azeri, Armenian, Chechen and other "mafias" share the region with an equally impressive collection of "armies," "national guards," and provisional armed groups ostensibly associated with states, factions, and criminal organizations—but which is which is far from evident in most cases.[37] Similarly, Central Asia's rapidly developing status as a world-class drug transit, cultivation, and export region (as well as an arms trafficking center) is closely linked to factional conflict there.[38] The view that "it is not just coincidence . . . that ethnic conflicts in Central Asia, as a rule, flared up during the opium poppy harvesting season." has been expressed by more than one spokesman.[39] A third example is provided by continuing confrontations in the former Soviet republic of Moldova, which are characterized by an intermixing of ethnonational conflict and criminal activity, replete with charges and countercharges of corruption and crime among all participants involved.[40]

Criminal activity in Moldova is widespread and profitable and includes drug and arms trafficking.[41]

In the former Yugoslavia, ethnonational conflicts and organized criminal activities have merged in ways that seem little appreciated by those international representatives engaged in the peacekeeping and conflict resolution processes there. The past, lingering, and potential conflicts in the former Yugoslavia have had many consequence for organized criminal activity of all types, to include in particular the closer association of many parties in the disputes with organized crime. As in other regions around the world, a combination of pressing military requirements, economic disarray, the disruption of existing institutions and organizations, expanded opportunities for many types of criminal endeavors, and the potential for enormous criminal profits, have all appeared at the same time. Because these developments have provided the opportunity to observe just how rapidly organized criminal activity can grow and mutate, they deserve a brief review.

Yugoslav criminals, of course, were quite active in a variety of regional smuggling activities well before the state began its slide to dissolution and active conflict. Smuggling and banditry in many forms had been a traditional feature of the area long before there had been a Yugoslav state, and the reemergence of banditry and the activities of "brigand groupings"—with modern twists—recalls the eighteenth and nineteenth century bandits and groups who operated throughout Bosnia, Dalmatia, Montenegro, Serbia, and elsewhere.[42] Indeed, E. J. Hobsbawm's Balkan "haiduk" model of primitive, cruel, rebel bandits has made a strong comeback in modern, more lethal variants.[43] Lengthy coastlines and borders together with a location along traditional smuggling routes continue, to guarantee Yugoslavia a prominent place in the illegal movement of goods of all types.

The accelerated development of a brisk trade in drugs and arms jointly took place hand-in-hand with the start of shooting conflicts in late June 1991.[44] Local mafias in every former province cut out territory for their criminal activities and developed international ties as well. A feature of these groups has been their ethnic orientation, centered on Croats, Serbs, Bosnians, Albanians, Montenegrans, Macedonians, and others. The war also created, in the words of one especially knowledgeable observer in the region, "a wonderful opportunity for all sorts of criminals in uniform."[45]

In Serbia, the often-violent random and mafia criminal activities in Belgrade run the gamut of crime, including drug trafficking. Criminal groups increasingly began to compete for spheres of influence and pursued in particular their extortion and protection rackets as law enforcement efforts unraveled amidst the general economic and societal disarray generated by continuing regional turmoil.[46] Ethnic Albanians were singled out for their potential involvement in organized crime by Serbian spokesmen because of their "patriarchal ties to one another."[47] In a relatively short time, some observers pointed to a national "psychosis" where high-profit state crime (the sale of oil and other high-priced commodities) existed with drug and arms trafficking, protection and extortion, robberies, and a host of other criminal actions committed by a variety of players.[48] The Serbian leadership—widely accused of direct involvement in these activities—may be among the most egregious offenders.

Montenegro, which remains aligned in a federal "Yugoslav" state with Serbia, is a hub of smuggling, particularly along the Adriatic coast. In addition to the trafficking in profitable items like tobacco, as well as the major commodities of heroin, arms, and ammunition,[49] new banking and commercial establishments have been set up in Montenegro (and elsewhere) to facilitate the illegal trading. One specialist in Belgrade—speaking about the role of Montenegran and other organized criminal activity in the conflicts—noted that "states in the territory of the former Yugoslavia are accepting crime as a source of funding and emerging as partners of the underworld."[50]

Representatives of the "Croatian diaspora" around the world are repeatedly accused by the Serbs, in particular, of undertaking arms purchasing and drug trafficking deals in behalf of the Croatian state and for personal profit as well.[51] Macedonia, Slovenia, and Bosnia have all developed mafias and profitable criminal trafficking that have benefited or taken advantage of conflict and tension in the region.

Bosnia remains a continuing center of active conflict and as a consequence of its geographic location, has been particularly hard hit by the arms embargo, local transportation blockades, and the besieged status of Muslim forces and populations in particular. Materiel support to Bosnian Muslims from Islamic states abroad has been widely rumored, but organized crime seems to have been of far greater consequence. Even with the hardships, atrocities, and extreme military difficulties, criminal organizations and elements are believed to be actively involved with influencing the course of operations, as will be discussed below.

Ex-Soldiers and Criminality

One of the historic consequences of the demobilization of armies upon the end of a war, breakup of an empire, or other event that removes soldiers from armies faster than they can be absorbed is the growth of crime and banditry. Examples from the past are numerous and include the most diverse countries and regions.[52] In virtually all cases, ex-soldiers and deserters have been "natural material for banditry" because of reduced community ties and prospects and their possession of skills that lend themselves to criminal enterprise and armed action or coercion.[53] Like mercenaries, their motivations then and now have been a combination of money, political cause, religious conviction, and adventure.[54]

More recently, the phenomenon of soldiers turning to crime or banditry has been observed in El Salvador, where both demobilized army members (coming from a force reduced by one half) and members of the Farabundo Martí National Liberation Front (FMLN) have engaged in organized criminal activity of various types to include kidnappings, robberies, and murder.[55] Analogous developments have occurred elsewhere in Central America, Nicaragua being a particularly good case in point.[56] The prospects for analogous developments in Peru remain a concern as well, where scattered Sendero Luminoso and MRTA factions have turned increasingly to crime, and Peruvian armed forces reductions may also put large numbers of personnel at loose ends. Large numbers of discharged Cuban military and security forces may pose analogous problems for the region when the Castro regime is dissolved or removed.

In Eastern Europe and the former Soviet Union, discharged (and active duty) soldiers and security personnel have become closely associated with a range of criminal enterprise. The active recruitment of discharged soldiers by organized crime groups in Russia is now common, while former security service personnel throughout the East European and Central Eurasia region have been linked to criminal groups with international affiliations. The numerous examples from current and past times, and other parts of the world, all suggest that shrinking or disrupted military establishments will continue to provide a recruiting base for organized crime.

Crime and Peacekeeping

Because areas to which peacekeepers are sent are often centers of linked crime and conflict, deployed peacekeepers confront criminal endeavors and their complications along with their other missions. Multilateral and unilateral peacekeeping efforts have been marked often by the presence or allegations of corruption and crime on the part of peacekeepers, a development that is the consequence of opportunity, flawed selection criteria, or the endemic corruption of the forces deployed. Diversion of resources and smuggling by peacekeeping personnel are among the most frequent charges.

Russian troops deployed beyond Russian borders and in areas of ethnic conflict or civil war, for example, are judged by Russian military spokesmen to be in a "special risk zone" insofar as their involvement in organized crime is concerned. In the Central Asian state of Tajikistan—formerly a Soviet republic— Russian military and border guard units are engaged in peacekeeping activities aimed at controlling a civil war involving the Tajik government, internal opposition groups, and militant Islamic partisans from neighboring Afghanistan. As noted earlier, however, the area is also the center of opium poppy cultivation and trafficking, as well as a central transit point for heroin and other opium products leaving Afghanistan. In

this environment, Russian troops have been charged with deep involvement in the drug trade, moving opium products to Russia aboard military
transportation.[57]

Charges of war–profiteering and drug-trafficking have been leveled at
French peacekeepers in Sarajevo. These are two problems that abound in
the area. A number of Ukrainian troops had been sent home from the same
area for involvement in heroin trafficking.[58] In Somalia, where petty crime
of all types abounded, the more systematized smuggling of the widely used
drug khat under ostensible United Nations (UN) protection has been the
object of media attention, with Somali warlords thought to earn considerable revenue from khat trafficking.[59]

Dealing with a criminal environment characterized by high levels of
crime or thievery also presents special problems ranging from physical
security to active countermeasures. In Somalia, the problems encountered
by U.S. military planners in dealing with rampant "thievery" were of such
a level that they required special attention. They also generated a number
of lessons for future deployments in humanitarian assistance or peacekeeping operations where U.S. forces can expect to encounter conditions similar
to those found in Somalia, and where special attention to civil affairs,
psychological operations (PSYOP), and military police components may be
needed.[60]

Crime and Conflict Termination

There are a number of instances in which criminal interests seem to have
complicated or prevented the termination of an active conflict. In most
cases, it appears that the potential disruption of lucrative criminal ventures—which could be sustained only in the midst of conflict—has sparked
the opposition of criminal interests that were parties to the conflict or merely
its beneficiaries.

In Colombia, the conclusion some analysts reached is that profit has
become far more important to the Colombian guerrillas than ideology.
Peace negotiations may become more difficult because "if the FARC and
ELN effectively have converted themselves into such profitable criminal
enterprises, how could a process of reincorporation appear attractive to
them?"[61] Other Colombian spokesmen have suggested that the loss of
ideological vigor and a dependence on "sharing the spoils" to maintain
group cohesiveness is harming guerrilla effectiveness and recruiting.[62]

In Central Asia, where drug-trafficking groups appear to exercise considerable power, one commentator has suggested that "the rivalry of
criminal clans for control of the sale of narcotics may in turn become a
serious obstacle for a peaceful settlement of the Tajikistan conflict."[63] It is
widely believed—with more than a little justification—that the conflict is
actively manipulated by drug-trafficking interests. As a consequence, in the

view of one Russian observer, "striving to regulate the Tajik conflict by purely political means will encounter resistance from the opposition, which is fed by money from smart narcotics operators."[64]

The former Yugoslavia, as is in so many instances of intertwined crime and conflict, seems to exemplify suspicions about the role criminal interests are playing in shaping or prolonging conflict. Indeed, the situation in the former Yugoslavia reminded one Russian commentator of a torturous Middle East conflict. As he put it:

> The situation is mindful of the civil war in Lebanon, where Shiites, Sunnis, and Maronite Christians in conflict with one another have continued to cooperate in the narcotics trade. *Money is more important than war and interethnic hatred.*[65]

As noted earlier, there are considerable indications that senior Serbian officials have taken advantage of the criminal opportunities available amid Yugoslavia's troubles. There is also a popular belief that the conflict is deliberately prolonged in order to sustain proceeds from profiteering. As one Serbian source noted about the political leadership in this regard, "they are not only in a position to take advantage of the war, but they are also in a position to maintain it 'so long as it brings in income.'"[66]

The ease which unknown parties—criminal and paramilitary—can disrupt or even end humanitarian or peacekeeping efforts has been demonstrated time and again in recent years. Shots fired at relief aircraft or casualties inflicted by sniper fire can bring UN activities to a halt, as occurred in mid-March 1995 in Bosnia.[67] Suspicions have long abounded that such actions are committed by criminals seeking to ensure high prices, captive markets, and unhindered criminal opportunities. Clearly, the impact of crime on the Bosnian conflict has been particularly visible to UN peacekeepers and Bosnians alike. In early 1993, the then-Chief of Staff of the Army of Bosnia-Herzegovina Sefer Halilovic pointed to the existence of "an assorted criminal-political mob" composed of Serbian, Croatian, and Muslim members. He charged that even Muslim criminals had an interest in keeping Sarajevo under siege in order to ensure criminal profits.[68] Such charges have been echoed frequently and heard in other states of the former Yugoslavia, the former Soviet Union, and far more distant areas as well.

Crime and Postconflict Stability

As noted, organized crime develops rapidly in areas where the social and political order are in disarray, and where police and security institutions are ineffective. This is the case for many states following the end of a conflict or some other crisis. The cases of El Salvador, Peru, Panama, and Guatemala were mentioned specifically in this regard, but there are many other illustrations as well. Crises promoting organized crime do not have to be well-developed shooting conflicts, as the proliferation of crime in parts of Eastern Europe and the former USSR illustrates. Similarly, Venezuela has been subject for some years now to simmering tensions, riots, a strong military coup potential, and severe economic problems. In this environment there has been an increase in violent crime and other criminality. A two-dozen person murder rate for a weekend in Caracas is thought now to be relatively light.[69]

Once organized crime has become established—and particularly when there are interregional or international criminal linkages—creating or rebuilding strong national institutions is a far more complex undertaking. This is being illustrated in the former Yugoslavia, where crime promises to be an enduring problem long after "peace" has returned—if indeed it does. In this regard, the prospects for postconflict crime were likened by one spokesman to back-to-back motion pictures:

> This is a double feature. The war film is nearly over and the crime film is just beginning. We know from the beginning who the murderer is, but it is not clear who is on the side of the law, who will be caught, and for whom we are rooting.[70]

As another specialist from the region put it when considering the prospects for dealing with the enduring consequences of criminality: "The mess created by this war will be so huge that it will take decades to sort things out."[71]

There are many countries dealing with active conflicts and sustained crises—or their aftermaths—that could characterize their problems in this way. The problem of institutional corruption is a most important component of restoring government effectiveness and legitimacy. Several dimensions of this will be examined below.

Crime and Institutional Corruption

Institutional corruption is one of the most serious manifestations and consequences of organized crime. It undermines the very basis of state structure, effectiveness, and legitimacy, while providing criminal enterprise broad opportunities to grow and develop. Sustained high levels of corruption result in even long-established states being governed by what one observer termed a "natural selection of thieves and scoundrels" that ultimately inflicts severe wounds on the affected government.[72] In Mexico, where corruption has long been endemic, charges that the country has become a "narco-democracy" in which drug traffickers are the "promoters" and "even pillars" of Mexican "socioeconomic growth and development" are neither uncommon nor implausible.[73]

Colombia, with world renowned levels of corruption, has frequently been characterized as a narco-democracy as well. Allegations against Colombian President Samper for accepting Cali cartel drug money in his campaign only constitute the most recent, highest level illustration of Colombia's real and perceived corruption problems.[74] Chechen President Djokhar Dudayev gave a seemingly candid response when questioned about corruption in the Chechen government in 1992 after a year in power. He noted that it was a widespread attitude among educated Chechens in government that "anyone who did not take bribes was regarded as God's fool."[75] The recent and continuing series of corruption investigations, indictments, and trials in Italy—including the indictment of former Italian Prime Minister Giuliano Andreotti and the conviction for fraud and corruption of former Prime Minister Bettino Craxi—have given more definite form to what was long alleged about the Italian Mafia's penetration of government.[76]

Corruption raises special problems for security planners when it fundamentally affects the military and law enforcement establishments of governments with which we are engaged. A number of military and security establishments on every continent have been associated with—or accused of—narcotics and arms trafficking together with other forms of criminality. One particularly troublesome aspect of institutional corruption is the continuing penetration of military and security establishments in both Eastern Europe and the former Soviet Union by criminal enterprise. This growing criminality reflects the overall high levels of corruption and crime permeating the region and provides a disturbing view of how rapidly crime can consume institutions.

In 1994 official Russian estimates of organized criminal penetration of state institutions assessed that organized criminal groups controlled some 40,000 state and private organizations, including hundreds of state enterprises, joint-stock companies, cooperatives, banks, and markets. Senior Russian law enforcement figures also estimated that 2,500 or more organized criminal groups existed in Russia alone, many with international connections and structures that are increasingly sophisticated.[77] Other new states in the region are subject to analogous problems.[78] Indeed, an explosion in the variety, intensity, and scope, of "military crime" has justified the designation of "mafias in uniform" for some regional military establishments.[79]

Criminality and corruption in the Russian military and security forces— key institutions of a state occupying a high priority in U.S. foreign policy— are illustrative of the progress of "uniformed crime" generally. The Russian armed forces—whose pitiful performance in Chechnya continues to highlight publicly its profound lack of military capability—had been repeatedly wounded by force reductions, withdrawals, restructuring, budget cuts, and profoundly reduced popular and official status since its official creation in May 1992.[80] As a consequence of this—and the dissolute legacy of seven decades of Soviet power—the Russian armed forces have also been pushed to near–disintegration by high levels of military criminality and corruption that are now embedded in the army at every level. The frequent small–scale pilfering of unit equipment and supplies by military personnel that characterized Soviet garrison life for decades in just a few years has become a sophisticated, multidimensional series of criminal enterprises.

Russian military crime is now directly associated with the Russian Ministry of Defense and other senior staffs; transportation, construction, and logistic organizations; combined arms units and commands; technically oriented and highly trained aviation and air defense formations; military research organizations; and military-educational components. Individual military criminals range from general and field grade officers to the newest conscripts.[81]

Security service corruption—within the Ministry of Internal Affairs (MVD) and the successor organization to the KGB—parallels that in the military establishment. By the early 1990s, some 20,000 MVD militia (police) were proved to be cooperating with the various mafias in Russia, and the situation has deteriorated since. As one 1994 appraisal by a Russian presidential analysis group put it, "bandit formations have informers everywhere in the militia organs, traffic police, and banks." The authors further judged that "the growth of organized crime which is intertwined with the Internal Affairs Ministry [MVD] organs and local executive authorities, threatens Russia's political and economic development and creates real conditions for national socialists to come to power."[82]

As 1995 progressed, poorly paid, badly housed, and demoralized Russian military forces at home and abroad are deeply involved in criminal activities. Domestically, the widespread "commercialization" of key military components like the Central Military Transportation Directorate, Military Transport Aviation, Military Trade Directorate, and Military Construction Directorate in an effort to generate operational revenues or meet other military support requirements, is bringing Russian military personnel into a host of criminal ventures including close linkages with organized crime groups outside the military.[83] Military financial crimes and schemes involve a spectrum of banks and financial organizations, real and dummy corporations, so-called joint ventures with foreign partners, and overseas money laundering schemes that in the past would more readily be associated with Latin American drug cartels than a military establishment.[84]

Among the most recent examples of controversy centering on the diversion of military resources is the question of how armed groups in Chechnya acquired such large stocks of arms. The intensity of fighting in Chechnya suggests that Chechen stockpiles were substantial. Although the existence of large Chechen arms inventories is presented by some Russian govern-ment officials as a consequence of Chechen looting and stealing from Russian military depots in Chechnya, other voices assert that the arms were sold by Russian officials instead. More specifically, Russian presidential advisers Emil Pain and Arkady Popov assess in a February 1995 report that Chechen President Dudayev acquired arms by buying them from "smart traders in military uniforms," and that other criminal actions by officials in Moscow may have taken place as well.[85]

Illustrations of military crime in and out of Russia abound, and ties with criminals abroad have been in evidence for some time.[86] For example, a large Russian emigré criminal infrastructure with links to the departed Russian military has been left behind in Germany following the August 1994 withdrawal of Russian troops there.[87] In Central Asia, Russian military involvement in the drug trade has sparked charges that the "main route of transit of Afghan opium is . . . the military transport aviation of Russian troops based in Tajikistan."[88]

Overall, amid a society and state institutions that are increasingly under-mined by crime, the Russian military establishment itself is faced with a combination of powerful criminal incentives, opportunities, and resources that are facilitating the development of institutionalized military-criminal organizations. This situation raises profound questions about the stability, motivations, and reliability of the Russian armed forces. Russian military performance in Chechnya—to include the most severe, continuing viola-tions of humans rights—points to an institution disintegrating rapidly.

The crime and corruption faced by other military and security institu-tions in the FSU and parts of Eastern Europe suggest that in some of these states, at least, organized crime could have an impact analogous to that in the Russia armed forces. More broadly, however, institutional corruption is a threat around the world. Its impact in the military and security arena, in particular, is a serious and growing threat to democratization, economic development, and stability.

Conclusion

Organized crime is closely associated with other security problems and goals that the United States has described as paramount. Organized crimi-nal groups—often cohesive, well financed, internationally or regionally linked, and with access to new technologies that enhance their effective-ness—have demonstrated a capability to thrive amid the turmoil that so far has defined the post–Cold War world. Crime threatens the national security of every state but is especially disruptive and damaging in areas where state institutions are fragile, economic resources limited, and interethnic ten-sions high. Thus, many new democracies, or other states dealing with multiple internal or external challenges, have proved particularly vulnerable to the penetration and influence of criminal groups.

In addition, there is a deepening association of organized crime with conflict. This association is reflected in the high criminal content found in insurgencies, ethnonational conflict, and separatist movements in many parts of the world. In many cases, criminal agendas and personal profit have come to play a more central role in these conflicts than political or ideological goals. The long-standing historic phenomenon of ex-soldiers turning to crime has been widely evident in recent years, a development that has more effectively fused criminal and paramilitary groups.

Organized crime has in some respects become a factor in concluding conflict, or sustaining the peace in the wake of a cease–fire or accord. Because the goal of some combatants may be more criminal in nature than political, criminal enterprise has the potential for frustrating international efforts to broker lasting political solutions. The sustained growth of organized crime in states emerging from war or conflict—or facing other internal difficulties—shapes the desirability or form of security assistance provided, peacekeeping or humanitarian assistance programs instituted, and postconflict stability efforts undertaken.

The extraordinary criminal penetration of crime into state institutions and private enterprise has in some cases accelerated in the early post–Cold War period. The proliferation of corrupted officials in the former Soviet Union and Eastern Europe has in some cases exceeded the more familiar institutional corruption observed in Latin America, Asia, and elsewhere. The "criminalization" of military and security establishments has been particularly harmful, because it is these very institutions that are expected to provide the environment in which democratic reform and economic growth is to take place.

The implications for U.S. national security are manifold and particularly notable in their military, law enforcement, and foreign policy dimensions. In particular, U.S. military "operations other than war" (OOTW) promise to be a major focus for U.S. armed forces planning and employment in the decade ahead. As conceived by defense planners, OOTW constitute joint, interagency military-political undertakings involving armed forces, law enforcement, foreign policy, economic, and other organizations. The range of OOTW activities includes support for insurgencies and counterinsurgencies (a number of which have growing organized crime associations and activities); combating terrorism (with terrorist groups now often supported by criminal enterprise to include an expanding narcoterrorism dimension in some regions); peacekeeping operations (where organized crime represents a major consideration and potentially disruptive influence in conflict areas where U.S. and UN peacekeeping and peace enforcement contingents may be engaged; counterdrug operations (against that organized criminal activity most often characterized as the major threat to U.S. national security, values, and institutions); and a host of other contingencies that include security assistance, humanitarian assistance, population control, and disaster relief (where the illegal diversion of resources, criminal violence, and other criminal undertakings undermine the effectiveness or intent of U.S. programs).

As a consequence of the criminal dimensions of OOTW, international organized crime must become an increasingly integral consideration in broadened "threat assessments" in specific states and regions. This necessarily includes the physical and operational security of U.S. military bases abroad and assessing the effectiveness and reliability of states in regional security roles (e.g., Andean Ridge countries, Eastern European states, and states of the former Soviet Union.) This is true as well for assessing the type and quality of U.S.-foreign law enforcement cooperation and interaction deemed desirable or most effective, and levels of support and humanitarian assistance provided to states in many areas of the world. Shifting developments in terrorism and drug, arms, and strategic material trafficking should be similarly addressed in broadened threat assessments as well.

Planning and executing post-conflict activities clearly would benefit from considering the many organized crime dimensions involved, a view supported by a number of the situations discussed above. Organized crime considerations may require more attention in overall "campaign planning" for foreign security assistance programs involving military, law enforcement, and other U.S. Government agencies supporting U.S. policies abroad. These include in particular a determination of how organized crime may affect regional security, the strengthening of democratic institutions, the support of economic and social progress, curtailing drug cultivation and trafficking, and other such continuing U.S. goals.

It is evident in many areas of the world that regional and international organized crime is increasingly influencing the stability, effectiveness, and reliability of foreign regimes and institutions. As a consequence, organized crime is clearly a potential factor in any decisions regarding the type and quantities of foreign aid that should be provided; the structure of the "Country Team" in U.S. embassies and the kinds of support provided in and out of the host country; and decisions associated with U.S. immigration policy and screening processes among other considerations. Government and private attention to the physical security of U.S. business enterprises abroad will continue to be an issue, with higher levels of official corruption and bribery already emerging as factors in business decisionmaking in new areas. Electronic and computer security issues, along with other technological innovations, are facilitating industrial espionage and other criminal agendas, while a range of financial crimes (money laundering, funding of criminal activities, counterfeiting, etc.) with links worldwide through the international financial community are evident even in relatively backward countries.

Overall, the need to consider the influence of organized crime as an integral part of planning and policy formulation for a number of political, economic, and military issues has grown in importance. There are new intelligence requirements generated by organized crime, many of them being addressed by intelligence and law enforcement agencies. They include the collection and analysis of criminal intelligence and the new challenges posed by developments like worldwide electronic computer linkages and the acquisition of black and gray market technologies with criminal applications.[89]

It should be emphasized, however, that organized crime in its ethnic- and conflict-associated variants has generated special requirements for military and law enforcement personnel with regional and cultural skills. Although the day may have passed when, as at the turn of the last century, United States navy officers "who happened to be cruising in the China Sea knew the difference between a Macao *lorcha* and a Canton junk, and in the Sulu Sea never mistook a Moro proa for a Visayan *Banca*," there nevertheless is a requirement for engaged personnel to better understand the context and perspectives of criminal groups and armed factions that now shape many conflict areas.[90]

U.S. policies and assistance should clearly be aimed at strengthening state structures and preventing organized crime and accompanying corruption from gaining a foothold. It is necessary also—in light of the inroads that crime has made and is making into state structures—to consider what the proper policy should be toward states with extraordinarily high levels of crime and institutional corruption. This includes carefully balancing U.S. interests, goals, and diplomatic imperatives against the consequences of minimizing or ignoring rampant corruption and its impact on our own programs and international status. The criminal challenge to legitimacy promises to be formidable in every respect.

In this regard—given that many states are dealing with security environments characterized by organized crime groups, ethnic and national paramilitaries bent on plunder and profit, bandits, and pirates—it is worth returning to St. Augustine and critically considering how best to defeat, win over, or otherwise deal with modern-day variants of the pirate captured by Alexander the Great in the fourth century B.C.:

> The answer which a captured pirate gave to Alexander the Great was perfectly accurate and correct. When that king asked the man what he meant by infesting the sea, he boldly replied: "What do you mean by warring on the whole world. I do my fighting on a tiny ship, and they call me a pirate; you do yours with a large fleet, and they call you a Commander."[91]

Neutralizing organized criminals and their widening circle of associates—who have the same view of state power as Alexander's pirate—may present even more difficult challenges than those faced when security policies were formulated largely on the basis of an ideologically divided world dominated by two superpowers.

Notes

1. "Organized crime" has been defined variously in the United States and abroad, with a number of new democracies currently grappling with their own views of what constitutes a rapidly maturing and expanding criminality that is increasingly structured and sophisticated. A recent, succinct U.S. effort—that is in close accord with those used by most Western specialists and will guide the discussions in this chapter—defines organized crime as "a more or less formal structure that exists over time and is directed towards a common purpose by a recognizable leadership operating outside the law, quite often based on family or ethnic identity, and prepared to use violence or other means to promote and protect common interests and objectives." See Roy Godson and Wm. J. Olson, International Organized Crime: Emerging Threat To US Security, (Washington, D.C.: National Strategy Information Center, 1993), pp. 3–7.

2. St. Augustine, *The City of God*, ed. Vernon J. Bourke and trans. Gerald G. Walsh, Demetrius B. Zema, Grace Monahan, and Daniel J. Honan (Garden City, New York: Doubleday and Company, Inc., 1958), p. 88. St. Augustine was addressing the linkage of "justice" and "sovereignty" by raising the question: "In the absence of justice, what is sovereignty but organized brigandage?"

3. Historian E. J. Hobsbawm's review of "social banditry" over the centuries in his still-pertinent study *Bandits*, (London: Weidenfeld and Nicolson, 1969) pp.17–18, made this point well. Although Hobsbawm focused principally on one form of banditry, his observations and arguments are extremely useful for assessing more modern forms of the outlaw, guerrilla, or criminal.

4. The U.S. analogy was drawn by a senior State Department official in a presentation delivered to an international conference on organized crime, September 1994, Vienna, Virginia on a nonattribution basis, while an illustrative Russian assessment of the same type was made by a Russian presidential analysis group in the document "Organized Crime and the Prospects of National Socialists Coming to Power in Russia," cited in "Rossiyskaya mafiya sobirayet dos'e na krupnykh chinovnikov i politikov," *Izvestiya*, January 26, 1994.

5. See, for example, Godson and Olson, *International Organized Crime*. In the two years since the publication of this comprehensive assessment of organized crime and its consequences, most specialists would agree that the United States and its friends and allies—despite some limited successes—have lost more ground in countering the development of international organized crime in its many dimensions.

6. This includes the phenomenon of armed gangs formed from former Farabundo Martí National Liberation Front (FMLN) guerrillas and discharged government

soldiers. See, for example, NOTIMEX, 0239 GMT, April 16, 1994, as translated in FBIS–LAT–94–075.

7. Some analysts have postulated that drug profits may similarly undermine Sendero's revolutionary idealism, a process that seems to be underway in the wake of Abimael Guzman's September capture, the arrest or surrender of other Sendero Luminoso leaders, and Peruvian military successes in the field. See Arnaldo Claudio and Stephan K. Stewman, "Peru, Sendero Luminoso, and the Narcotrafficking Alliance," *Low Intensity Conflict and Law Enforcement* 1, no. 3 (Winter 1992): 279–292. For Peruvian views of Sendero after Guzman's capture, see the pertinent chapters in Enrique Obando Arbulu, ed., *Nuevas Amenazas a La Seguridad y Relaciones Civiles Militares en un Mundo en Desorden* (Lima: Centro Peruano de Estudios Internacionales, 1994), especially Carlos Tapia's "La subvercion en el Peru, la situacion actual," pp. 141–146.

8. Criminal activities ranging from cattle rustling and illegal border crossings to arms and drug trafficking, for example, have generated a requirement for joint military and police patrols. See Foreign Military Studies Office, "Foreign SOF," *Special Warfare*, Spring 1995, forthcoming.

9. One of numerous examples of this is the arrest of Raul Salinas de Gortari, brother of former President Carlos Salinas de Gortari, for the murder of the politician and then PRI (Institutional Revolutionary Party) Executive Committee Secretary General, Jose Francisco Ruiz Massieu. Early speculation on personal, political, and criminal motives, complex personal and organizational relationships, and broader involvement by narcotraffickers and others—as with the leading PRI presidential candidate, Donald Colosio, murdered earlier— touched virtually every base. Few of the theories seemed totally implausible, given Mexico's extraordinary problems. See Tim Golden, "Salinas' Accused Brother: Mexico Searches for a Motive," *New York Times*, March 2, 1995; and Pierre Thomas and Daniel Williams, "Graft in Mexico a U.S. Dilemma," *Kansas City Star*, March 12, 1995.

10. All India Radio Network, 1530 GMT, July 7, 1994, as cited in JPRS–TDD–94–030–L, p. 55.

11. Departamento de Informacion y Divulgacion del Ejercito (DIDE—Department of Information and Dissemination of the Guatemalan Army, *Threats to the Consolidation of the Democratic System in Guatemala* (Guatemala: DIDE, January, 1994), p. 12, as edited for *Low Intensity Conflict and Law Enforcement*, 3, no. 3 (Winter 1994).

12. See, for example, the article by Roberto Garduno and Juan Jose Guadarrama in *La Jornada*, July 25, 1994, as translated in JPRS–TDD–94–034–L, pp. 12–14, under the JPRS title "Formation of New Guerrilla Group, Drug Cultivation in Guerrero Detailed."

13. Francis W. Belanger, *Drugs, the U.S., and Khun Sa* (Bangkok: Editions Duang Kamol, 1989).

14. See "Drug Runners of the Golden Crescent," *Moscow Times*, February 18, 1995, for an account of Alyosha's activities and his own December 1994 assassination.

15. Ibid., pp. 24–25.

16. Vinita Damodaran, "Azad Dastas and Dacoit Gangs: The Congress and Underground Activity in Bihar, 1942–44," *Modern Asian Studies* 26, no.3 (1992): 417–450.

17. Statesman, September 3, 1992, as translated in JPRS–TDD–92–044–L, p. 26.

18. Presentation and supplemental remarks by a former senior Indian security official to "Radicalism: International Conference on Terrorism and Violence," Office of International Criminal Justice, University of Illinois at Chicago, Chicago Illinois, August 1–3, 1994.

19. See Richard W. Slatta, ed., *Bandidos: The Varieties of Latin American Banditry* (New York: Greenwood Press, 1987), with a useful introduction (pp. 1–9) and conclusions (pp. 191–199) by Richard Slatta.

20. For a particularly interesting illustration of this, see Richard L. Maullin, *The Fall of Dumar Aljure, A Colombian Guerrilla and Bandit*, Rand Corporation Memorandum RM–5750–ISA, November 1968, Santa Monica, California.

21. Interview with Colombian government minister Humberto de la Calle Lombana, et al, on Santa Fe de Bogata *Emisoras Caracol*, 1130 GMT, November 10, 1992, as translated in FBIS–LAT–92–219, p. 31.

22. For an excellent U.S. examination of this topic that sets out indications of guerrilla-drug trafficking linkages, see Geoffrey B. Demarest, "Narcotics Trafficking and the Colombian Military," forthcoming in *High Intensity Crime—Low Intensity Conflict*, published by the Office of International Criminal Justice, University of Illinois at Chicago. Additionally, in the view of a British Petroleum security officer assigned to Colombia, the guerrillas are deeply involved in organized criminal activity but still use the old ideological approaches and revolutionary idealism to recruit new members. Discussion between the author and BP representative, Miami, Florida, February 1993.

More specifically, the arrest of the ELN finance minister in north central Colombia in early 1992 and the recovery of computer records and documents detailed ELN money-making operations throughout northeastern Colombia that included a list of ransom payments and victims, extortion schemes involving businesses and individuals, and an assessment of guerrilla front expenses. Colombian authorities also claimed to have intercepted FARC secretariat mail, seized documents, and debriefed a number of defectors and collaborators. All of this documentation was said to reveal an extraordinary amount of information on FARC and ELN financing, and indicated that the two guerrilla groups had become the "largest, best organized, and most profitable criminal activity in the country."   Further, the Colombian authorities determined a close correlation between the deployment of the various guerrilla fronts and the centers of economic enterprise of one form or another, especially oil, gold, coal, bananas, coca, and—most recently—poppies. Guerrilla deployment shifted to these areas where revenues were greater. Today the most active and belligerent guerrillas occupy the petroleum zones of Arauca, Casanare, Huila and Barrancabermeja; the gold zones of western and northwestern Antioquia; the coal zones of Cesar; the coca zones of the Caqueta, the Meta, the Sierra Nevada, the Putumayo, and the poppy–growing areas of the Huila, the Tolima, Narino and Cauca. In addition, the FARC allegedly intends to take over the land abandoned by the demobilized Popular Liberation Army (Ejercito Popular de Liberacion—EPL) in the Uraba banana area. See "El gran negocio de la guerrilla," Semana, July 7–14, 1992, no. 531, pp. 26–29; and Arnaldo Claudio, "Heroin—the Colombian Cartels Diversify," *Low Intensity Conflict and Law Enforcement* 1, no. 1 (Summer 1992): 3–13, for more discussion of these issues.

23. Ibid. See also Santa Fe de Bogata INRAVISION Television Cadena 1, 1630 GMT, September 7, 1992, as translated in JPRS–TDD–92–038–L, p. 18, for a discussion of the FARC's alleged drug trafficking involvement in the eastern plains region of Colombia; and *El Tiempo*, November 16, 1992, as translated in JPRS–TDD–92–048–L, p. 9, for a reported FARC and ELN role in protecting coca and poppy crops in 10 Colombian Departments. See also, Arnulfo Barroso Watson, "'Police Source' Says FARC Owns Coca Plantations in Darien," *El Panama America*, November 28, 1993, as translated in JPRS–TDD–93–048–L, p. 17.

24. "El gran negocio," p. 30.

25. Michel Demelin, "ETA Money Laundered in Switzerland," *Le Figaro*, May 16–17, 1992, as translated in JPRS–TOT–92–022–L, pp 42–43.

26. Jimmy Burns, "Dealing In the Business of Fear," *Financial Times*, January 7, 1992, as translated in JPRS–TOT–92–003–L, p. 39.

27. For an excellent treatment of the participation of IRA and Loyalist paramilitaries in crime of all types, see Paul K. Clare, *Racketeering in Northern Ireland: A New Version of the Patriot Game* (Chicago: Office of International Criminal Justice, University of Illinois at Chicago, 1989).

28. Murat Yetkin report on PKK narcotics trafficking in *Turkish Daily News*, February 3, 1993, as translated in JPRS–TDD–93–007–L, pp. 23–24; and *Anatolia*, 1535 GMT, November 24, 1992, as translated in JPRS–TOT–92–042–L, p. 24.

29. Ankara TNT Television Network, 1800 GMT, October 2, 1992, as translated in JPRS–TDD– 92–041–L, p. 39.

30. Gunaydin, April 12, 1993, as translated in JPRS–TOT–93–016–L, p. 51.

31. Yetkin, *Turkish Daily News*, February 3, 1993.

32. "PKK Is ASALA's Extension," *Hurriyet*, December 1, 1992, as translated in JPRS–TOT–92– 044–L, p. 33; and TRT Television Network, 1700 GMT, September 18, 1992, as translated in JPRS–TOT–92–033–L, p. 36.

33. See, for example, *Anatolia*, 1625 GMT, March 11, 1992, as translated in JPRS–TOT–92–009–L, p. 17. Reports in the late Fall of 1993 noted the dispatch of PKK "strike teams" to Ankara, Istanbul, and other major cities to create the impression that attacks such as those that swept some European cities "might come at any time at any place" in large Turkish cities. Muyessar Yildiz, untitled, *Yeni Gunaydin*, November 6, 1993, as translated in JPRS–TOT–93–044–L, p. 80.

34. USSR Ministry of Internal Affairs, 6th Main Directorate, "Organized Crime Survey Response," 1991, p. 1.

35. INTERFAX, 1345 GMT, September 8, 1992, as translated in FBIS–SOV–92–175, p. 25.

36. USSR Ministry of Internal Affairs, "Organized Crime Survey Response."

37. Narcotics trafficking, arms smuggling, robbery, and extortion are intermixed with ethnonational political or tribal agendas. Tensions and conflicts in Georgia proper, separatist Abkhazia, North and South Ossetia and the bloody war in Chechnya beginning in December 1994 have all involved a substantial criminal dimension incorporating drug and arms trafficking, other contraband smuggling, and financial crimes that extend well beyond the immediate area and in some cases are truly international. One notable illustration of the mix of crime and conflict in the Caucasus described, centers on activity around the South Ossetian city of Tskhinvali, Georgia in the summer of 1993. Judged to be on the verge of exploding "following

the slightest provocation" by separatist or government factions, the region never-theless flourished as a center of drug trafficking, with Georgians traveling from various parts of the country to buy drugs with dollars, rubles, automobiles—and guns. Kakha Shengelia, "Georgian 'Chekists' in Tskhinvali," *Rezonansi*, June 15–16 1993, as translated in JPRS–TDD–93–026–L, p. 27.

38. David M. Hart, *Banditry in Islam: Case Studies From Morocco, Algeria and the Pakistan North West Frontier*, Menas Studies In Continuity and Change in the Middle East and North Africa (Cambridgeshire: Middle and North African Studies Press Limited, 1987), examines the Islamic and regional context of what has been called "social banditry." Traditional smuggling activity by some Central Asian peoples—now expanded far beyond traditional levels—would also fall into this category.

39. "Whom are the Compradors Trying to Save," *Sovetskaya Rossiya*, March 27, 1991, as cited in Joseph Serio, "Organized Crime in the Former Soviet Union," Master of Arts Thesis, University of Illinois at Chicago, Chicago, Illinois, 1993. Russian observers have emphasized that "the on-going and maturing conflicts in Central Asia constantly demand financial support and insistently push the oppos-ing sides towards the source of the drugs." Vladimir Gubarev, "The Gold Mine of Drug Trafficking," *Moscow News*, no. 37, September 10, 1993, p. 15.

40. It should be emphasized that linkages between ethnonational groups and organized crime—like issues of drug trafficking, illegal arms sales, and interna-tional terrorism generally—often rest on assertions and evidence that need to be considered critically and skeptically.

41. "Moldova: New Center of Drug Trade," a July 14, 1993 Novosti report by a Moldovan police captain translated in SOVSET Computer Bulletin Board, Radio Free Europe/Radio Liberty, *Daily Report*, July 16, 1991. Western Moldova, in particular, has become prominent as a poppy-growing and opium production area with competing drug trafficking groups. There were thought to be some 30 orga-nized, national criminal groups operating in Bulgaria, Turkey, and Romania, which because of their proximity to Moldova and the lack of effective enforcement, easily cross its territory. See Moldovan MVD report on INTERFAX, 1444 GMT, November 20, 1991, as translated in JPRS–TDD–91–048–L, p. 43; and Svetlana Gamov, "Prestupniki iz Moldovy perekhodyat granitsy," *Izvestiya*, February 25, 1993; and Vladimir Zaynetdinov, "The Invasion of Drugs Into Russia," *Rabochaya Gazeta*, as translated in JPRS–TDD–92–014–L, p. 53.

42. Hobsbawm, *Bandits*, treats a numbers of these bandit figures in their historical context.

43. Ibid., pp. 61–71.

44. See Dr. Timothy L. Sanz, "The Yugoslav Conflict: A Chronology of Events," *Military Review*, December 1992, pp. 21–24, for a most useful overview of events and developments up to the late fall of 1992.

45. "Yugoslav Sleuth Tracks Spoils of War," Associated Press Report, November 13, 1993, presents the candid views of former Yugoslav police inspector and subsequent private investigator Mladen Lojovic.

46. Uros Komdenovic, " "A Second Front," *Nin*, September 13, 1991, as translated in JPRS– EER–91–149, p. 40.

47. Ibid. The autonomous Serbian province of Kosovo and Metohija, with a predominately Albanian ethnic population and strong separatist leanings, has by

many accounts some of the most active criminal groups in the region as well as armed groups associated with the separatist cause. Criminal links among ethnic Albanians in Serbia, other provinces, and Albania itself are widely reported. The Italian Mafia and other groups compete for influence and a share of the market at Albanian ports like Durrazo, while Italian police believe that Albanians are actively working Western narcotics trafficking routes.

48. For Western accounts of crime and profiteering, see Carol J. Williams, "A People Poisoned by Chaos," *Los Angeles Times*, March 27, 1993; Blaine Harden, "Serb Smugglers Turn Sanctions Into a Boom," *Washington Post*, November 5, 1992; and "Young Gangs Rule Belgrade Streets," *Christian Science Monitor*, November 6, 1992.

49. Branko Vojicic, "Montenegro, 'Black Marketeering,' and the State Leadership Itself: Montenegro on Mafia Payroll, " *Novi Vjesnik* (Zagreb), October 25, 1992, as translated in JPRS–TDD–92–047–L, p. 34.

50. Ibid.

51. For typical early reporting on this dimension, see *Tanjug* (Belgrade), 1355 GMT, June 25, 1991, as translated in FBIS London 251602Z June 1991; *Tanjug*, 1632 GMT, November 16, 1991, as translated in JPRS–TDD–91–049–L; *Tanjung*, 1018 GMT, July 28, 1992, as translated in FBIS London, 281517Z 1992; and Steve Coll, "In the Balkans, A Balance of Terror," *Washington Post National Weekly Edition*, March 1993.

52. Hobsbawm, *Bandits*, p. 27.

53. Ibid., p. 27

54. Gary R. Perlstein, "The Mercenary as Social Bandit: A Preliminary Look," *International Journal of Offender Therapy and Comparative Criminology* 32, no. 3, (December 1988): pp. 201–207, reviews the history of mercenaries and discusses their mixture of motivations.

55. NOTIMEX, 0239 GMT, April 16, 1994, as cited in FBIS–LAT–94–075 report, "Army Awaits Orders To Engage Armed Gangs."

56. In addition to former soldiers, contras, and recontras turning to crime, the diversion of weapons collected during disarmament has been a concern. At least some of these arms evidently have been acquired by drug traffickers. David Gutierrez Lopez, *Barricada*, March 7, 1994, as translated in JPRS–TDD–94–011–L under the title "Diversion of Weapons to Drug Traffickers Detailed," pp. 25–26.

57. Lyubov Latypova, "Report From Tajikistan," *Trud*, June 10, 1994, as translated in JPRS–TDD–94–028–L, p. 59.

58. AFP, 1308 GMT, August 26, 1993, as translated in JPRS–TDD–93–035–L, p. 54; and AFP , 1313 GMT, August 28, 1993, as translated in JPRS–TDD–93–036–L, p. 29.

59. Francois Misser, " Somalia: United Nations 'Covers' Drug Trafficking—UN Peacekeeping Forces, Including Belgians, Do Not Have Mandate to Halt Sales of 'Khat' That Finance Warlords," *La Libre Belgique*, June 19–20, 1993, as translated in JPRS–TDD–93–0126–L, p. 24.

60. Colonel F.M. Lopez, USMC, "Confronting Thievery in Somalia," *Military Review*, August 1994, pp. 46–55.

61. "El gran negocio," p. 32.

62. Interview with the Commander of the Colombian Armed Forces General Ramon Emilio Gil Bermudez, *El Tiempo*, February 28, 1993, as translated in FBIS Chiva Chiva messages 031752 March 1993, and 031753Z March 1993. This kind of

question may increasingly be applied to other insurgencies as well. Peru's Sendero Luminoso, for example, has long been alleged to earn money from its relationship with Peruvian coca growers and Colombian traffickers. Some analysts have postulated that drug profits may similarly undermine Sendero's revolutionary idealism. See Arnaldo Claudio and Stephan K. Stewman, "Peru, Sendero Luminoso, and the Narcotrafficking Alliance," *Low Intensity Conflict and Law Enforcement* 1, no. 3 (Winter 1992): 279–292.

63. Vladimir Gubarev, "The Gold Mine of Drug Trafficking," *Moscow News*, no. 37, September 10, 1993, p. 15.

64. Andrey Borodin, "Narcotics: Danger From the South," *Segodnya*, August 10, 1993, as translated in FBIS–TDD–93–036–L, p. 38.

65. Kovalenko, "Slav Mafia." (Emphasis added)

66. Stojan Cerovic, "The Serbian Awakening: Nightmare on Pirates' Island," *Vreme*, March 15, 1993, as translated in FBIS–EEU–93–069, p. 41.

67. "Aid Plane Hit By Gunfire; U.N. Suspends Sarajevo Airlift," Associated Press Report, March 12, 1995.

68. Interview with Sefer Halilovic by Miljenko Jergovic "Wars Here Last Three, Four Years," *Nedjeljna Dalmacija*, February 3, 1993, as translated in FBIS–EEU–93–031, p. 52.

69. Ed McCullough, "Venezuela Lives From Crisis to Crisis," Associated Press Report, March 1, 1994.

70. Cerovic, "The Serbian Awakening," p. 41.

71. "Yugoslavian Sleuth."

72. Cerovic, "The Serbian Awakening," p. 41.

73. In this instance, the charges were leveled by an adviser to the Mexican Attorney General's Office, Eduardo Valle Espinoza, who resigned in May 1994. *Reforma*, May 11, 1994, as translated in JPRS–TDD–94–021–L, p. 17. As addressed in Thomas and Williams, "Graft in Mexico," systemic Mexican corruption raises complex questions for U.S. diplomacy.

74. Michael S. Sherrill, "The Narco-Candidate," *Time*, July 4, 1994, p. 49.

75. Interview by Lyudmilla Leontyeva with Djokhar Dudayev, *Moscow News*, no. 14, April 5–12, 1992. In that same interview, the Chechen president was asked about his ties to the mafia, and if he had surrounded himself with Chechen mafia members. He answered that it was the other way around, that mafia members had surrounded him in the same way they had linked themselves to Boris Yeltsin and other leaders of the Commonwealth of Independent States in the transition period. He acknowledged that getting rid of them would not be easy. When asked how, he said he was "working out a scheme designed to rid the mafia of its specific characteristics and qualities so that in the long run this whole sector is converted to a new outlook and brought to serve the Chechen people."

76. "Craxi Says Vatican, Not Mafia, Backed Andreotti," Reuter New Service, March 11, 1995.

77. See Dmitry Alyokhin, "Law and Order: Head of the Chief Administration for Combatting Organized Crime Discusses Organized Crime—and the Rector of the Russian Ministry of Internal Affairs' Institute Talks About That New Educational Institution," *Segodnya*, as translated in *The Current Digest*, vol. XLVI, no. 20 (1994): 16. For excellent treatments of organized crime in Moscow and the former Soviet Union

as well as its implications, see Joseph Serio, "Organized Crime in the Soviet Union and Beyond," *Low Intensity Conflict and Law Enforcement* 1, no. 2 (Fall 1992): 127–151; and Mark Galeotti, "Organized Crime in Moscow and Russian National Security," *Low Intensity Conflict and Law Enforcement* 1, no. 3 (Winter 1992): 237–252.

78. More than two years ago, Ukraine's President L. M. Kravchuk expressed dismay at the levels of organized crime and how "corruption and bribes are penetrating into the structures of our ministries and departments." The situation has worsened substantially since that time. See *Imenem Zakonu*, January 15, 1993, as translated in FBIS Vienna message 251340Z, January 1993.

79. Vitaliy Chechilo, "Financial Leapfrog: Ukrainian Officers Union Funds Are Being Spent in a Controlled Manner," *Pravda Ukrainy*, December 21, 1992, as translated in JPRS–UMA–93–002, p. 25.

80. By January 1995, the authorized strength of the Russian Armed Forces was to be at around 1.5 million personnel—the remnants of a Soviet military establishment that stood at more than three times that size during its Cold War high point in the 1980s. Interview with Russian Defense Minister Pavel Grachev, Mayak Radio Network, 1830 GMT, August 19, 1994, as translated in FBIS–SOV–94–162, pp. 30–31.

81. For a review of the scope of military crime in mid-1994, see Yelena Sizova, "Warning: Would You Step on a Rake?" *Krasnaya Zvezda*, June 3, 1994, as translated in JPRS–UMA–94–027, pp. 1–2. For earlier allegations of high-level military corruption see Julia Wishnevsky, "Corruption Allegations Undermine Russia's Leaders," *RFE/RL Research Report* 2, no. 37, September 17, 1993, p. 18.

82. "Rossiyskaya mafia."

83. Yuriy Deryugin, "Trevozhnye tendentsii v Rossiyskoy Armii," *Nezavisimaya gazeta*, August 24, 1994.

84. Among many discussions of military financial crime, see the article by the murdered reporter Dmitriy Kholodov, "And Service There, Will Seem To Be Honey . . . a Military Mafia Exists in Moscow," *Moskovskiy Komsomolets*, June 30, 1994, as translated in JPRS–UMA–94–031, pp. 7–9; Robert Fisk, "Moscow's Mafia Finds an Island in the Sub," *The Independent*, August 3, 1994, as translated in JPRS–TDD–94–034–L, pp. 44–45; and Stanislav Baratynov, "When the Generals Are Bluffing: The Financial Mafia Is Making Millions From the Military Budget," *Moskovskiy Komsomolets*, April 22, 1994, as translated in JPRS–UMA–94–022, pp. 3–6.

85. Robert Orttung, "More Revelations About Beginning of Chechen War," *OMRI Daily Digest*, no. 28, Part I, February 8, 1995.

86. Allegations of high and low-level thievery began long before the Western Group of Forces (WGF's) withdrawal in August 1994. The unattributed article, "How People Are Warming Their Hands On Army Supply," *Rossiyskaya Gazeta*, September 25, 1991, as translated in JPRS–UMA–91–026, pp. 34–35, discusses the waste and diversion of military supplies, among other issues.

87. Peter Scherer, "Russians Leave Behind 'Criminal Bridgehead'," *Die Welt*, June 3, 1994, as translated in FBIS–WEU–94–108.

88. Lyubov Latypova, "Report Form Tajikistan," *Trud*, 10 June 1994, as translated in JPRS–TDD–94–028–L, p. 59; and Vladimir Gubarev, "The Gold Mine of Drug Trafficking," *Moscow News*, no. 37, September 10, 1993.

89. The use of the Internet by the Zapatista Liberation Army and its supporters, Chechen separatists, conflict participants in the former Yugoslavia, and other

irregular groups with limited resources, serves to illustrate how accessible such global communications are to any group with a criminal agenda. Tod Robberson, "A Peasant Uprising Via Internet," *The Washington Post National Weekly Edition*, February 27–5 March 5, 1995.

90. David Potter, *Sailing the Sulu Sea: Belles and Bandits in the Philippines* (New York: E. P. Dutton and Company, 1940), p. 13. Asian piracy, and piracy in other areas, has emerged as a security concern in recent years. In some of these instances, criminal profits may combine with the desires of states to use "piracy" as a covert means of asserting territorial or other agendas.

91. St. Augustine, *The City of God*, p. 88. It may be noted in passing that modern territories once part of Alexander's ancient Macedonian homeland, now play host to a wide selection of nonstate entities that fundamentally influence the region's security environment.

13

Strategic Intelligence in the Coming Years: Foreign Policy and Defense Asset

Roy Godson

This chapter adapts general principles of intelligence to the emerging security environment of ungovernability in which non-state actors play expanded roles in world politics. Although the global environment is experiencing rapid change, the intelligence community (IC) can still rely on fundamental precepts about politics and intelligence to better shape its mission, orientation, and organization.[1]

Perhaps the most significant new challenges to U.S. interests come from the increasing number of weak governments and from the rise of sub- and transstate actors increasingly able to undermine governance.[2] The new threats are as varied as they are potentially dangerous. Criminal and terrorist organizations take advantage of weak governments and modern communications technologies to transnationalize their operations, giving them economies of scale with their increased reach. The world's highly interconnected financial system is also threatened; few international safeguards protect financial institutions from assault by non-state actors. Ethno-religious groups challenge the legitimacy and sovereignty of numerous nation-states. In some cases these groups launch coups or secessionist movements; in others they simply undermine states' capacity to govern. Finally, the looming proliferation of weapons of mass destruction threatens global security. Altogether, these seemingly disparate phenomena are making the world increasingly ungovernable.

The State-Centric Model

The nation-state has long been the basic unit of activities that define or threaten the interests of political communities. Since the early sixteenth century, when modern nation-states emerged, political theorists have explained global politics in terms of states' policies.[3] Throughout the ensuing centuries, strong nation-states demonstrated their vigor by consistently triumphing against peoples organized into other associations such as tribes or ethno-religious groups.[4] Commentators of world politics have continued to rely (often unselfconsciously) on a state-centric model. They did so with good reason. By the turn of the twentieth century, few regions outside of Europe and the Americas were not under state rule. As colonial peoples gained political independence, they looked to this model. Yet, developing nations continually encountered the Cold War's two countervailing forces. The first was the integration of new states into one of the two contending security communities; the competing Soviet and Western spheres each sought to combine people and to organize resources on ever larger scales. The second force was the disintegrative energy of local power struggles: Who was to rule at home? On what basis?[5] In the four-and-a-half decades of the Cold War, many of these issues were subsumed under the simpler conflict between the First and Second Worlds. In many ways, the Third World was viewed by many outside and within the region as merely the battleground in the state-centered global strategic conflict.[6] With the end of the Cold War, however, the balance began to change.

The Relative Decline of State Sovereignty

Although the Cold War divided the world into an essentially bipolar geostrategic system, a number of trends were under way that generated profound changes in the nature of the international system. Some older states saw their governance deteriorate because of domestic political and technological forces. This trend was accelerated by the emergence of a host of new states that had little experience in self rule and often lacked the basics of social consensus that otherwise underlie civil order and political cohesion.[7] Many of these states incorporated minorities harboring claims to self-determination that challenged the sovereignty of the new states.[8] In several cases, these claims became central concerns to the East-West rivalry, but overall the Cold War contained the centrifugal force of the new states.

Since the end of the Cold War, many of the constructs that had held countries together have been lost, while long-term trends promoting a new species of self-determination have matured.[9] Many of the new states have begun to unravel, some spectacularly. Wars, insurgencies, collapsing economies, and violence against civilian populations have created unstable environments that defy governance.[10] In extreme cases, government has either ceased to exist or has become just another element in a swirling complex of competing forces whose constant struggle embitters civil life and fosters an insecurity that hinders economic development or political stability. In this environment, relatively easy access to arms has enhanced the operational effectiveness of sub-state actors, further eroding the states' monopoly on violence.

The international system has been based primarily on the assumptions that nation states cover virtually all territory, and that within their respective territories their authority is sovereign. This sovereignty is defined most importantly by monopolies on violence, taxes, and border controls, as well as by a high degree of primacy for emotional affiliation (i.e., patriotism and civic duty). These measures of sovereignty have been undermined significantly of late. First, the massive decolonization of the 1960s and 1970s created numerous states that failed, with governments incapable of governing. Second and ironically, the recent spread of liberal democracy promoted openness and discouraged state repression, thereby diminishing their capacities to govern. Third, the demise of the Cold War reduced the overwhelming threat states faced, allowing them to "let down their guards" by, among other things, weakening border controls. Fourth, the disintegration of the Soviet Union left approximately half of the Eurasian landmass considerably less governed, allowing organized crime, drug smuggling, and arms trading to spread where the old regime would once have halted it. Fifth, the emergence of transstate actors has also contributed to undermining state sovereignty in myriad if sometimes subtle ways. Some transstate actors are legal — the United Nations, the European community (and other regional groupings), human rights organizations, and financial organizations (both nongovernmental agencies like the World Bank, the International Monetary Fund, and the World Trade Organization, as well as multinational corporations). Sixth, technological change has accelerated each of these trends, allowing people to communicate, travel, move money, and even wage war over greater distances with increased economy, ease, assurance, and accuracy. It seems, then, that states are losing the very monopolies that have defined them and the international system for several centuries.

Sub-State Actors

Sub-state actors are those groups organized for political, financial, or ethno-religious reasons that generally confine their activities to the territory of one country. Sub-state actors fall into three basic if sometimes overlapping categories: criminals, secessionists, and nonsecessionists pursuing internal or civil war to change the basis of sociopolitical order (revolutionaries). The first group includes all major criminal organizations whose actions are generally limited to the subnational level but who sometimes cross borders to conduct business, launder money, or punish enemies. This category includes Japanese Yakuza, Sicilian Mafia, and Chinese Triad crime organizations. The second category, those associations that would secede from an existing country for ethno-political reasons, includes such groups as the Basques, Biafrans, Zapatistas, and Quebecois.[11] Where once only the remnants of colonial Africa and Asia faced serious secessionism, similar movements now threaten mature and wealthy states. The third group, those seeking to gain control of their country's government, includes such recent actors as Zviad Gamsakhurdia's successors in Georgia, Peru's Sendero Luminoso, or any number of groups in Liberia. Since 1945 there have been more than 100 secessionist movements across the globe, of which 39 have become guerrilla or civil wars.[12]

Transstate Actors

Transstate actors who operate illegally are also threatening regional and global security. Transstate actors are those groups that act in more than one and frequently in many countries. Criminal organizations (such as the Colombian cartels), militant religious movements (e.g., Islamists), and sometimes corrupted financial networks all operate across borders. The burgeoning technologies of communication, computation, transportation, and war-fighting facilitate the activities of these transstate actors. Although some groups do not pose direct threats to state sovereignty or integrity, others, such as major criminal organizations and religious and ethnic movements, have demonstrated a growing capacity to challenge directly the right and ability of governments to govern in some regions. Some of these groups are also developing interconnections among themselves to improve their operational capabilities, to strengthen their ability to resist governmental or international control efforts (the Colombian cartels are the most notorious example). These linkages that combine to pose serious threats to security and the commonweal.

The Nature of Intelligence

These changes are part of a process of evolution, rather then revolution. Their ramifications for the state-centric system are still far from evident. Thus, policy necessarily remains ill-defined and unclear. In a perfect world, intelligence managers would have a clearly defined cohesive policy to implement. To a great extent, containment provided such an policy, particularly during the first decades of the Cold War. The demise of the Soviet Union removed the most salient and easily identified threat, leaving the United States uncertain of its threat environment. There are some things we do know, however. An effective intelligence community includes four elements of intelligence, each working symbiotically with the others and related to policy. These elements are: (1) collection (2) analysis (3) counterintelligence and (4) covert action.[13] For all four elements to function effectively both as inputs into policy and as instruments of policy implementation, they require guidance from policymakers.

There is an unfortunate and growing absence of policy pertaining directly to emerging ungovernability. In theory, the IC takes its orders regarding collection and action from the policymakers. In practice, however, the IC attempts to come to terms with the policy agendas and then suggests a plan which is, in turn, approved by the policymakers. Given the vicissitudes of contemporary world politics and the proliferation of actors, threats, vulnerabilities, and opportunities, this practice inevitably leads to tension, as the IC cannot possibly anticipate every need of the policymakers. This tension is further exacerbated by the fact that intelligence assets, human or technical, frequently require years to develop. These are investments that cost-conscious legislators are increasingly hesitant or unwilling to make. Such investments were easier to justify during the cold war when the targets were relatively fixed and hard and resources were abundant. As the actors proliferate and metamorphosize and as resources shrink, it is much more problematic. Finally, a full-service community will have to consort with some disreputable individuals and organizations. These associations may appear unseemly, yet they remain an important source of secret information and unparalleled opportunities to effect change on the ground.[14] Indeed, because of the shifting nature of ungovernability's threats and opportunities, the IC's ability to effect change might be considerably enhanced through such assets.

Intelligence may be defined as the information, activities, and organizations that result in (1) the collection, analysis, production, dissemination, and specialized exploitation of information relating to any other government, political group, party, military force, movement, or other association that is believed to relate to the group's or government's security; (2) the neutralization and countering of similar activities by other groups, governments, or movements; and (3) the covert activities undertaken to affect the composition and behavior of such groups or governments.

Allowing for differences in form and emphasis, the four distinct elements of intelligence might be defined as follows:[15]

- Clandestine Collection — Obtaining valued information through the use of special, usually secret, human and technical methods. The major components are signals or sigint; imagery (overhead- and ground-based, including especially photography) or imint; electronic emissions particularly from computers or elint; human collection or humint; and frequently open-source materials or oscint.[16]
- Counterintelligence (CI) — Identifying, neutralizing, and possibly

exploiting other states' or groups' intelligence activities. Despite being crucial for evaluating and using intelligence, this element is often slighted by modern, democratic intelligence systems.

- Analysis and Estimates—Assessing the fruits of collection along with other data and delivering to policymakers finished products that have more clarity than is inherent in the data alone. As targets and opportunities proliferate, analysis must increasingly become opportunity-oriented.[17]

- Covert Action (CA)—Activities to influence political, economic, or military conditions abroad, where it is intended that the actor's role will not be apparent or acknowledged publicly.[18] CA may include political action, propaganda, intelligence assistance, and offensive or defensive paramilitary operations.

While the elements of intelligence are here separated, it is important to recognize the symbiotic relationship between and among them. For example, effective CI is necessary for the success of all other components of intelligence. Without effective CI, an organization cannot be sure that the data it is collecting are not the products of an adversary's attempt at deception. If what is collected is faulty, it is likely that flawed analysis and misguided policy will follow. Effective collection and analysis also provide the basis for successfully conducting covert action, and counterintelligence operations can be used for positive collection purposes. In general, the elements of intelligence, while theoretically distinct, are often closely related operationally.[19] Historically, when states have failed to understand and operationalize the truth, they are disadvantaged.

Matching Intelligence to Ungovernability

This section examines ways of applying intelligence to the problems of ungovernability. It does so by applying the four elements of intelligence to historical examples. History abounds with lessons for providing governance in difficult situations.[20] However, the utility of these lessons is limited by America's unique situation and sensibilities. In few previous cases has a hegemon been constrained by the pluralistic and human-rights sensibilities that strongly shape U.S. policy. Furthermore, the United States is the only true global power. As such, it is the only state capable of addressing the transstate linkages that distinguish emerging global ungovernability from traditional security issues.

Intelligence Collection

History evinces the importance of collecting information from a variety of sources. One need look no further back than Somalia in 1993-1994 or Iran in 1979 to see the pitfalls in failing to collect information widely on non-state actors. In each of these cases, strong militaries were humbled by non-state actors. On the other hand, history is replete with examples of operations that have succeeded in part because collectors cast their nets widely. For important examples, see the U.S. campaigns against the Philippine revolutionaries between 1898 and 1901 and again during the 1950s. The various counterinsurgency campaigns in Bolivia (1960s) and Peru (1990s) have brought home this point more recently.

In the cases of Operations Restore Hope in Haiti and Desert Storm in Iraq and Kuwait, aggressive collection sometimes produced insufficient data, but the opposite is far more likely to occur. Vacuuming all elint produces prodigious amounts of data—far more than could reasonably be culled to separate the wheat from the chaff. Roberta Wohlstetter has called this a signal-to-noise problem in reference to the alleged intelligence failure at Pearl Harbor in 1941. The signal-to-noise problem is incalculably exacerbated in an era of proliferating actors, communications, and capacities for collection. Yes, the National Security Agency could conceivably record every phone call made via satellite, but it would only provide phenomenal amounts of noise until some sort of clues or keys were found to focus the search on truly significant signals. These keys have frequently been found in the form of humint.

Collecting secrets directly from human beings, or from proximity to significant individuals, is critical. Humint can provide invaluable information on opportunities and vulnerabilities, as well on planned terrorist attacks or on the organization of a criminal or terrorist group. It may be easier to penetrate, say, the Serbian, Rwandan, or Haitian leadership than it was the Soviet Union. Infiltrating a family-based criminal organization, on the other hand, is extremely difficult. Nevertheless, experience, in Italy for example, shows that it is not impossible to break the code of silence that surrounds such criminal enterprises.

IC collection in foreign areas has long operated at considerable (and frequently unnecessary) disadvantage because of the nation's reluctance to use collectors who are not under official cover or attached formally to the foreign service or the military. Operating against cold war hard targets, official cover humint made more sense. Generally only officials of the regimes knew state secrets, and the way to meet these officials was at diplomatic events. Having most of our intelligence officers under official cover makes them easier to deploy, administer, pay, and protect, but official cover collectors are also far less likely to infiltrate an unfriendly group successfully—even to the level of being able to collect its pamphlets or newspapers. Working out of an embassy or consulate marks the officer, making him or her immediately suspect both to local security services and to non-state actors.

The IC needs a great deal of non-official cover (NOC) collection capabilities. As with other forms of intelligence, it requires organization, perhaps a Non-Official Cover Corps (NOCC). The organization would include regular case officers who could operate under nonofficial cover, some living in targeted areas and some mobile. They would carry out most of the dangerous work of espionage. For instance, these officers might operate out of a "discreet" air charter service, so that they would be targeted to meet individuals knowledgeable about illegal transactions of arms, drugs, or fissionable materials. This group of officers would also run the more passive networks critical for successful operations. For instance, military planners and operators require "tour" guides. Planning an assault requires good maps of buildings and streets and lists of telephone numbers. To carry off such an assault, one might wish, therefore, to use hotel managers, airline ticket agents, and taxi dispatchers.

The proposed NOCC offers several advantages. First, by creating a core of true regional or local specialists, the IC would have access to the types of qualitative intelligence most crucial for making realistic threat analysis—based on intentions as well as capabilities. Some of the kinds of information one might wish to collect are reports of clandestine meetings and reports of government or police corruption.

In the new world disorder, U.S. presence appears to be spreading overtly as we take on more humanitarian, aid, and policing roles. Another method of humint collection, then, could be debriefing U.S. and friendly foreign personnel working abroad. For example, local women and children in particular are inclined to speak frankly with a doctor or medic—even if he or she is wearing a U.S. Army or a UN uniform. One major obstacle to this kind of collection lies in the culture of the medics themselves; they believe that they are caregivers and not soldiers, so they might not collect aggressively. They are required to complete after-action reports that include any information potentially relevant to operations, but they do not like to be tasked to ask specific questions. Special Forces medics, on the other hand, are usually cross-trained in intelligence and are far more useful.

Collection is an increasingly complicated chore, one that requires a great deal of flexibility and creativity. For instance, one can only begin to wonder at the possibilities for targeting collection on biological threats to national security. The vast preponderance of biological threats are not subject to human will; they are simply viruses or bacteria that mutate or are transmitted in such a way that they could potentially prove deadly on awesome, if not unprecedented, scales.[21] Collection on these threats generally falls into the domain of the scientists, doctors, and epidemiologists at the Centers for Disease Control and Prevention (CDC) and other biomedical research centers. A variety of countries and non-state actors are also examining the possibility of harnessing biological agents for political purposes, however.[22] Although banned by virtually universal international agreement, biological agents may well be used in the future by non-state actors as inexpensive, deniable, and widely lethal alternatives to nuclear weapons.[23] Indeed, one recent Department of Defense study anticipates that in addition to state-sponsored and -assisted terrorism, we will be faced with non-state groups acting in relatively unconstrained ways using weapons of mass destruction.[24] The means for generating or harnessing them are readily available, signifying a tremendous challenge for collection.

Collection on nuclear or chemical agents is likely to cause similar challenges. These agents are far easier to obtain and control. A variety of states are known to be stockpiling nuclear or chemical weapons, but this is an issue left over from a more governable era. The complications arise from the non-state actors increasingly gaining access to these materials. Much of the problem is related directly to the disintegration of the Soviet Union and the subsequent proliferation of access to fissionable materials. In 1994 and 1995, for instance, the U.S. and German governments were able to trap several groups of criminals engaged in the trafficking of nuclear materials that presumably originated from the former Soviet Union.

Nuclear materials, of course, need not be used exclusively for complicated weapons. They can also be fashioned into radiological weapons. Had a couple of pounds of fissionable material been included in the World Trade Center or Oklahoma City bombs, the downtowns of these cities would have been rendered uninhabitable for decades.

Collecting information on nuclear, chemical, or biological agents used intentionally to harm or threaten is a complicated process that illustrates the importance of close coordination of the elements of intelligence. Technical or signal collection may well provide some initial leads, for example, on the names and locations of front organizations and individuals that might be making purchases. Resourceful analysis, however, would be required to make use of this information and to target the further collection of useful information that would otherwise be ignored as useless. For instance, export lists, shipping manifests, and customs receipts might provide crucial information about the agents, or about the media and tools for processing, handling, and delivering them, but one needs to know what to search for in the first place.

Counterintelligence

Because of the possibility of foreign deception, we need clandestine collection and functional counterintelligence systems. We need to protect our secrets and we need to be able to learn the secrets of others, especially when they are using their intelligence capabilities to mislead us. Proponents of open source collection and analysis make few or no provisions for the intentional and frequently elaborate efforts to deceive us.[25] It is difficult to distinguish between hiding and deceiving. Nonetheless, we must recognize the fact that multi-billion dollar weapons projects can be constructed underneath the ground, hidden from image sensors, or hidden in plain sight as the Iraqi nuclear program was for years. Terrorist groups use false names and front organizations to channel funds from legitimate public interest groups into murderous activities. Criminal cartels launder billions of dollars, easily evading the capacity for bank regulators or open sources collectors to trace them. Criminal organizations suborn local law enforcement and intelligence services through bribes or intimidation, neutralizing them or using them to send us deceptive information. They also use electronic communications, sometimes expecting that their signals will be intercepted; these signals can also be part of deception campaigns. Intelligence requires good CI simply because it is secrets that we are interested in, and people will go to extraordinary efforts to deny their existence or to deceive us of their capabilities.

Another useful tool in the campaign to contain ungovernability is information warfare (infowar). The definition of this emerging category of conflict is contentious, but the following may prove useful: infowar seeks to influence an adversary by denying him information, or by influencing, degrading, and or destroying his information systems. It also includes denying, negating, or turning to friendly advantage an adversary's efforts to deny us his information and to disrupt ours. The U.S. and other states can develop the capacity to use infowar to disrupt, destroy, or deceive the enemy's information systems. Infowar must be founded on a coherent strategy or policy and must be buttressed by an orchestrated plan; disruption for disruption's sake serves little purpose.

Clever infowar operations use a variety of techniques—sigint, humint, diplomacy, media, rumors, and propaganda—to prevent the enemy from learning a plan in its entirety; in other words, to keep him scrambling after pieces of the puzzle. To lead the target to draw certain conclusions, verbal, written, or illustrative information may be planted on agents known to be working for the adversary, or on those technical sources known to be intercepting communications, or on imagery sources. A reliable feedback channel to gauge the adversary's reactions is helpful, if not essential, so that future messages can be constructed to reinforce any conclusions.

If other states or non-state actors are seeking to control or alter perceptions by manipulating the IC's collection and analysis (or even that of Western media or academics), CI analysts can respond with counterdeception analysis. By mirroring the setups involved in enemy perception management, CI analysts protect their own government and people from manipulation. They may try to identify any enemy objectives that could be furthered by a deception plan. Military operations usually (and economic and diplomatic operations often) employ a deception plan to achieve surprise and thereby to increase the chance of success. CI analysts need to examine their own government's collection modus operandi to determine its vulnerability to foreign deception.

Examples of the need for CI abound: Iraq was able to deceive its opponents for years, even after the Gulf War, about the extent of its programs for weapons of mass destruction.[26] Such deception is not, however, limited to states. Apparently, Aum Shinrikyo, the group responsible for the deadly chemical attacks on Tokyo subways in the spring of 1995, long denied its intentions and hid its capabilities, deceiving the Japanese press and government. The Bank of Commerce and Credit International (BCCI) was able to put up a legitimate front for many years, in part through clever use of such respected men as Clark Clifford and Robert Altman. Deception comes naturally to terrorists or criminal groups. They have little new to learn from Sun Tzu.

Analysis

To be successful, analysis must take place at several levels: in the region, at the area desk, at the agency level, and at the national and international levels as well. Each of these efforts should be coordinated and interactive, to create opportunity-oriented analysis.[27] The analysis must concentrate on identifying individuals, groups, linkages, and coalitions and should attempt to delineate their strengths, assets, and vulnerabilities. Analysis should also suggest plans of action in order to give policymakers the tools they need to formulate informed, proactive policies. Among the most important tasks is identifying groups and their coalitions. Study of the structures of criminal organizations or ethno-political groups, for instance, will provide useful insights into their strengths, weaknesses, and intentions. Such groups are unlikely to publish organizational charts or annual reports, however. In fact, some consider their organizational fluidity to be a key feature of their structure. Criminal organizations, for example, succeed in part because they are so flexible in responding to new opportunities as presented, crossing borders and developing new operations as required.[28] The same could be said for ethno-political terrorist groups, such as Hizbollah. Their arcane structures may hold many secrets about their capabilities and their intent, but accessing and assessing this information are severe challenges. This makes the analysts' job more difficult but no less critical.

The case of Lebanon provides several important lessons. Lebanon, particularly since the outbreak of civil war in 1975, has been a textbook case of regional ungovernability.[29] Assad's successes in Lebanon in the 1980s and 1990s suggest important lessons for the use of intelligence to cope with localized ungovernability. First, he appears to have made great use of humint for understanding the Byzantine intergroup dynamics in this region. Second, Assad evinced little interest in the Sisyphian task of creating a governable Lebanon. The lesson here might be that Israel and the United States could not succeed in Lebanon because they were not sufficiently focused on one of the major targets—Damascus. If true, then the proper role of intelligence (including possibly active measures) should have been to concentrate on the major player in the area's ungovernability, again on Damascus. "The Syrians instigated a problem (in Lebanon)—smuggling, drug trafficking, ethnic conflict, attacks on Israel—then rushed in with a solution that served their interests. Perhaps the most evident example of this pattern was Assad's complex ploy through the 1980s of gaining freedom for hostages he had caused to be captured in the first place."[30] This case should not be read as a briefing in favor of terrorism, drug trafficking, and duplicity. Rather, it presents an assessment of the tools and levers one authoritarian ruler was able to use, given insightful analysis, to make ungovernability work in his favor.

Covert Action

The United States generally does not have, nor does it desire, the ability to behave as ruthlessly as Syria. In fact, for the most part, its foreign actions can be carried out overtly, frequently with the support of interested legitimate parties. Yet, in dealing with ungovernability, it is likely to face situations that call for actions that could plausibly be denied, either to ensure operational success or to protect U.S. national security interests.

As noted above, covert action (CA) has four components: political action, propaganda, intelligence assistance, and paramilitary operations. In collaboration with the other elements of statecraft, such as diplomacy, military force, and economic assistance, CA can assist in disrupting the groups that encourage ungovernability while also bolstering our allies.

Overt and covert political action holds much promise for containing ungovernability. It can strengthen those governments engaged in holding the lines, much as covert action was used as an adjunct to the economic support of Western Europe and Japan in the late 1940s and early fifties. Curiously, most historical literature on CA focuses on its efforts to destabilize governments, rather than on its constructive efforts.[31] During the early cold war, the United States overtly and covertly supported non-Communist trade unions and political parties, supplying funds for publicizing, campaigning, and coalition-building. Similar efforts could well be made to support governments and non-state players struggling, for example, to contain a vehement Islamist movement intent on overthrowing legitimate authorities or to assist moderate Muslim forces struggling against Islamism. Political action could also be made available for governments besieged by criminal organizations (e.g., Colombia, Russia, or Mexico). Such action includes providing expertise on police and criminal prosecution techniques or in providing witness protection assistance.[32]

In addition to political and intelligence assistance, a covert action agenda might include propaganda. Again, it might be used to bolster a government besieged by Islamist or criminal organizations. It could come in the form of expertise (providing advice on propaganda techniques), hardware or simply financial support earmarked for such enterprises. During the cold war, the United States developed a large propaganda capability, opening fronts across the globe.

Disrupting one's adversaries can take several forms. It must be part of a coherent strategy, and it can require international cooperation. Possibilities include (1) stopping or at least minimizing travel and transfers of money for the would-be perpetrators (2) publicizing their secret bank account balances to stir jealousy and rivalry within or among adversary organizations (3) tampering with their communications capabilities (4) discrediting particular actors, for instance, by showing doctored photographs or videotapes or copies of Swiss bank account ledgers with embarrassingly large sums or simply by instigating unflattering rumors.

Finally, one can use paramilitary operations to thwart terrorist acts or to disrupt criminal operations. Such campaigns could include raids on terrorist bases; bombing attacks on large drug labs; spraying coca fields with herbicides or planting a fungus on the crops themselves; or launching a commando raid to capture a specific leader. Although covert action in general and paramilitary operations in particular are not magic bullets, they do sometimes prove useful. CA can only work as part of a concerted effort, however. That effort means means not only coordination inside the intelligence community, through wide collection, careful analysis, and attentive counterintelligence, but also coordination throughout the government to achieve well-thought-out policy objectives via political, diplomatic, and crypto-diplomatic campaigns so that the effort is not doomed before it commences.

In sum, the United States faces myriad security threats and opportunities in the post–Cold War world. The relative decline of many states' ability to govern is leading to zones of ungovernability. Non-state actors—sub- and transstate-criminal or revolutionary forces—are becoming increasingly powerful. These forces menace security and threaten the stability of global political, economic, and social systems. Along with diplomacy and military force, intelligence offers numerous useful tools to understand and confront this emerging ungovernability.

Both as an input into policy and as tools of policy implementation, the four elements of intelligence should be used symbiotically. Effective collection and analysis can play a significant role in policy formulation. Counterintelligence and covert action are not only important to collection and analysis; they also can play significant policy support roles. The IC ought not be excessively timid, ceding the realm of action to proponents of other tools of statecraft. Intelligence alone cannot do the job, but it can be one of the pillars of policy success.

Notes

1. The author would like to thank the following for their assistance: Jeffrey Berman, Mark R. Shulman, William J. Olson, Eliot Cohen, Col. William Flavin, Robert Jenks, Walter Jajko, Martin Libicki, Col. William McDonald, Col. Alfred Paddock Jr., Peter Probst, Stephen P. Rosen, Col. Bryant Shaw, Brian Sullivan, and Col. John Waghelstein.

2. See, for example, Roy Godson, Ernest May and Gary Schmitt, editors, *U.S. Intelligence at the Crossroads: Agenda for Reform* (Washington: Brassey's, 1995).

3. Some of the more interesting works to discuss the evolution of the threat environment are historical, including John Keegan, *History of Warfare* (New York: Knopf, 1993); Martin van Creveld, *The Transformation of War* (New York: Free Press, 1991); Michael Howard, George Andreopoulos, and Mark R. Shulman, editors, *The Laws of War: Constraints on Warfare in the Western World* (New Haven: Yale University Press, 1994).

4. Other important works on the evolving threat environment include: Max G. Manwaring, editor, *The Gray Area Phenomena: Confronting the New World Disorder* (Boulder: Westview, 1993); Daniel Patrick Moynihan, *Pandaemonium: Ethnicity in International Politics* (Oxford University Press, 1993); Zbigniew Brzezinski, *Out of Control: Global Turmoil on the Eve of the Twenty-First Century* (New York: Scribner, 1993); Samuel Huntington, et al. *The Clash of Civilizations* (New York: Council on Foreign Relations Press, 1993) and Alvin and Heidi Toffler, *War and Anti-War: Survival at the Dawn of the 21st Century* (Boston: Little, Brown and Co., 1993). An interesting article on the subject is Robert Kaplan, "The Coming Anarchy," *Atlantic Monthly* (February 1994).

5. Much of the state-centered security paradigm is laid out in the classic studies of nationalism: Louis L. Snyder, *The Dynamics of Nationalism: Readings in its Meaning and Development* (Princeton: Princeton University Press, 1964); Hans Kohn, *The Age of Nationalism* (New York: Harpers, 1962). As Richard Shultz writes, "As a conceptual category . . . 'national security' suggests a perspective on security issues that looks out from a national capital. The primary concern is the well-being if not the survival of a particular state." Richard Shultz, Roy Godson, and Ted Greenwood, *Security Studies for the 1990s* (Washington: Brassey's, 1993), 1–2.

With their origins in Thucydides' *History of the Peloponnesian War*, the classics of security studies include: Arnold Wolfers, *Discord and Collaboration* (Baltimore: The Johns Hopkins University Press, 1962); Frank Trager, "Introduction to the Study of National Security," in *National Security and American Society*, edited by Frank Trager and Philip Kronenberg (Manhattan, KS: University Press of Kansas, 1973) 35–48; Helga Haftendorn, "The Security Puzzle: Theory Building and Discipline Building in International Security," *International Studies Quarterly* 35 (March 1991): 3–18; and Robert Jervis, "Cooperation Under the Security Dilemma," in *The Use of Force*, edited by Robert Art and Kenneth Waltz (New York: University Press of America, 1988), 67–97.

6. See Bruce Porter, *War and the Rise of the State: the Military Foundations of Modern Politics* (New York: Free Press, 1994); Peter Paret, editor, *Makers of Modern Strategy* (Princeton: Princeton University Press, 1986), especially chapters on Machiavelli and the Napoleonic Wars. Also see Paul Kennedy, *The Rise and Fall of the Great Powers* (New York: Random House, 1987); Geoffrey Parker, *The Military Revolution* (New York: Cambridge University Press, 1986); Robert H. Jackson, *Quasi-States: Sovereignty, International Relations, and The Third World* (Cambridge: Cambridge University Press, 1990); and Grant T. Hammond and Bryant P. Shaw, "Conflict, The Rise of Nations, and the Decay of States: The Transformation of the International System?" *Conflict Studies* (Spring 1995).

7. This disintegrative force split several major former colonies, including Palestine (into Israel, Jordan, and the territories), India (into India, Pakistan, Bangladesh, and Ceylon), and French Sudan (into Mali, Mauritania, Niger, and Chad).

8. For analyses of the emerging chaos, see: Brzezinski, *Out of Control*; Moynihan *Pandaemonium*; and Kaplan, "The Coming Anarchy." Huntington disagrees, seeing, instead of anarchy, order along the lines of *The Clash of Civilizations*. See: Roy Godson and William Olson, *International Organized Crime: Emerging Threat to U.S. Security* (Washington: National Strategy Information Center, 1993); Manwaring, *Gray Area Phenomena*; and Richard Shultz and William Olson, *Ethnic and Religious Conflict* (Washington: National Strategy Information Center, 1994).

9. For works illustrating the importance of national sovereignty and its requirements (e.g., the capacity to govern domestically and to carry on foreign policy), see Robert J. Lieber, *No Common Power: Understanding International Relations*, 2d ed. (New York: HarperCollins, 1991); Samuel Huntington, *Political Order in Changing Societies* (New Haven: Yale University Press, 1968); William Pfaff, *The Wrath of Nations: Civilization and the Furies of Nationalism* (New York: Simon and Schuster, 1993); Karen Rasler and William R. Thompson, *War and State Making: The Shaping of Global Powers* (Boston: Unwin Hyman, 1989); Michael Howard, *War in European History* (Oxford: Oxford University Press, 1976) and Kennedy, *Rise and Fall of the Great Powers*.

10. The literature on ethno-nationalism is burgeoning, but see the following: Anthony Birch, *Nationalism and National Integration* (London: Unwin Hyman, 1989); Michael E. Brown, *Ethnic Conflict and International Security* (Princeton: Princeton University Press, 1993); Walker Connor, *Ethnonationalism: The Quest for Understanding* (Princeton: Princeton University Press, 1994); Gidon Gottlieb, *Nation Against State: A New Approach to Ethnic Conflicts and the Decline of the Sovereignty* (New York: Council of Foreign Relations Press, 1992); Ted Robert Gurr, *Minorities at Risk* (Washington: United States Institute of Peace, 1992); Donald L. Horowitz, *Ethnic Groups in Conflict* (Berkeley: University of California Press, 1985); Mark Juergensmeyer, *The New Cold War? Religious Nationalism Confronts the Secular State* (Berkeley: University of California Press, 1993); Joseph Rothschild, *Ethnopolitics: A Conceptual Framework* (New York: Columbia University Press, 1981); and Anthony Smith, *The Ethnic Origins of Nations* (Cambridge: Blackwell, 1993).

11. These trends include rapid urbanization, growing disparities between the "haves" and "have nots," a proliferation of communications and war-fighting technologies, and anti-imperialism.

12. This decline of governance is discussed widely, but most notably in Brzezinski, *Out of Control*; Robert Jackman, *Power Without Force* (Ann Arbor: University of

Michigan Press, 1983); Jackson, *Quasi-States*; and Walter B. Wriston, *The Twilight of Sovereignty: How the Information Revolution is Transforming Our World* (New York: Charles Scribner's Sons, 1992).

13. This list is in contrast to those secessionist groups that are essentially transnational because their ethnic group crosses national boundaries: Albanians, Armenians in Nagorno-Karabah, Kurds, Macedonians, Ossetians, Romanians, or Russians (of the near abroad).

14. Ted Robert Gurr, *Ethnic Minorities in Conflict* (Washington: U.S. Institute of Peace, 1993), 98 and Gurr, "Peoples Against States: Ethnopolitical Conflict and the Changing World System," *International Studies Quarterly* 38 (1994): 347–377. While Gurr argues that ethnic conflict is not on the rise, he appears to believe that the secessionist movements are generally one-time only events, rather than steps in a process of disintegration.

15. For a summary of the literature, see Roy Godson, "Intelligence and Security," in Shultz, Godson and Greenwood, *Security Studies for the 1990s*.

16. This point was brought home in spring 1995 with Rep. Robert Torricelli's claim that the Central Intelligence Agency had recruited a Guatemalan army colonel who was implicated in the deaths of a U.S. citizen and a spouse of a U.S. citizen. If true, this type of association is unfortunate and embarrassing but does not diminish the importance of gaining strategic, military, and political insights into other countries and cultures, as well as gaining the capability to influence major players in these regions.

17. Until recently few attempts could be found in the literature to define systematically each element of intelligence, to identify how each is associated with others, and to understand the products, process, and organization of each element. The series by the Consortium for the Study of Intelligence, *Intelligence Requirements for the 1980s*, was the first attempt to approach intelligence in this manner. Its system was adopted in a textbook by two participants in the Consortium's work: Abram N. Shulsky, revised by Gary J. Schmitt, *Silent Warfare: Understanding the World of Intelligence*, 2d rev. ed. (Washington: Brassey's, 1993).

18. These categories are simplifications and can be contentious. For instance, one could easily include the information intercepted from telemetry data as a separate category. Given, however, the relative unimportance of these systems in non-state oriented conflict, we include telint under elint.

Oscint is, on the other hand, a category that appears to be of growing importance. Consider, for instance, the company order forms, shipping manifests, and tax forms, any of which might prove useful for understanding the links among criminal groups or for discerning front organizations purchasing weapons components for ethnic or religious groups that would otherwise be prohibited from owning them. While many of these forms are proprietary, they are not actually secret. Perhaps a new category of "Somewhat Open Sources" should be used to define them.

19. Two schools debate whether the IC should function as a worldwide think tank or whether it should be more specifically opportunity-oriented. For a discussion of how the two models differ, see Shultz, Godson, and Greenwood, *Intelligence Requirements for the 1990s* and Jack Davis, "Analysis and Policy: The Kent-Kendall Debate of 1949," paper presented at the International Studies Association Convention, March 1991. For an important enunciation of the doctrine of opportunity

analysis, see Douglas J. MacEachin, "The Tradecraft of Analysis" in Godson, May, and Schmitt, editors, *U.S. Intelligence at the Crossroads*. MacEachin was the CIA's deputy director for analysis from 1993 to 1995.

20. This definition is derived from the wording used in the U.S. Congress, *Intelligence Authorization Act of 1991*. For elaboration see Roy Godson, "Intelligence: An American View," in K.G. Robertson, ed, British *and American Approaches to Intelligence* (New York: St. Martin's Press, 1987). For many illustrations, see Roy Godson, *Dirty Tricks or Trump Cards* (Washington: Brassey's, 1995).

21. Despite the explanatory value of a state-centric paradigm, countries have perennially dealt with some forms of ungovernability, generally on a local basis. While it might be said that great empires such as those of Rome or London have dealt with one form or another of global ungovernability, even they addressed the problems on localized, case-by-case, bases. Lessons learned from the following numerous (and by no means comprehensive) cases provide some insights into possible means for addressing ungovernability in the twenty-first century. A partial list of experiences with varying degrees of success worth examining includes the Roman Empire; the English in Wales, Scotland, and then Ireland; the British on Indian frontiers, including Pakistan and Burma; the Japanese in Manchuria; the Germans in France, Poland, and central Europe and the Balkans, 1939–1945; the U.S. in the border and Confederate states during the Civil War and Reconstruction; the American conquest of the Great Plains; and the Russians in the trans-Dniester and Siberia during much of the nineteenth and twentieth centuries. These conflicts range from border wars and imperial conquests to counterinsurgency campaigns and proxy wars. To this list could also be added those countries that have faced serious challenges from criminal organizations, a long litany that would include the Mediterranean and Caribbean nations that faced pirates in the seventeenth and eighteenth centuries; China during its century-long campaign to stop the opium trade; Britain during its century-long campaign to halt the African slave trade; and Italy over the past century.

22. The various plagues that have swept through societies over the ages have caused death and destruction on scales that no human could have planned—at least until the era of nuclear weapons. Among the most notorious examples are the plague that nearly destroyed Periclean Athens; the Black Death that wiped out a third of Western Europe's population in the 1340s; and the 1918–1919 influenza that swept the globe, killing an estimated 20–30 million people. Several recent studies have pointed to the possibility that such a disaster might happen again, on an even larger scale.

23. Iran, Iraq, and possibly Libya are among those states in apparent contravention of the biological weapons agreements. The Japanese religious sect *Aum Shinrikyo* is the first named non-state actor apparently attempting to gain use of biological agents per se, as evidenced by their stockpile of biological media. They are also the first group accused of devising and implementing a covert delivery system. In an unrelated event a few years ago, however, the biological agent ricin was discovered during a police raid on an illegal drug laboratory in the U.S. The ricin apparently was to be used against law enforcement personnel in Minnesota.

24. For the ban, see the 1925 Geneva Protocol on gas and bacteriological warfare, cited by Adam Roberts, "Land Warfare," in Howard, et al., *Laws of War*, 127.

25. Marvin Cetron, *Terror 2000: The Future Face of Terrorism* (Washington: Department of Defense, 1995), chap. 8.

26. One such group is Open Source Solutions (OSS). Although OSS makes a convincing case for using more open sources and even for some privatizing of collection and analysis, their literature appears to fail to account for deliberate deception and the need for counterdeception capabilities.

27. For some background, see David Kay, "Denial and Deception," in Godson, May, and Schmitt, *U.S. Intelligence at the Crossroads*. On opportunity analysis, see Douglas J. MacEachin, "Tradecraft of Analysis."

28. For some important works on the structure of criminal organizations, see the summary in Roy Godson, "Transstate Security," in Roy Godson, Richard Shultz, and George Quester, *Security Studies for the Twenty-First Century* (Washington: Brassey's, 1995).

29. See Stephen Pelletiere, *Hamas and Hizbollah: The Radical Challenge to Israel in the Occupied Territories and Assad and the Peace Process: The Pivotal Role of Lebanon* (Carlisle Barracks: U.S. Army War College, Strategic Studies Institute, 1994). Quotation is from *Assad*, v.

30. Daniel Pipes, "Understanding Assad," *Middle East Quarterly* 1:4 (December 1994): 51.

31. For another view, see Godson, *Dirty Tricks or Trumps Cards*.

32. Roy Godson, "Devising Strategy to Counter Organized Crime," testimony before U.S. Senate, Foreign Relations Subcommittee on Terrorism, Narcotics and International Operations, Recent *Developments in Transnational Crime Affecting U.S. Law Enforcement and Foreign Policy*, S. Hrg. 103–606, 103rd Congress, 2d session, April 20–21, 1994 (Washington: GPO, 1994).

14

Final Thoughts on Lessons Learned and Conflict Management

Max G. Manwaring

War is a matter of vital importance to the State; the province of life or death; the road to survival or ruin. . . . Therefore appraise it in terms of five fundamental factors. . . . The first of these factors is moral influence. . . . By moral influence I mean that which causes the people to be in harmony with their leaders, so that they will accompany them in life and unto death without fear of moral peril.

Sun Tzu

"Lessons learned" are not just a simple matter of careful analysis of past errors or successes. A more difficult matter is that of assimilating the lessons that should have been learned and incorporating them into policy and planning processes. A quick look into one example from history can illustrate the danger of attributing victory to one particular factor or technological advantage and forgetting about the more fundmental "pillars of success" in conflict management.

Much has been made of the technological breakthrough represented by the stirrup in tenth and eleventh century warfare in Western Europe. The stirrup provided stability, balance, and leverage for a horseman. As a result, it has been asserted that the stirrup gave the Norman cavalry a decisive advantage in the conquest of England.

As early as 1066, William the Conqueror took full advantage of the technological superiority that the stirrup provided his cavalry as a type of "launching platform." Clearly, William understood the value of appropriate weapons systems. What seems to have been forgotten is that William also understood and applied the concepts of "end state" and "unity of effort." He knew exactly what he wanted to accomplish, and he applied a management structure that ensured there was never any question as to who was in charge or the objectives of the effort. Every military action was calculated to achieve the psychological objectives that would lead to ultimate political success.

Probably the most salient lesson that should have been learned from William's conquest of England, however, is that the most important weapon or instrument of power that he took with him was a certain legitimacy. That legitimacy was provided by the blessing of the pope himself. The invasion of England and the ascendancy of William to the monarchy became a holy endeavor. William could offer land to his leaders and booty for everyone. The church would offer absolution for anything to anyone involved in the holy cause.

At the same time, King Harold had been excommunicated for reneging on a solemn oath to allow William to become king of England. The papal edict that condemned Harold to Hell forever threatened all his followers with the same fate if the English crown was not surrendered to the pope's choice. Harold's own confidence in himself and his cause—and that of the English church, the army, and the people—can only have been shaken to its foundations.

The only appeal was to God himself through a trial by ordeal that would declare His judgment. The Battle of Hastings in October of 1066 was that trial. The result was a foregone conclusion, however. Everyone, including Harold, knew he was guilty as charged. The outstanding valor, initiative, and aggressiveness Harold and his followers demonstrated against a Scandinavian invasion force in the north only a few weeks previously were not evident at Hastings. In comparison to the battle at Stamford bridge, Harold's effort in particular and the army's actions in general at Hastings could only be described as "halfhearted."

When Harold lost and died at the Battle of Hastings, the fate of England and William was sealed. Duke William of Normandy, with about 8,000 troops, became King William "the Conqueror" of all England. William's moral influence and Harold's lack of legitimacy were the crucial factors in the Norman invasion of England—not stirrups or cavalry.

A legitimacy approach, appropriate instruments of power, and an organizational structure to ensure the achievement of a desired political end state are not radical relics of the Cold War era. These pillars of success are basic foreign policy and military asset management.

About the Contributors

Col. Dennis F. Caffrey, USAF (ret.) is an international consultant based in Miami, FL. He has served in various posts including the Secretary General of the System of Cooperation Among the American Air Forces (SICOFAA); the Director of Plans, Policy and Politico-Military Affairs and Deputy Chief of Staff at the United States Southern Command in Panama; and the Chief of Western Hemisphere Division, Plans and Policy Directorate, Headquarters United States Air Force. Colonel Caffrey's published work includes "The Inter-American Military System: Rhetoric versus Reality" and "Insurgency and Drug Trafficking: Have the Peruvian Armed Forces Become an Unrecognized Casualty?"

Col. Bruce B.G. Clarke, USA (ret.) is an international consultant based in Saudi Arabia. He has served in various posts including director of United States National Security Studies at the U.S. Army War College, Commander of the 2d Brigade of the 1st Infantry Division, and as a staff officer at the Arms Control and Disarmament Agency. Colonel Clarke's published work includes "Conflict Termination: A Rational Model."

Ambassador Edwin G. Corr, whose diplomatic career under both Republican and Democratic administrations includes ambassadorships to Bolivia, El Salvador, and Peru, and Deputy Assistant Secretary of State for International Narcotics Matters, is currently the Henry Belmon Professor of Public Service at the University of Oklahoma. Ambassador Corr is the recipient of several U.S. and foreign awards, and has written various articles and books including *Low-Intensity Conflict: Old Threats in a New World.*

General Wayne A. Downing, USA, is the Commander in Chief of the United States Special Operations Command, headquartered at MacDill Air Force Base, FL. As Commander in Chief, he is responsible for the readiness of all United States special operations forces of the Army, Navy, and Air Force, both active duty and reserve. Prior to assuming his present position, General Downing served as Commanding General, United States Army Special Operations Command, Fort Bragg, NC, Commander of a Joint Special Operations Task Force assigned to the United States Central Command during Operation DESERT STORM in the Persian Gulf War, and Commander of the Special Operations Forces of all Services during Operation JUST CAUSE in Panama. The general's awards and decorations include the Defense Distinguished Service Medal, the Distinguished Service Medal, the Silver Star with oak leaf cluster, the Defense Superior Service Medal, the Legion of Merit with three oak leaf clusters, the Soldier's Medal, the Bronze Star Medal with "V" device and five oak leaf clusters, the Purple Heart, and the Combat Infantryman Badge.

Dr. John T. Fishel is Professor of National Security Affairs at the U.S. Army Command and General Staff College. As a reserve officer on active duty LTC Fishel served in several military staff positions in the United States Southern Command's Directorate for Plans, Policy, and Politico-Military Affairs. After Operation JUST CAUSE he was responsible for planning post conflict activities in Panama and establishing the Panama National Police. Dr. Fishel's published work includes *1989-90 Restoration of Panama and Liberation. Occupation, and Rescue: War Termination and Desert Storm.*

Dr. Roy Godson is associate professor in the Department of Government at Georgetown University and president of the National Strategy Information Center. He has served as a consultant to the President's Foreign Intelligence Advisory Board, the National Security Council, and related agencies of the U.S. government. Dr. Godson has written, co-authored, or edited 18 books on intelligence and national security.

Dr. Max G. Manwaring is a political-military affairs consultant based in Carlisle, PA. He has served in various civilian and military positions including the United States Southern Command's Small Wars Operations Research Directorate, the Defense Intelligence Agency, and the United States Southern Command's Directorate for Plans, Policy, and Politico-Military Affairs. Dr. Manwaring is the author of several articles dealing with political-military affairs and is editor of *Uncomfortable Wars: Toward a Paradigm of Low Intensity Conflict* and *Gray Area Phenomena: Confronting the New World Disorder.*

Ambassador David C. Miller, Jr. is President and CEO of Par Ex, Inc., a privately held investment company located in Washington, Baltimore and Warsaw, Poland. His diplomatic career included ambassadorships to Tanzania and Zimbabwe, and an appointment as Special Assistant to the President for National Security Affairs. His published work includes "United States Government Organization and Capability to Deal with Low-Intensity Conflict."

Dr. Wm. J. Olson is Staff Director for the Senate Caucus on International Narcotics Control and a Senior Fellow at the National Strategy Information Center, and served most recently as a Deputy Assistant Secretary of State for International Narcotics Matters. He has also served as the Director of the Low-Intensity Conflict Organization of the Assistant Secretary of Defense for Special Operations and Low-Intensity Conflict. He is the author and co-author of numerous articles and books including "Low-Intensity

Conflict: The Challenge to the National Interest," *Guerrilla Warfare and Counterinsurgency, and U.S. Strategy in the Persian Gulf.*

Ambassador David Passage is Political Advisor to General Wayne A. Downing, Commander in Chief of the United States Special Operations Command. A career member of the United States Foreign Service, Ambassador Passage has served in England, Vietnam, Ecuador, Australia, El Salvador, and as U.S. Ambassador to Botswana. He was also Special Assistant to Secretary of State Henry Kissinger; Spokesman for the State Department under Secretaries Vance, Muskie, and Haig; and Director for Africa on the National Security Council Staff. Ambassador Passage has also received numerous State Department honor awards and three Presidental Performance Awards.

Dr. Graham H. Turbiville, Jr. is a senior analyst and research coordinator with the U.S. Army's Foreign Military Studies Office, Fort Leavenworth, KS. Before joining the Foreign Military Studies Office, Dr. Turbiville was Chief of the Defense Intelligence Agency's Soviet/Warsaw Pact Strategic Operations Branch, and served in a variety of other DIA assignments. His current research addresses transnational security issues and associated problems of civil-military relations. Dr. Turbiville is the editor of *The Voroshilov Lectures: Materials from the Soviet General Staff Academy*; co-editor of *High Intensity Crime—Low Intensity Conflict*; and is also the editor for the international journal *Low Intensity Confict and Law Enforcement.*

About the Book

Departing from conventional policy rhetoric on the unconventional "new world disorder," Max G. Manwaring, Wm. J. Olson, and their colleagues here build upon Ambassador David C. Miller, Jr.'s three pillars of success for foreign policy and military management. They provide a sound intellectual road map through the dense fog of the contemporary international threat environment. This seasoned group of contributors, from diplomatic, military, and intellectual circles, offers a wide range of pragmatic and theoretical perspectives on emerging regional security issues.